THE
HALF-MAD LORD

HOLT, RINEHART and WINSTON
pub date: July 27, 1979

Nikolai Tolstoy

THE HALF-MAD LORD

Thomas Pitt
2nd Baron Camelford
(1775–1804)

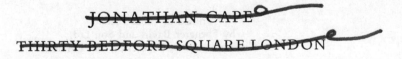

JONATHAN CAPE
THIRTY BEDFORD SQUARE LONDON

First published 1978
© 1978 by Nikolai Tolstoy

Jonathan Cape Ltd, 30 Bedford Square, London WC1

British Library Cataloguing in Publication Data

Tolstoy, Nikolai, *Count*
The half-mad lord.
1. Pitt, Thomas, *Baron Camelford*
2. Great Britain. Royal Navy – Biography
1. Title
359.3'3'20924   DA87.1.P/

ISBN 0–224–01664–4

Printed in Great Britain
by Ebenezer Baylis and Son Ltd.
The Trinity Press, Worcester, and London

*This book is dedicated with permission
to my fellow Brothers,
past and present, of
the Sublime Society of Beef Steaks*

Finn ... felt some palpitation at the heart ... knowing well the fiery nature of the man he expected to see. It might be that there would be some actual conflict between him and this half-mad Lord before he got back again into the street.

Anthony Trollope, *Phineas Finn*

Therefore, omit him not; blunt not his love:
Nor lose the good advantage of his grace,
By seeming cold, or careless of his will.
For he is gracious, if he be observ'd;
He hath a tear for pity, and a hand
Open as day for melting charity:
Yet notwithstanding, being incens'd, he's flint;
As humorous as winter, and as sudden
As flaws congealed in the spring of day.
His temper, therefore, must be well observ'd.

King Henry IV, Part II

Contents

	Acknowledgments	xiii
I	'Wellcome little Stranger'	1
II	The Caning in Conduit Street	17
III	Blood on the Quayside	38
IV	A Secret Expedition	66
V	The Lion Tamed: Lord Camelford in Love	84
VI	Politics and Prize-fighters	99
VII	Dangers and Disguises	119
VIII	The Peer and the Pugilist	134
IX	A Controversial Character	142
X	The Prisoner in the Temple	150
XI	A Dangerous Challenge	171
XII	Pistols for Two	180
XIII	Envoi	190
	Appendix	195
	Notes	203
	Index	231

Illustrations

PLATES

Between pages 10 and 11

1 Thomas Pitt, second Lord Camelford
2 Cushion made on Lord Camelford's birth
3 Lady Camelford, *née* Anne Wilkinson
4 Boconnoc House, Cornwall
5 The first Lord Camelford
6 Lord Grenville
7 Henri de Meuron's school at Neuchâtel
8 Anne Pitt, later Lady Grenville

Between pages 74 and 75

9,10 The wreck of the *Guardian*
11 Matavai Bay, Tahiti
12 The *Discovery* in Queen Charlotte's Sound
13 Captain George Vancouver
14 Captain Robert Barrie
15 The Caning in Conduit Street
16 The shooting of Lieutenant Peterson
17 English Harbour, Antigua

Between pages 122 and 123

18 Lady Hester Stanhope
19 The Union Club. Cartoon by Gillray

xi

20 Camelford House
21 The Old Sarum Election. Cartoon by Gillray

Between pages 186 and 187

22 Joe Bourke
23 Jem Belcher
24 Belcher, afterwards Trusty, the bulldog
25 Celebration of the Peace of Amiens
26 In the watch-house. Engraving by I. R. and G. Cruikshank
27 Lord Camelford's duelling pistols
28 The death of Lord Camelford
29 The Île de St Pierre on the Lac de Bienne

ILLUSTRATIONS IN THE TEXT

The house of Pitt and the family arms	*page* 3
The Windward and Leeward Islands	43
The French passport issued to Lord Camelford	125
Note from Lord Camelford to his sister	163
Altar erected where Lord Camelford fell	189
Lord Camelford's magazine pistol	196

ENDPAPER MAPS

Front: The West End of London, from *Bowles's One-sheet Plan of the Cities of London and Westminster with the Borough of Southwark*, published by Carington Bowles in 1803
Back: New Bond Street, from R. Horwood, *Plan of London, Westminster, Southwark, and Parts Adjoining, shewing every house*, 1799

❧❧❧❧❧❧❧❧❧❧❧❧❧❧❧❧❧❧❧❧❧❧❧❧❧❧❧❧❧❧

Acknowledgments

In compiling material for the writing of this book I received generous assistance from many people. I trust I have acknowledged every instance in the Notes, but I would like to single out several cases where the help was of a more general nature. Mr Tom L. Brock has been long preparing a biography of Lord Camelford's lifelong friend Robert Barrie, in the course of which he compiled an original and highly interesting typescript monograph on Camelford. This he generously placed at my disposal, so drawing my attention to material I might otherwise have overlooked. Mr John Ehrman, F.B.A., author of a celebrated biography of Pitt the Younger, placed his unequalled knowledge of the manuscript sources at my disposal on several occasions, and assisted me with much other invaluable advice. My stepfather, Patrick O'Brian (himself the author of a distinguished series of novels set in the period of Lord Camelford's career), first suggested the idea of my writing this biography, and later read and criticised in detail the first three chapters. His suggestions were particularly fruitful, resulting in many improvements to my original text. My old friend and fellow member of the Beef Steak Society, John Yeowell, loaned me his unique grangerised copy of Reade's *Belgravia* article of 1876, and stimulated my researches during numerous discussions. Mr E. K. Timings of the Public Record Office directed my attention to some important manuscript material; while the staff of the London Library aided me throughout with the same courtesy and industry that I have experienced for the past twenty years. I am also grateful to my copy-editor, Margaret Stevenson, for all her help. Lastly I should like to thank Lady Margaret Fortescue and Captain Desmond Fortescue for hospitality and help afforded me during my visits to Cornwall and Devon.

xiii

To these and other friends of Lord Camelford and myself I would like to place on record my heartfelt thanks.

As for the illustrations, I am indebted to the following: Mr John Yeowell for Plates 1, 28 and 29; Captain Desmond Fortescue for Plates 5, 6 and 8; the Service Cantonal des Monuments et des Sites, Neuchâtel, for Plate 7; the National Maritime Museum for Plates 9, 10, 11 and 17; the London Library for Plate 12; the National Portrait Gallery for Plate 13; Mr Tom L. Brock for Plate 14; the British Library for Plates 15, 19, 21, 22 and 24; the Radio Times Hulton Picture Library for Plate 16; the British Museum for Plates 20 and 25; the Mansell Collection for Plate 23.

The endpaper maps come from the Greater London Council Map Collection. The map of the Windward and Leeward Islands, from *West India Commonplace Book*, came from the London Library.

Lord Camelford's French passport is reproduced by permission of the Archives Nationales in Paris. The British Library supplied a microfilm of Lord Camelford's note to his sister (Addn. MS. 59491, p. 33), and a copy of the article in *A Journal of Natural Philosophy, Chemistry, and the Arts* about Lord Camelford's pistol, which forms the Appendix.

Finally, the engraving of Lord Camelford reproduced on the title page comes from *London und Paris*, vol. XIII, Halle, 1804, lent by the British Library.

xiv

I

'Wellcome little Stranger'

On a September morning in 1796, people strolling in Conduit Street in the West End of London were astonished to see a tall young man dash across the road towards two older men who were walking peaceably on the other side, and start to thrash one of them with his cane. All three were involved in a scrimmage, in the course of which severe blows were received on all sides. Despite this, the assailant announced furiously that if he and his victim were ever to meet again in a public place, he would repeat the performance.

Not surprisingly, this fracas attracted widespread public attention. The speech and dress of all three proclaimed their status in the upper levels of society. The angry young man was in fact a naval officer; much more than this, he was a peer, the inheritor of great wealth and a vast estate in Cornwall: the second Lord Camelford. The man he had attacked was also a naval officer. He was the captain under whom Lord Camelford had served as a midshipman.

For a 21-year-old officer, even one of Lord Camelford's rank, to assault a senior officer in public is, to say the least, unusual. In fact, the Caning in Conduit Street, as the episode came to be called, was far from being the greatest or most scandalous of the young lord's eccentricities.

His life was short: only twenty-nine years. But it was full of bizarre incidents. He was responsible for the death of more than one man, and he himself died in violence. He was handsome, athletic, arrogant, immensely sensitive on the subject of his honour, and, with pistols or swords, ever ready to meet an opponent on a lonely spot at dawn. He was constantly in physical and legal conflict with others. Some doubted his sanity, but none his courage.

Despite his impetuosity, and his frequent recourse to violence, he was capable of gentleness and generosity, particularly to those far below his own station in life. He was extreme, both in his failings and his virtues. Inevitably, in his lifetime it was the failings which, because of their often sensational consequences, came to be the basis for judgments of his character. Perhaps, after the greater part of two centuries, it is now possible to form a fuller and more charitable assessment.

The second Lord Camelford was born Thomas Pitt on 19 February 1775. The Pitts were the wonder and glory of the eighteenth century. In the brief space of a century a single family produced two of Britain's greatest prime ministers and received the accolade of four distinct peerages: the earldoms of Londonderry and Chatham, and the baronies of Rivers and Camelford. The family fortunes were established in large part in the early years of the eighteenth century: by the second decade of the nineteenth the family was virtually extinct in the male line. Their splendour was extinguished as suddenly as it had arisen.

The Pitts first came to national prominence in the reign of Queen Anne. Thomas Pitt, the younger son of a country parson, had sailed to India in search of a fortune. He eventually rose to become governor of Fort St George at Madras, and returned to England a nabob. Nabobs— men with fortunes acquired in the service of the East India Company— were familiar figures in England at the time, but Thomas Pitt's achievement was held remarkable even then. In 1702 he had purchased from a native an enormous diamond, known thereafter as the Pitt Diamond. On his return home he entered into negotiations with the Regent of France, who agreed to buy the magnificent stone for the then princely sum of £125,000. Part of the French Crown Jewels were pawned to meet the price.[1]

With the money he received, Pitt settled down in accordance with the custom of the time to establish himself as a country gentleman. He bought lands in several counties of southern England, but settled principally upon the beautiful wooded estate of Boconnoc, near Lostwithiel in Cornwall. Boconnoc had come on the market following the death of its previous owner, Lord Mohun, in a duel. Coincidentally, the house was eventually to pass from the Pitt family as the result of another duel.

Despite savage quarrels with his eldest son (also characteristic of the period), when Thomas Pitt died in 1726, he left the estate in the senior

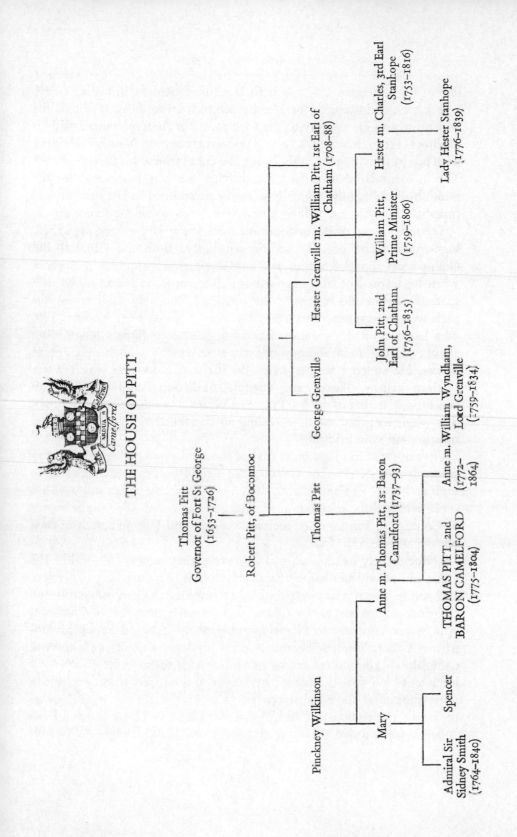

THE HOUSE OF PITT

Thomas Pitt
Governor of Fort St George
(1653–1726)

Robert Pitt, of Boconnoc

Thomas Pitt   Hester Grenville m. William Pitt, 1st Earl of Chatham (1708–88)

George Grenville

John Pitt, 2nd
Earl of Chatham
(1756–1835)

William Pitt,
Prime Minister
(1759–1806)

Hester m. Charles, 3rd Earl
Stanhope
(1753–1816)

Lady Hester Stanhope
(1776–1839)

Anne m. William Wyndham,
Lord Grenville
(1759–1834)

Pinckney Wilkinson

Anne m. Thomas Pitt, 1st Baron
Camelford (1737–93)

Mary

THOMAS PITT, 2nd
BARON CAMELFORD
(1775–1804)

Anne m. William Wyndham,
(1772–
1864)

Spencer

Admiral Sir
Sidney Smith
(1764–1840)

line of his descendants. The heir to Boconnoc, Robert Pitt, died barely
a year later, and his successor Thomas fell into severe financial difficulties
which forced him to retire to the Continent for three years to avoid his
creditors. From these straits he was rescued by his son (another Thomas,
born in 1737), who generously broke the entail to pay his father's debts.[2]
The indigent father died in 1761, leaving his heir to re-establish the
position of the family, which had nearly succumbed to the quarrels and
financial difficulties bedevilling the two successors to old Governor Pitt.

The new owner of Boconnoc was a man of stately presence, well bred,
high-minded and of deep artistic sensibility. Both the Classical and
Gothic tastes appealed to him, and he was viewing antiquities in Florence
when he learned of his father's death. Boconnoc he found to be in a
state of neglect and disrepair: the furniture had been sold, whilst the
park was overgrown and marred by savage tree-felling. Thomas Pitt,
who later acquired a reputation as a fine landscape-garden designer, set
about restoring house and grounds to a state worthy of their magnificent
setting. He added a further wing, on the upper floor of which was a
spacious gallery. There hung portraits of Mohuns and Pitts, and an
enormous painting of the late Prince of Wales, a benefactor of the family.
The windows gazed south, providing an unrivalled view of the lake and
surrounding wooded hills.[3]

Pitt's life was in many ways that of the archetypal eighteenth-century
grand seigneur portrayed by Gainsborough and Romney. He corresponded
with architects and antiquaries, designed impeccable villas and gardens,
spoke with urbane restraint on leading questions of the day in the House
of Commons, and travelled to France, Spain and Italy in search of men
of taste and objects of vertu.

Unfortunately he also suffered from recurring bouts of ill-health. His
father's improvidence had nearly deprived him of a university education,
and young Thomas was only enabled to continue at Cambridge through
the generosity of two uncles. One of these was the great Earl of Chatham,
who wrote regularly to his neglected nephew. Abandoned by his un-
natural father, Thomas became a prey to depressive fits and nervous
complaints. 'The violent emotions with which these scenes affected me
left a sensible impression upon my health, and nervous disorders, which
some time after increased upon me to a very alarming degree, owed
their origin to anxiety of mind,' he wrote in later years. He suffered from
epileptic fits, though these ceased as he entered middle age. As a result

of this incapacity he was prevented from taking up as active a political career as he might have wished, and was obliged to sojourn for prolonged periods in southern Europe.[4]

With his natural gifts, social position and family connexions he might otherwise have hoped for high office in the state. In 1783, indeed, he was approached by King George III with a view to becoming prime minister, but was obliged to decline. Possibly as a compensation for this, he was raised to the peerage in the following year at the request of the new prime minister, his cousin the younger William Pitt. Thomas Pitt was now Lord Camelford and Baron Boconnoc.[5] All in all, the picture provided by his contemporaries is that of an intelligent, aesthetic man of refined tastes, of gentlemanly address, generous and serious; but at the same time correct and formal almost to the point of being precious. He was fastidious and held his emotions under restraint. perhaps a result of generous affections unreciprocated in childhood.

Lord Camelford's marriage followed an established convention of the age. The entail had preserved his inheritance from being too seriously ravaged by his father's insolvency, and he was a wealthy man. In 1771 he married the daughter of a rich London merchant, Pinckney Wilkinson. Anne Wilkinson was thirty-three, and brought with her a splendid dowry of £40,000.[6] The marriage itself was a happy one, though it brought unlooked-for troubles which involved the Camelfords in un-welcome scandal and intrigue.

Anne had an elder sister, Mary. An impoverished Guards captain named John Smith had struck up an acquaintance with her at the spas of Bath and Tunbridge Wells, and they eloped in 1760. Old Mr Wilkinson was outraged, regarding Smith as an adventurer. The ruthless old man cut off his once favourite daughter from all but a token part in the inheritance of his wealth. He also swore never to see her again.

One's sympathies would be entirely with Captain Smith, were it not for the fact that he began to quarrel with Mary, threatened her with physical violence, and finally drove her in despair to seek refuge with her family. Lord Camelford had married her sister Anne in the previous year, and willy-nilly found himself playing a part in the distasteful affair. It was in large part due to his influence that Mr Wilkinson was induced to pay Smith a small annuity to keep him quiet, and (very grudgingly) to contribute to the education of the Smiths' three sons.

Smith later began to claim larger sums for himself and the children;

recourse was had to the law, and wild accusations flew about. It was even alleged that Lord Camelford, as an interested party, had not been unhappy to see the major part of the inheritance pass to his wife Anne. This was unjust: Camelford had in fact paid money of his own to help his three nephews, and had played no part in his father-in-law's decision. So persistent were the slanders, however, that Lord Camelford was obliged to take the unusual step of publishing a book defending his conduct.

The matter was eventually resolved, though not to anyone's great satisfaction. Mary and the Smith grandchildren were eventually bequeathed £10,000; a handsome sum in itself, but paltry in comparison to that received by the Camelfords. No blame for this arrangement can be attributed to them; it was Mr Pinckney Wilkinson who decided everything. He indeed behaved discreditably; for, whatever he thought of John Smith, there could be no justification for discriminating between two sets of grandchildren.

However, subsequent events were to redress the balance. The favoured grandson, with every imaginable material advantage placed at his disposal, achieved neither success nor happiness; while the slighted Smith grandsons, spurred perhaps by the injustices to which they had been subjected, were brilliantly successful. One indeed went on to gain distinctions which the sordid wealth of his grandfather could never have bought; he was the intrepid Admiral Sir Sidney Smith, the hero of Acre. He was to have a strong influence on the subject of this history, which is the reason for relating the story of this unhappy family squabble.[7]

Lord Camelford and his wife Anne had spent the first months of their marriage on his Cornish estate at Boconnoc. Just over a year later, when they returned to London, their first child was born. 'About half an hour after one this afternoon Mrs Pitt made me a present of a fine girl after about an hour of pretty serious business. Thank God both She and the child are well, and myself happier than I can describe.'[8] The daughter was called Anne, after her mother.

The Camelfords still required an heir to the name and property. They must have been overjoyed when the next child duly proved to be a boy. This time the birth took place at the ancestral home in Cornwall, and Lord Camelford proudly recorded in the family Bible: 'Thomas born the 19:th of February 1775 ¼ after 5 o'clock in the morning.'[9] The baby, who was to become the second Lord Camelford, was baptised with his father's name next day in the church next to the house at Boconnoc.[10]

The family was delighted, and Lord Camelford wrote to his aunt, Lady Chatham, of 'the Birth of our little Cornishman'.[11] There is still in existence a charming little silk cushion, embroidered at the time with the words *'Wellcome little Stranger'*.

After more than half a century's vicissitudes, it seemed the senior line of the Pitts had succeeded in establishing its dynasty on a secure footing. They had great wealth, a famous name, and now an heir to bear all this glory on his sturdy little shoulders. For, unlike his parents and sister, little Thomas was from the beginning exceptionally strong and healthy; 'the young Cornish Hercules,' Lady Chatham called him soon after his second birthday.[12]

The christening took place at the height of the summer, and the Rector of Boconnoc despatched an account to a friend on 27 August.

> Since I answered your last, we have had all the bustle of a christening, with its appendages of concert, and ball, and wrestlings, and a great supper of shew to 107 gentlemen and ladies; and the great house so dressed up and bedizened on the occasion, that my hermitage became the retreat for two days of lordings and high dames of honours. I wished to see the wrestling; but just before it began Frank Dixon was taken very ill on the downs, and I was obliged to bring him home in a carriage. Report talks of it as the most famous wrestling that was ever seen in this wrestling county. A silver bowl of fifteen guineas value was the prize of the victor (the first who threw five falls); and about fifty pounds worth of silver was distributed amongst the vanquished wights. They tell me that there is some account of our great doings in the newspapers; so I hear from my brother Tom and from Yorkshire, but it is in no paper that has reached our neighbourhood. If you can procure it from some pamphlet-shop or coffeehouse, it would be an acceptable present here.[13]

Tom Pitt passed his childhood days at Boconnoc. There were occasional visits to the other family properties, Petersham Lodge near Richmond and Camelford House in London.[14] When he was three, he and the family were taken by Lord Camelford to Italy;[15] but apart from these rare intervals, Tom knew little of the world beyond the pales of the great Cornish estate until the age of ten or eleven.

The great house at Boconnoc faced southwards from the summit of a hill in the centre of the park. A great area of grassland, cropped by sheep, stretched below. Beyond, and on every side, undulated to the skyline dark woods of beech and oak. Herds of deer roamed the wilderness, whose forbears had been hunted by the Courtenays, the Carminows and the Mohuns, ancient families formerly dwelling at Boconnoc. Today it is a haven distant from the world; in the eighteenth century it was remote and enchanted indeed.

To little Thomas it must have been a land of adventure, romance, and fear. The house was great enough to become lost in: there were the huge state rooms, the cavernous underground kitchens and cellars, and the broad staircase, winding up to gloomy passages with their rows of empty rooms. Beyond was the hundred-foot gallery, where Pitt ancestors and Mohun predecessors gazed forbiddingly down on the solitary child.

Just across the lawn was the church, where Thomas, his tutor, the steward and the servants attended every Sunday. Great yews and laurels spread an oppressive gloom over the interior. Inside the shadowy building the boy's wandering gaze would frequently have rested upon a grim image, whose sinister significance had long passed from memory. An arch framed the mouldered representation of a child sleeping in a cradle. Over it loomed a gigantic, menacing figure bearing a scythe, whilst Death himself hovered nearby.

Out of doors, in contrast, all was light and green splendour, at least in summertime. A rivulet ran brightly down the vale below the house, onwards to the distant sea. A six-mile drive had been set out at Lord Camelford's orders through the woods, and successive vistas opened on to waterfalls, rustic bridges, grottoes, and lush hollows banked with hart's-tongue and wild garlic, where all beneath the leaves was of a subaqueous greenness. Even in summer, though, thick sea-mists could come stealing up the valley, leaving Boconnoc alone on its knoll like a floating fairy castle.

In winter mists and fogs pressed round the house, hiding all but the closest trees. Heavy rain-clouds passing up the Channel brought incessant downpours lasting days or weeks; often must Thomas have pressed his nose to a window in the great gallery, looking out on sodden verdure, the rain drumming without pause on the roof above and splattering dully on the gravelled drive and ornamental pond below. Occasionally fearful gales raged across the hills; one March, when Tom was just eight, the trunk of an enormous oak behind the house broke off nine feet above the ground, in the midst of one such tempest. It bore an ill-boding reputation;

its leaves were held to have changed colour ever since an attempt had been made to assassinate King Charles I at its base.[16]

It must surely serve as some explanation of his subsequent conduct that Thomas Pitt scarcely knew a family. 'His education was conducted by a private tutor alone in the seclusion of Boconnoc', the mentor being a clergyman named Wyat, who unfortunately does not appear to have fulfilled his difficult role satisfactorily. As Thomas's closest friend and confidant wrote years later:

> ... His early years no sage Instructor knew
> No friendly monitor with [tear in MS] hands
> Might ope the Book of Nature to his view.
>
> Thus as with ripening years his mind matured
> His lofty spirit burn'd without controul,
> And self directed no restraints endured
> While passion oft time shook his fervid Soul.[17]

It is unlikely that the young heir was at all amenable to discipline; except in the case of unusually diligent pupils, the sons of the nobility and gentry at that time generally managed to escape learning more than the elements of reading and Bible stories before first attending school.[18]

Lord and Lady Camelford were rarely at Boconnoc. Their days were spent abroad or at Petersham and London. Tom's sister Anne ('Annette', as the family affectionately knew her) was also away from home most of the year. In 1783 she had nearly died, an event that greatly upset his parents and which very likely had a lasting effect on Tom, who adored her.[19]

Communication with both children was on a formal and, at times, forbidding level. One of Thomas's earliest surviving letters pleads (in French): 'Forgive, my dear father, my little faults; always consider the excuse of my youth.' In return the father would despatch a long excursus on family history (this to a six-year-old child), or a homily on Christian prayer. His concern was almost wholly with the duties of the children to the parents; that these were at least reciprocal does not seem to have occurred to him. His daughter Anne, who by all accounts was goodness personified, received in response to some childish lapse a four-page rebuke. Informing her at length of her duties, of which he presumed she was aware, her father added coldly: 'If I believ'd otherwise I should never think it worth my while to throw away a thought upon you again as long as I live.' At Boconnoc there were servants, ponies, guns; but not, it seems, that which a child requires above all else. This neglect was frequently to be found among all the splendour of aristocratic households of the period.[20]

Not much is known of those early years. At five Tom was described as 'boisterous', and 'fond of his Papa'.[21] A letter to his mother tells her how he is learning chess so as to be able to play with Annette; he thanks her for the present of a watch, and rejoices in the downfall of Mr Fox, the family's great political rival. There are new goldfish in the pond at Boconnoc, and he is setting off for the seaside.[22] Despite the presence of a tutor, Tom Pitt seems to have largely taught himself. His handwriting remained a mere scrawl all his life, and his enthusiastic search for knowledge suffered from lack of disciplined purpose. Many rewarding hours were perhaps spent in the library beyond the long gallery. Among his father's books he could find that wonderful liberation of the spirit which literature provides for lonely children.

When Thomas was about eleven his parents decided to subject him to proper schooling. They took him to Switzerland, where he shot woodcock and enjoyed himself with the excitement of his new surroundings. He was less happy, however, when he arrived at the establishment of his parents' choice. The school was at Neuchâtel, and the new pupil arrived

> half dead with the heat. There is only one Englishman in the house of about 17 or 18 years old who cannot be my companion as you may conceive. But I like him very well he is not in the least Proud as I should have expected. As to Mr Meuron I have a little more to do with him than I should wish at Present; Because as the Masters cannot comme till the Beginning of the Month he gives me all My lessons. I think he is a very good natured man but he has the Most detestable manner you ever saw he never seems contented with anything; & you know there is nothing I hate more.

Long years in the solitary wilderness of Boconnoc had left Thomas emotionally vulnerable. Strangers were necessarily expected to be 'proud' towards him; personal criticism was something so wounding as almost to incapacitate him.

Nevertheless it seems likely that Tom came to revise his opinion of his host. Henri de Meuron had gained a lasting reputation as a philosopher and teacher. Ordained in 1773, his voice and health proved too weak to

1 A caricature of Lord Camelford, published by R. S. Kirby in 1805

2   The cushion made on the birth of the
    second Lord Camelford in 1775

3   Lady Camelford, *née* Anne Wilkinson

4   Boconnoc House, Cornwall

5 Thomas Pitt, first Lord Camelford,
by Romney

6 William Windham, Lord Grenville,
by Hoppner

7 Henri de Meuron's school at Neuchâtel (white-fronted building at centre)

8   Anne Pitt, later Lady Grenville, by Vigée Le Brun

conduct services, and instead he became a schoolmaster. He established his academy in a handsome building, the former Hôtel de la Couronne, which can still be found in Neuchâtel at number 23 rue du Château. Many of Monsieur de Meuron's pupils later achieved distinction in various fields, and bore testimony to the patience and kindliness of his teaching, as well as to the extent of his scholarship. Literature, natural history, physics and philosophy were his specialities; subjects in which Thomas was to sustain a lifelong interest.

In later years Thomas was to remember his brief stay in Switzerland as the one really happy period of his life, and it seems some of the credit for this must go to the gentle Swiss pastor whose body was so weak and mis-shapen, and whose mind was so deep and generous.[23] Thomas had found a momentary haven from an unsure and potentially hostile world. Among the lakes and mountains of this beautiful country, he could turn to nature and books for comfort. One work in particular seemed to epitomise all that had assailed his wounded sensibility.

Years later, when Thomas Pitt came to make his will, he was to request that his body be buried on an island on the Swiss lake of Bienne, beneath one of three prominent trees. It was 'at the foot of this tree he formerly passed many hours in solitude contemplating the mutability of human affairs'.[24] It can scarcely be a coincidence that this spot had also been the favourite refuge of Jean-Jacques Rousseau. To romantic and rebellious youth in the late eighteenth century, Rousseau's writings and life expressed the vernal stirrings of generous and violent emotion that were soon to burst the sage bonds of the Age of Reason.

Pilgrimages to the sylvan spots where the author had depicted his own or his characters' passionate outpourings were frequent amongst the young at that time. It might have been Edward Gibbon, whom the Camelfords visited at Lausanne in 1788, who introduced the boy to the philosopher's writings. Gibbon, despite differences, admired and pitied Rousseau and himself knew the Lac de Bienne. In any case, Lord Camel-ford himself is recorded as having visited Rousseau's island in 1786, and from subsequent events it seems likely his eleven-year-old son had accompanied him.[25]

Ten years previously Rousseau had completed his *Rêveries du promeneur solitaire*. The opening paragraphs summed up at a glance the predicament of Thomas Pitt:

Here I am, alone upon the earth, having no more brother, neighbour, friend or company than myself. The most sociable and affectionate of men has been banished by unanimous agreement ... Detached, I know not how, from the natural order of things, I find myself thrust into an incomprehensible chaos, where I can grasp nothing and the more I think of my present situation, the less I can understand where I stand.

Like Thomas, Rousseau suffered from a persecution mania that many ascribed to insanity. No one appreciated his honesty, his desire to please, his inner goodness. All watched eagerly for a chance to strike a treacherous blow.

Oh, how could I have foreseen the destiny awaiting me? ... Could I in my right senses have supposed that one day I, the same man I had always been, the same that I am now, would pass for and be held, without the slightest doubt, a monster, a poisoner, an assassin; that I would become the horror of the human race, the plaything of the rabble; that the only greeting accorded me by passers-by would be to spit on me; that a whole generation would unite in amusing itself by burying me alive?[26]

Thus Rousseau lamented his turbulent past; Thomas Pitt was to experience exactly parallel miseries, and already his excessive sensitivity made such sentiments strike home. He too was alone on the earth, like a man on a strange planet. At Boconnoc he had been left among the beech-woods and sea-fogs, his parents and sister far from home. Now he was abandoned amid strangers in an alien land. Like Rousseau, he felt himself an innocent being, subjected to unjustified punishment.[27] To a sensitive and intelligent child, absence of love is not a passive state of suffering, but a conviction of being actively rejected, shunned, hated.

Rousseau's book had an effect on Thomas Pitt that lasted all his life. The sufferings of the great philosopher were so close to his own, and the measures he took to allay them so congenial and apt, that he never forgot them. The Lac de Bienne, moreover, was only a couple of hours' walking distance from Monsieur de Meuron's school at Neuchâtel. There, on the Île de St Pierre, like Rousseau he found for the only time in his troubled life real peace of mind. On a ridge was a pretty pavilion, where peasants from villages on the lakeside gathered on Sundays to dance during the *vendange.*[28] Nearby grew the three trees, beneath one of which the boy would sit to ponder on what life had in store for him.

This Swiss interlude seems to have come to an end about the spring of 1789. Thomas's father intended him to receive a more regular education at an English public school. In July he arrived at Charterhouse. Nine days later he had run away, never to return.[29] Why is not known, but the harsh discipline of the place would certainly have repelled him. Thirty-five years later the school authorities' cruelty was notorious (Thackeray was to term it 'Slaughterhouse'), and it is unlikely to have been much better in the earlier period.[30]

Dislike of the school's restrictive discipline may not have been the only consideration. Eight years previously, when only six, Thomas had been taken from Boconnoc on a visit to Plymouth. This excursion took place 'at a time when naval preparations were in full activity', and the sight of many stately men-of-war anchored in the Sound aroused the boy's sense of adventure: 'He acquired a passion for the sea so strong and rooted, as not to be overcome by all the efforts of authority or advice.'[31] The fleet he saw was probably that fitting out for the relief of Gibraltar; by chance it included the great 74-gun *London*, on which Thomas was to serve fifteen years later.[32]

It was presumably as a result of his pressing entreaties that Thomas had been, on 25 September 1781, enrolled as 'Captain's Servant' on board H.M.S. *Tobago*.[33] His 'service' lasted two months, but it must not be imagined that the little boy actually set foot on board the ship, which was at that time moored in Port Royal Harbour, Jamaica.[34] It was then common practice to enter boys in this way on to a ship's muster, in order to shorten the six years' service necessary to qualify for a commission;[35] and Thomas did eventually include this two months' 'service' when submitting his qualifications for promotion to lieutenant. But the brevity of his enrolment seems to suggest some other motive. Possibly his father, who seems at first to have opposed his naval aspirations, had the boy registered for a few weeks to still his eager demands to be allowed to go away to sea.[36]

Now Thomas Pitt was more eager than ever to enter the service. Desire for glory and public recognition based on personal achievement was his most marked characteristic, and no career offered a better opportunity than the Royal Navy. His cousin, Sidney Smith, had adopted the same career when even younger, had fought with gallantry against the

French in the American War, and was already a post-captain.[37] Faced with his son's absolute refusal to return to Charterhouse, Lord Camelford acceded to his request to be allowed to go to sea. On 9 September of the same year (1789) he went on board the *Guardian* sloop, armed en flute (partly armed), at Spithead.[38]

Three days later the ship sailed westwards down the Channel. It bore a cargo of plants, passengers and convicts destined for the newly established British settlement at Port Jackson, New South Wales. Its commander was Captain Edward Riou, an officer of Christian character and distinguished gallantry, who took a fatherly interest in the welfare of young midshipmen.

To the fourteen-year-old Tom Pitt the voyage must have been one of exhilarating excitement. Past Ushant the ship veered southwards, and on 26 September touched in at Santa Cruz in the Canary Islands to take on board 2,000 gallons of wine for the Australian settlers. Four days later they sailed again, arriving at the Dutch colony of the Cape on 24 November. After again taking on supplies, the *Guardian* plunged onwards into the wintry wastes of the Southern Ocean, in order to take advantage of the westerly winds south of latitude 40 degrees. Five or six thousand miles lay before them, during which time they were unlikely to sight a single sail.

As the ship moved southwards the temperature steadily dropped. Christmas Eve found them floating in a still, icy sea. All day a heavy fog had surrounded them; it now began to disperse fast, revealing a blood-red sun sinking in their wake. But not long after, the mist gathered up and began again to swirl around. It grew thicker and thicker until the sloop became completely enveloped in a dense fog. Then, suddenly, the curtain parted, presenting the crew with a terrifying sight. Immediately ahead loomed a giant wall of ice, twice as high as the *Guardian*'s mainmast. The ship must strike it in a moment, and what made the prospect if possible even more horrific was the appearance of a colossal chasm, into which the sloop was driving like a dinghy into a whale's mouth. The ship juddered from bow to stern as she struck the ice at the very edge of the cave. The situation was appalling. At any moment they might be driven into the dreadful cavern; yet where they lay the danger was if anything more terrifying. A projecting pinnacle of ice hung over them. At any moment it might detach itself and hurtle down through the ship's decks and bottom. The rudder had been torn away, and water pouring through a hole below was gaining fast on the ship's pumps. The darkness of night was fast closing round them.

Riou ordered everything movable to be thrown overboard: guns, anchors, water-butts. The cattle taken on at Cape Town were thrust off the deck, to struggle among a mass of broken spars and fragments of ice. All that night and much of the next morning (Christmas Day) relays of men worked themselves to exhaustion in an unavailing struggle to keep the water from rising. Eventually the Captain realised that all hopes were failing. He ordered the sloop's boats to be made ready, but was agonisingly aware that they could hold only a portion of the crew. Riou calmly resolved to remain on board with those unable to escape.

The preparation of the boats was the signal for panic to break out. Many of the men had already broken into the stores and deliberately drunk themselves into oblivion, believing they were doomed. Drunken mishandling resulted in the swamping of the jolly boat, and only about thirty or forty men were able to embark. They rowed away into the fog, but the cutter returned shortly, its drunken crew demanding a new sail. Immediately twenty terrified men sprang from the *Guardian*'s deck into the sea and attempted to scramble aboard. The fog closed over the suicidal struggle, and the cutter was never seen again.

Only one of the boats survived the abandoning of the ship. The launch, with a handful of men on board, was picked up by a French merchantman and taken into Table Bay on 18 January 1790. They bore with them a farewell letter from Riou; also among those whom they had left on the wreck of the *Guardian* had been Tom Pitt.

Four months later the news reached England. Tom's cousin, Lord Chatham, was First Lord of the Admiralty and it was to him the message was delivered. Lord and Lady Camelford were informed of the tragedy: their only son and heir had been drowned on his first voyage. At Windsor Castle, King George expressed his deepest sympathy.

Then, a bare four days later, there arrived a fresh message. The *Guardian* itself had sailed out of the blue into Table Bay! The truth of this incredible event could not be doubted, for the message came in the form of a letter from Captain Riou himself.

What had happened can be described here only in the briefest outline. As soon as the boats had departed, the Captain had led those remaining in patching up the ship, which they managed to detach from the iceberg and set wallowing precariously on its way. With a smashed stern and

15

a gaping hole beneath the bows, the *Guardian* was awash from end to end below decks. But this had had the effect of sweeping out the ballast; at the same time a number of empty barrels in the hold remained buoyant. With her sails patched with blankets and all pumps working unceasingly, the shattered hulk had blundered precariously through the freezing ocean for two months before putting into Table Bay. The news reached England within a week of the first, false alarm. King George wrote at once to Lord Chatham:

> I never received more real joy than on reading Lord Chatham's note enclosing the letter from Capt Riou with the account of the safe arrival of the Guardian at the Cape of Good Hope; I desire Lord Camelford may be acquainted how sincerely I rejoice the change of his situation.[39]

That night Lord Chatham himself set off post to Boconnoc to bear the joyful tidings to Tom Pitt's parents.[40] Not everyone was content with the boy's conduct, however. Seven years later Captain Riou was to decline signing Thomas's certificate for promotion to lieutenant, 'as during the time he was under my Command his Conduct was such as not to entitle him to it'.[41]

II

❧❧❧❧❧❧❧❧❧❧❧❧❧❧❧❧❧❧❧❧❧❧❧❧❧❧❧❧❧❧

The Caning in Conduit Street

The *Guardian*, with an overjoyed Tom Pitt on board, had staggered into Table Bay on 23 February 1790. It was not until September of the same year that he was enabled to return home, arriving at Harwich in the packet *Prince of Orange*.[1] He had been away for exactly a year. At the age of fifteen he had become a hero in his family's eyes.

His adventures on the *Guardian* had but whetted Tom's appetite for further exploits on the high seas. His parents were probably delighted at the brilliant début he had effected in a profession so suited to his energies and ambitions. With connexions such as theirs, there should be no difficulty in placing the boy on another voyage offering suitable opportunities for him to make his mark in the profession. Lady Camelford wrote to her husband's cousin, Lord Buckingham, 'in great anxiety' to see if a place could be found. Buckingham in turn asked his brother William Grenville, then Home Secretary, whether Thomas could be included in an expedition then being fitted out for the north-west coast of America.[2] As Grenville's department was closely concerned with the planned expedition,[3] this presented no difficulty.

Aside from family feeling, the Home Secretary had a more particular reason for being interested in the Camelfords. The previous winter Lord and Lady Camelford had been in Rome, together with their daughter. Anne was then seventeen, and had her portrait painted by Madame Vigée Le Brun, who had fled to Italy from the disturbed atmosphere of revolutionary Paris. She described Anne as 'extremely pretty', and portrayed her as Hebe offering a drink to an eagle. The latter was taken from the life, and terrified the artist by suddenly flying at her.[4] The painting still hangs at Boconnoc, and does indeed represent Tom's Annette as an adorable young lady. William Grenville was thirteen years older, and had known her since childhood. He was grave and wise beyond his years, becoming Home Secretary at the age of thirty, but he now found himself falling fast in love with his charming cousin.

Anne's young brother was accordingly entered on the complement of H.M.S. *Discovery*, a sloop of war preparing to sail for the Pacific. Its captain was George Vancouver, who had sailed in Cook's great voyages of exploration. His instructions were to establish a British presence in the disputed settlement at Nootka Sound and to conduct a thorough survey of the Pacific coast of North America. Nootka Sound had long been the subject of dispute between the British and Spanish governments, but a compromise agreement had at last been concluded, and it only required the appearance of a British ship to complete arrangements on the spot.[5]

In March 1791 the whole Camelford family travelled down to Falmouth to watch Tom embark. The *Discovery* arrived shortly after from Plymouth, and Vancouver wrote:

> I found my Lord Camelford here with his family all very well. They had been waiting a few days with some anxiety for the arrival of the Ship. I have as yet in course been able to see but little of my young Shipmate; however, I cannot avoid observing that I was extremely pleased with his appearance and deportment.[6]

Vancouver's 'young Shipmate' came on board the *Discovery* on 12 March,[7] but the ship did not set sail until 1 April. It was necessary to await the arrival of her companion vessel, the *Chatham*, which appeared at the end of March.[8]

On the *Discovery* Thomas Pitt found he had fourteen companions in the midshipmen's mess.[9] Understandably, some were at first prepared to resent the presence of the heir to Boconnoc. Robert Barrie was a similarly high-spirited boy, known on his previous ship as 'one of our finest Midshipmen'. He had written to his mother a month before that 'our Cpt rejoins us at Falmouth as does Pit a mid. he who was in the *Guardian*. I don't like his character therefore sh'ant court his acquaintance'. This prejudice was, however, soon dispelled, and the two struck up a friendship that was to last a lifetime. They had much in common: Barrie was only a year older, and had like Tom run away from school to join the navy.[10] Another 'mid' in their mess who became a warm admirer of the young nobleman was a Scottish boy of the same age named John Stewart.[11]

For the next three years these were to be Thomas's only friends, and the dark 'cockpit', the midshipmen's quarters, his only home. Thomas Pitt, of course, was by now familiar with the routine of a midshipman's life at sea. From nine a.m. till noon and from two p.m. till four there were lessons for the fifteen 'young gentlemen' with their schoolmaster. If Thomas was one day to achieve his ambition and receive a lieutenant's commission, he must prepare to pass the Admiralty's searching examination. There were

> two separate duties to learn—Seamanship and Navigation. The nautical expressions alone were nearly a language of itself: such (in the former) as bowlings, braces, backstays, bobstays, shrouds, buntlines, clewlines, tacks, sheets, earrings, reef tackles, luff tackles, brails, and many other names too numerous to mention: then again (in the latter) logarithms, sines, tangents, cosines, secants, cosecants, horizontal parallax, semidiameter, meridian altitude. Next came all the heavenly bodies, the planets ...

Then the midshipmen would tumble out of the stuffy gun-room, and emerge on the quarterdeck in their smart blue uniform coats, white breeches and dirks. There they crowded on the leeward side to watch and be instructed in the practical business of managing a man-of-war. Opposite, at a decent distance on the windward side, the portly figure of Captain Vancouver paced the deck, accompanied by one or more of his lieutenants, Zachariah Mudge, Peter Puget and Joseph Baker.[12]

On 1 April the *Discovery* and her consort the *Chatham* set sail. Their first port of call was at Tenerife, in the Canaries. Thomas wrote to his sister Annette, telling her that 'everything is as pleasant on board as it can well be'; in fact, conditions were better than on the *Guardian*.[13] One Sunday a number of men from both ships were given leave to view the sights on shore. All went well until the afternoon, when one of the *Discovery*'s midshipmen came on shore to bring the men back on board. He became involved in a scuffle with some of the *Chatham*'s men; a Spanish sentry who attempted to intervene was disarmed by a British marine. Vancouver and some officers were hastily getting the men into the boats, when the Spanish guard, accompanied by a mob, arrived and without parley attacked the sailors. Immediately a wild brawl broke out, and Vancouver himself was pushed off the quay into the sea. 'The attack then became so general that the H'ble Mr Pit and some others jumped into the sea and swam to the boat to save their lives.' The next day the difference was patched up: the Spanish governor apologised, and four British sailors and a marine were flogged at their commanders' orders.[14]

After this excitement the ships set out on the next long leg of the voyage. They were following the same route as that taken by the *Guardian* two years before. Captain Vancouver's favourable impression of his 'young Shipmate' apparently continued, for on 1 June, when at sea in the South Atlantic, Thomas was promoted to master's mate.[15] This made him a senior member of the midshipmen's mess, and ultimately eligible for promotion to lieutenant.[16] By July he was once again at the Cape, scene of the miraculous arrival of the *Guardian*. On 19 July he wrote cheerfully to his father, saying that he 'was in good Health & Spirits'.[17]

This was the last letter the Camelford family was to receive from Thomas for over two years, for the expedition was now destined for the Pacific Ocean. Civilisation was left behind; in the whole of the North and South Pacific there was at the time only *one* European town of importance: the Spanish port of Valparaíso in Chile. Cook's great voyages, on which Vancouver had sailed earlier, had charted much that was previously unknown, but despite this vast tracts of the watery waste and the coasts bordering it had never been visited by any white man. The two ships were required to be virtually self-sufficient both in supplies and in conducting repairs. After six weeks' stay at the Cape they set sail again, the *Discovery* bearing stores sufficient for a year and a half in her hold. Also on board were quantities of beads and trinkets for trafficking with natives they might encounter.

The two ships ploughed their way across the southern ocean towards Australia. Part of the southern coast was fully surveyed for the first time (a project Vancouver had discussed with William Grenville, who had been raised to the peerage shortly before the expedition set sail). Next they passed round the south of New Zealand, and at the end of December 1791 the two ships anchored in Matavai Bay, on the north side of the tropical isle of Tahiti.

In the after cockpit excitement must have run high among the young midshipmen. As older hands, who had visited the island before with Cook in 1777, could tell, the island possessed a perfect climate, gentle and hospitable inhabitants, beautiful women: it was a veritable Land of the

Lotus-Eaters. Thomas and his friends crowding the ship's side could see white beaches shadowed by tall palms; above wooded slopes beyond, fantastic jagged mountains towered high into the sky, their shapes distorted by volcanic discharges in an earlier era. The air was still and balmy, and all was clear and bright save where a few wisps of cloud trailed from the higher peaks.

As the *Discovery* entered the bay a great flotilla of boats put off from the beaches and came swarming below the sloop's steep sides. Around the great high-prowed war-canoes of the King and chiefs, coming to pay their respects to Cook's successor, flocked myriads of canoes, their cheerful occupants holding up coconuts and brightly coloured articles of bark cloth. To the grinning sailors on deck, waving and shouting back, an infinitely greater attraction was to be glimpsed in the form of the women who had come out with their menfolk to welcome the white strangers. Since Cook's visits, it was known to every sailor in the fleet that there existed this paradise isle, where the women were as free with their favours as they were beautiful.

But these famous delights were not to materialise. Captain Vancouver issued the strictest instructions that no private trade was to be engaged in with the natives until the ship had completed its own renewal of supplies; that no man was to be allowed on shore during the whole of the visit except when on duty; and, above all, that no one was to enter into any communication with the women of the island. These orders Vancouver intended to see obeyed to the letter.

For the sailors there was no choice but to grumble privately and obey; the punishment for disobedience was too ferocious to be disregarded. To the young midshipmen, for the most part the dashing young sons of gentlemen, the restriction must have appeared if anything more galling. The excited anticipation of months was extinguished in a moment. And after Tahiti the *Discovery* was to head for the bleak, rain-lashed coast of north-west America, where some flat-nosed squaw, shivering in animal-skins, was likely to be the only woman for a hundred miles. Not for a year would they return to sunnier climes. To Tom Pitt, tall and well-built beyond his sixteen years, impetuous and romantic, Vancouver's order must have seemed particularly tyrannical.[18]

Chafing at the restriction, Pitt was idling on deck and gazing at the canoes bobbing below. Suddenly his glance was caught by the half-naked figure of a Tahitian girl. Their eyes met; the unspoken message and the lithe, barely covered figure overcame the young midshipman's fear of reprimand. Knowing that to the islanders iron represented wealth, Tom ran to the after cockpit and returned, bearing a piece of bent barrel-hoop that the midshipmen had used to grill their food over a charcoal fire. This he tossed down to the girl; but before they could exchange a word a shout rang out from the quarterdeck.

Captain Vancouver had witnessed the little exchange, and was furious. Thomas Pitt was instantly charged with infringing the captain's instructions ('purloining of His Majesty's Stores') and sentenced accordingly. The ship's officers were assembled to witness punishment. The boy was strapped across a gun and received from the boatswain's mate a flogging of two dozen lashes. After the first dozen, the first lieutenant, Zachariah Mudge, stepped forward and offered to intercede with the captain if Thomas promised not to offend again. In a choking voice the boy refused to be 'begged off' by Mudge, a man who owed much to the patronage of the Camelford family. He then received the remaining lashes and was released, to stagger off almost beside himself with pain, indignity and, as he felt, injustice. A Pitt to suffer such humiliation! The tears ran down his cheeks as he stifled sobs of shame and rage.

It does seem that Vancouver had grossly over-reacted to a trifling incident; to inflict so savage and humiliating a punishment on a boy of Pitt's social rank appears excessive. But it must be said that from Vancouver's point of view, the offence did not seem frivolous. Both he and Cook, on previous visits to Tahiti, had seen over-free relations between their sailors and the friendly Tahitian girls as harmful to discipline and good relations with the natives. And there had been the evidence presented by Captain Bligh at the *Bounty* court-martial, held in October 1790, just before Vancouver's departure from England, that the 'fascinating endearments' of 'the fair inhabitants of Otaheite' had been a prime cause of the mutiny.[19] Furthermore, Vancouver had prohibited the trading of iron in order to keep up the commercial value of the material he had brought to trade for ship's stores.

But as Joseph Whidbey, the ship's master, later pointed out, 'If such a construction as *Purloining* is applicable to the cutting up of an Iron hoop, I am afraid there are few Officers in the Navy that are not guilty of Purloining.'[20] The punishment may have been particularly mortifying and shaming for Thomas Pitt. It is unlikely that he had ever suffered physical chastisement at Boconnoc, and his abrupt flight from Charterhouse two and a half years before may well have resulted from revulsion at the possibility of being flogged.

George Vancouver's voyage was one of the greatest in the history of exploration, and he himself possessed exceptional qualities. His one failing appears to have been a propensity to violent fits of rage. He was a perfectionist, and could become violently angry if he felt those below him were not maintaining the same meticulous approach. His biographer, Admiral Anderson, has suggested that this excitability was aggravated by 'the gradual development of a hyperthyroid condition known as Grave's disease'. Whatever the cause, there are many independently attested accounts of Vancouver's frequent succumbing to ungovernable fits of rage, during which he often awarded punishments disproportionate to the offence provoking him.[21]

He seems to have been particularly ill-disposed towards the midshipmen. Shortly after arriving on board, one of them noted that 'Vancouver is in my opinion a verry good fellow, but verry passionate'.[22] Whidbey alleged that 'I never knew him put a favourable construction on any part of the follies of youth'; Thomas Pitt was a young man overflowing with energy, and in consequence involved in a number of harmless pranks. He was the natural leader and spokesman for his group, and the captain's disapproval now fell heavily on the 'young Shipmate' whom he had once welcomed.

All the midshipmen, however, seem to have hated and feared Vancouver. Robert Barrie vowed later he would not go through another such voyage 'if a Post Captain's commission was to be my reward'.[20] Another boy was so affected by Thomas Pitt's flogging that he told Vancouver that, if he ever did the same to him, he would commit suicide rather than submit to such a disgrace.

For Thomas the situation became intolerable. He spent three years on board the *Discovery*, with rare visits ashore, and then generally only when on duty. Since the major purpose of the voyage was to conduct a full survey of the North American coast from Alaska to California, this involved weary months of tacking up and down bleak, uninhabited headlands and inlets. To Vancouver the achievement was stupendous. A vast tract of the earth's surface was for the first time charted and made known to the civilised world. Countless islands, rivers, and mountains were named after Vancouver's fellow officers, patrons and associates, whilst the most prominent feature of all, the 285-mile-long Vancouver

Island, was named after the great explorer himself. But to the young midshipman, there could have been little to ease the tedium.

There was a fight with Indians, in which Thomas was engaged,[24] and there were heavily circumscribed visits to Spanish settlements in California and Mexico. But at Tahiti and Hawaii, where the two ships made prolonged stops, midshipmen were only allowed on shore in the company of officers.[25] These restricted visits were the only respite from three years spent on board the cramped living space of a vessel just thirty-three yards long and occupied by a hundred men.[26] Even the midshipmen's evening recreation was interfered with. Following one of his periodic outbursts Vancouver had ordered the canvas screen shielding their berth to be pulled down. This left them with no refuge from the jostling crowd of seamen on the same deck.[27]

Thomas Pitt had never really known a father or a family. Now, in the great empty spaces of the Pacific, he was completely cut off from home. General news took at least a year to filter from Europe to the other side of the globe.[28] Early in the autumn of 1792, Vancouver despatched First Lieutenant Zachary Mudge home with a report on the settlement of affairs at Nootka Sound. No reply was received to this, or presumably any other letters sent at the same time, for over two years – by which time Thomas had left the *Discovery*.[29]

Thomas's father had always been a remote, otiose figure; he had now faded from the son's life for ever. Thus Thomas may have looked upon Vancouver in some degree as a surrogate father – which made the captain's persecutions appear doubly wounding. He developed a conviction that Vancouver was actuated by personal malice, a belief shared by others on board.

Thomas was flogged twice more during the voyage. The second occasion arose from his breaking the glass of the binnacle compass when 'romping with another of the Midshipmen'; what caused the third is not known for certain, but it appears to have been some equally trifling incident. There was a further case of 'purloining', when he gave a pair of pistols to the ship's armourer in exchange for some scraps of copper. The pistols were thrown overboard, the armourer severely punished (presumably flogged), and Pitt publicly upbraided.

One night Thomas was conducting the forecastle watch with one of the mates. He lay down on his greatcoat for a while. After a time there was a shout for him from the quarterdeck. He did not hear and had to be called for a second time. This resulted in Vancouver's declaring he had been asleep: a charge both he and the mate denied vigorously. Vancouver ignored these protestations and, without further examination ordered him to be placed in irons. For nearly a fortnight he was chained up among the common sailors, and then summarily freed.[30]

The punishments young Pitt had received at Vancouver's hands were not in themselves exceptional. Midshipmen on Cuthbert Collingwood's ship, the *Mediator*, suffered very similar chastisement at about the same time. But Collingwood's discipline was remembered as firm and fair by one of the 'young gentlemen' who so suffered, and recalled his treatment with gratitude ('in so doing Captain Collingwood did his duty by me ... ').[31] But Vancouver appears to have been neither disinterested nor just, and other midshipmen besides Pitt (Barrie and Stewart) never forgot what they suffered at his hands.

Vancouver wrote home that 'the conduct of Mr. T. Pit has been too bad for me to represent in any one respect',[32] and on 1 June 1793 Thomas lost the rank of master's mate bestowed on him two years previously.[33] He had already written to a family friend in Cornwall, complaining of ill-treatment by Mudge and Vancouver, and expressing a longing to return home.[34] Finally Vancouver himself discharged Thomas from the *Discovery*. They were at Hawaii, fitting out for a return visit to the Alaskan coast, when on 7 February 1794 Midshipman Pitt was placed on board the supply ship *Daedalus* for return to England.[35]

The *Daedalus* sailed on the first leg of her journey to Port Jackson in Australia. There Thomas learned the astonishing news that he was no longer Midshipman Pitt, but the Right Honourable Lord Camelford, Baron of Boconnoc.[36] His father had been dead for well over a year without his son being aware of the fact. He had died on 19 January 1793 at Florence, where he had gone with Lady Camelford in a vain attempt to recover his health.[37] His body was brought back by sea and buried at Boconnoc.[38]

Thomas was now the owner of vast estates in Cornwall and Dorset, and heir to an income in excess of £20,000 a year. He was shortly to become a hereditary legislator of the parliament that ruled that enormous empire of which Port Jackson was the most remote outpost. The gilded glories of the House of Lords, of Boconnoc, of Camelford House must have appeared almost an unreal dream to the tall, sunburned young man in his faded, salt-stained uniform.[39] In England scores of servants were awaiting his arrival to fulfil his every wish; great houses, filled with price-less furniture and plate, would be his homes, to which he would travel in his own carriages. Yet here he stood, among the little wooden houses of Port Jackson, alone but for files of convicts trudging by under guard, watched impassively by aborigines squatting in the dust.

However, young Tom Pitt seems to have set little or no value on his new-found wealth and position. Some years later he was to confess that ambition was the spur of his life; ambition to achieve success independent of inherited rank and wealth. To be Lord Camelford was to rise as high as any man could reasonably hope. But Tom's father had achieved that for himself; Tom wished to surpass his father and compel the world to witness his personal qualities. Only then could he achieve recognition that would overcome the indifference, envy and hostility with which he fancied the world regarded him. He would make a further attempt to rise in the navy, this time unfrustrated by Vancouver's rancorous spite.

Besides, what was there to return to? His father was dead, and his darling sister Annette had left the family. On 18 July 1792 she had married her cousin, Lord Grenville, who had become Foreign Secretary in Pitt's government.[40] The next day Tom's father had written to inform him,[41] but it is questionable whether the letter ever reached its destination. Tom may not have learned the news until he heard of his father's death.

Lord Grenville had learned of the new Lord Camelford's quarrel with Vancouver.[42] He was anxious to see the new peer in England, where he could attend to his social and political duties. Imagining that Camelford was still on board the *Discovery*, he arranged with Lord Chatham for Lieutenant Mudge to return to the ship and accompany Lord Camelford home.[43] At the same time, he wrote in his official capacity of Foreign Secretary to the King of Spain's minister, Godoy, requesting that Lord Camelford and his suite be permitted to travel overland across Mexico.[44]

The young peer, however, had plans of his own. He was determined not to return to England without having proved himself worthy of promotion. Vancouver's reports would undoubtedly endanger his future prospects unless he could demonstrate by successful service else-where that he was not as black as he was being painted.

He resolved to cross the sea to Madras in India, where his great-great-grandfather had ruled as governor a century before. There he hoped to gain a berth on a man-of-war of the British fleet operating against the French in the Bay of Bengal. For eight months now he disappears from view. How he made his way across the great archipelago that stretches from Sumatra to New Guinea is not known. It was not until November that he found himself on board a merchant ship sailing from China to India. Passing through the straits dividing Sumatra from the Malay peninsula, the ship put in at the Dutch port of Malacca.

Below the impassive walls of the fortress, Dutch, Portuguese and British vessels rode alongside Chinese junks and Malay *proas*. And there among them lay at anchor a sight that set Thomas's heart beating faster: a Royal Navy frigate, the *Resistance*, of 44 guns. It was not long before he was able to strike up acquaintance with the ship's commander, possibly in one of the snug inns that looked down on the roads.[45] Captain Edward Pakenham proved to be the reverse of everything Vancouver had been. He at once took a liking to the young nobleman who had appeared so improbably in this remote spot, and on 8 December 1794 Lord Camelford found himself once again treading the deck of a King's ship. Three weeks later he was, to his inexpressible delight, promoted to acting lieutenant. What if Vancouver or his father could see him now, pacing the quarter-deck with the gentlemanly Pakenham!

He wrote to his mother to tell her the wonderful news, enthusing over 'the many marks of friendship and civility I have received'. Five months later his happiness was just as intense; a letter to his mother consisted of the single sentence: 'I am alive and well as usual, and bound upon a cruise the Lord knows where.'

Captain Pakenham continued to be equally delighted with his young protégé. He wrote to the Admiralty in January 1795, pointing out that Camelford would qualify in eight months' time to have his acting rank confirmed, and stressing that he 'is a most promising Officer, every way qualified for Promotion, and bids fair to prove a credit to the service'.

This was followed by a letter to Lord Grenville, who was informed that his brother-in-law would 'be an Ornament to his profession, and too honorable an Acquisition for the service to lose'. Pakenham respectfully urged Grenville to exert his influence to ensure that Camelford received his lieutenant's commission in due course. The boy was working very hard to pass the necessary examinations; above all 'his early attachment to a sea life has not been shaken by the most calamitous circumstance; nor by the estrangement from civilization'. Promotion meant more to him than most, and there was a danger that 'he may sacrifice more to disappointment than hardship'.

Pakenham wrote in similarly generous terms to Thomas's mother, assuring her that, 'after an absence of 4 or 5 Years, your Ladyship can hardly conceive his stature and form'. He had left home a sixteen-year-old schoolboy, and was now a handsome young man of twenty, sunburned, powerfully built and comfortably over six feet tall. He blossomed under the tutelage of his humane commander, and when the eight months had passed was confirmed by Admiral Rainier in the rank of lieutenant.

Lord Camelford served for nearly a year in the *Resistance*, and only left the ship because, as Pakenham generously stressed to him, there were no further opportunities for advancement in the squadron serving in the Indian Ocean. Prize-money—normally a prime consideration for a serving sailor, and of which the *Resistance* was receiving more than the average share[46] – was a small consideration to a young man of Camelford's wealth and ambition. On 24 November 1795, the two friends bade each other farewell. Third Lieutenant Lord Camelford had more than regained his lost credit in the service; he had displayed consistent devotion to duty, and had behaved with courage and distinction at the seizure of Malacca from the Dutch. Pakenham had 'not a doubt of his proving a Character of great promise in his Profession', and Thomas could be pardoned for feeling that at long last his childhood dreams on the Île de St Pierre were on the point of being realised.[47]

Lord Camelford left the *Resistance* at Malacca, where he had first encountered her. He travelled up the coast of Malaya to Prince of Wales Island, today known as Penang. There he bought a 'country ship', the *Union*, which he manned with a crew of twenty, drawn from the multifarious races plying the Andaman Sea. His intention was to sail to Bombay, and ultimately to reach the Mediterranean and home by way of the Red Sea and Egyptian desert. He was joined by two other navy men, a Lieutenant Thomson and Admiral Rainier's young chaplain, the Rev. Mr Owen.

The *Union* sailed across the Bay of Bengal in December, but it soon became apparent that Lord Camelford had made a very bad purchase. The ship's timbers were warped and old and she sprang a series of leaks. All hands worked night and day pumping and bailing until they were ready to collapse with exhaustion. By dint of extraordinary efforts they continued until they sighted a distant shore. The hold was filling fast and night came on. It was clear the ship was breaking up, and Lord Camelford gave hasty instructions for all to take to the boats. There was

28

no time to collect even the smallest possessions (Lord Camelford lost all his certificates of service and his precious commission), and the boats had only just won clear when the poor *Union* began to crack, and sink below the waves. The little party rowed ashore; it was midnight, and until morning they could do nothing but huddle together and wonder where on earth they were.

Next day they set off along the coast, and learned eventually that they had lighted on the island of Ceylon. Guided by natives, they made their way to Trincomalee. The town had recently been captured by British troops, its Dutch garrison being compelled to surrender. There Camelford and his comrades were able to replace their lost clothes and luggage and prepare for the next stage of their journey. He was in no way daunted by the danger they had barely escaped; he planned to sail as soon as possible to Madras, where he hoped to find a ship.

There was no ship to be had at Trincomalee, so the adventurous Chaplain Owen volunteered to press on through the jungle to the port of Jafna, at the northernmost tip of the island. Bidding farewell to his companions, he set off, accompanied by two natives. He had travelled some way when, passing through a great tract of paddy-fields near the sea, he came upon a middle-aged Scotchman, who was seated upon a chest and combing his hair. The two men shook hands politely and introduced themselves. Native servants spread out a meal, and the Rev. Owen and the stranger sat down to dine.

The Scot turned out to be a remarkable character. His name was Hugh Cleghorn; he was a native of Fife and had been for twenty years Professor of Civil History in the University of St Andrews. He was in the habit, however, of disappearing for prolonged periods, and in 1793 he had been in consequence obliged to resign his chair. There was a good reason for his absences, but not one he could declare to his fellow professors. He was in his spare time a secret agent, acting for the British government on important missions. He was at this very moment completing the greatest of all his exploits.

During visits to Switzerland he had come to know well a certain Count Charles de Meuron, a native of the city of Neuchâtel, and relative of Thomas's old schoolmaster. Count de Meuron was colonel of a regiment of Swiss mercenaries serving the Dutch government. In the winter of 1794–5, the French had conquered Holland, expelled the Prince of Orange, and set up a revolutionary puppet state known as the

Batavian Republic. Britain, being already at war with France, was in consequence at war with the new Dutch regime, a war that extended to Holland's colonial empire in the East.

The Dutch island of Ceylon occupied a crucially strategic position, potentially menacing British possessions in the Carnatic. It was resolved to capture the island; but the Dutch forts and towns were well garrisoned, and the forces at the disposal of the British East India Company scanty. It was then that Professor Cleghorn laid his scheme before Secretary of State Henry Dundas. Though the elderly Count de Meuron still resided at Neuchâtel, his regiment was now serving, under the command of his brother, as part of the garrison of the principal city of Ceylon, Colombo.

Cleghorn proposed to travel in disguise to Switzerland, persuade Count de Meuron to join the British, and then both men would travel in disguise to Ceylon, where the Colonel would persuade his regiment to change sides. Dundas accepted the imaginative plan with alacrity, and placed extensive funds at Cleghorn's disposal. All went as the professor had planned. Count de Meuron consented, and the two set off on their perilous journey. The adventures they underwent form another story; suffice it to say that all went well. A message from Count de Meuron to his brother was smuggled inside a Dutch cheese into Colombo, the de Meuron regiment marched out of the city, and the Dutch governor was shortly afterwards obliged to capitulate. Ceylon remained henceforward a British possession.

His mission accomplished, the spy-professor was preparing to return home, and proposed to Owen that his party accompany him. The clergyman at once agreed (Lord Camelford, he explained, was 'zealous to try what possible hardships may be encountered between India and Europe'), and a month later, on 22 February 1796, Cleghorn, Camelford, Owen and a Lieutenant John Davies, R.N. (who carried official despatches announcing the reduction of Colombo), sailed from Madras in the Company frigate *Swift*. They crossed the Arabian Ocean and sailed up the Red Sea in a 'tedious but uneventful' voyage, not arriving at Suez until 15 April. Lord Camelford, who was anxious to explore the deserts, had wished to disembark at Jeddah or Kosseir and travel to Cairo overland, but there was no opportunity to land. After some delay at Suez, the little party crossed the desert on camels to Alexandria. There they separated, Professor Cleghorn sailing in a neutral vessel to Malta, and so home to England with the news of his successful coup in Ceylon.[48]

Meanwhile Lord Camelford sailed to Zante, island haunt of pirates infesting the eastern Mediterranean, where on 30 May he chartered a boat for Venice. At Cattaro on the Dalmatian coast the Venetian authorities confined him and his companions in quarantine for forty days, on account of the plague that had been raging in Alexandria at their departure. After their release, Lieutenant Davies pressed on to London with his despatches, and there he was able to provide Lady Camelford with the first full news of her son since his departure from Boconnoc over five years earlier.[49]

It was in the quarantine at Cattaro that Lord Camelford found time to take stock of his situation. For over two years two related passions had burned unflagging within him: he must achieve promotion, and he must be revenged on Vancouver. It was to achieve these ends that he had crossed half the globe. Two letters were despatched to England. The first was to his mother, telling her to expect him in England by August. Explaining that he had already received his lieutenant's commission, he implored her, 'For God sake make haste to get me the Rank of Post Captain that I may not throw away any more time ... all depends upon the present moment.'

The second letter was addressed to Captain Vancouver. In burning phrases, he invited Vancouver – already back in England – to meet him, in order that he might obtain satisfaction for the injuries he had received on board the *Discovery*. If the captain declined to accept the challenge, then Camelford would see to it that 'the few surviving remnants of your shattered character' would be totally lost. He, Camelford, would be at Hamburg on 5 August with his seconds and would await Vancouver's arrival. In order that the expense of the journey would not provide an excuse for evading the meeting, he enclosed a draft for £200 to defray Vancouver's expenses.

Unfortunately Lord Camelford's impetuosity led to his naming a date for the duel which was, as it turned out, nearly a fortnight before Vancouver himself received the challenge.[50] But rumours of what was coming had been circulating in London since June. As Camelford's guardian and brother-in-law, Lord Grenville found himself reluctantly saddled with the task of preventing a scandal that must injure the whole family.[51]

Vancouver flatly rejected Camelford's suggestion. Directing his letter to Camelford House in London, rather than Hamburg, he replied firmly that Camelford's aggressive conduct when on board the *Discovery* fully justified the treatment he had received. In any case, no officer could be held personally liable for actions taken in his official capacity; if Camelford disagreed, Vancouver was prepared to submit the matter for adjudication to any flag officer in the navy.

By 1 September Lord Camelford was back in England, and an agitated Lord Grenville urged him to call at Dropmore (the Grenvilles' house in Buckinghamshire) to see his sister and himself as soon as possible. It was already too late. The same day a furious Camelford posted down to Vancouver's house at Petersham in Surrey. The captain had retired there after his return home the previous year in order to write an account of the voyage of the *Discovery*. No sooner was the young man shown in than he burst into an impassioned harangue. He demanded personal satisfaction for all he had suffered, refusing to listen to Vancouver's firm reiteration that he could not be held personally responsible for actions he had authorised as an officer. He also repeated his strictures on Camelford's conduct. The young peer could control himself no longer: he told Vancouver that they were now two men face to face – he could not hide behind his uniform – it was the thought of revenge that had kept Camelford alive through so many vicissitudes, and the duel *would* take place one way or another. With these threats he left.

Vancouver, wishing to ensure that the world would regard his refusal as honourable, at once consulted a number of people, including Lord Grenville. The Foreign Secretary fully endorsed Vancouver's action; he declined to hear any account of his brother-in-law's conduct while on the *Discovery*, but grounded his advice entirely 'upon the general principle that a commanding officer ought not to allow himself to be called upon to answer personally for his conduct in command'. Everyone else he consulted expressing a similar opinion, Vancouver wrote to Lord Camelford on 7 September. He repeated his reasons for refusing to fight, and again offered to submit to the judgment of any flag officer.

This letter was delivered the same day by Vancouver's brother Charles. Trembling with rage, Lord Camelford informed Charles Vancouver that, since his brother was continuing to skulk behind this pretext, he (Camelford) would seek him out in a coffee house and insult him publicly. In fact, if Vancouver refused to fight like a gentleman, he 'should meet him, box it out, and try which was the better man'. Next day the persecuted captain received a further note in the young peer's vigorous scrawl:

When a man of honor has the misfortune to be embroiled with a
Poltroon the line of conduct he ought to pursue is too obvious to
occasion him the smallest embarrassment.

It was abundantly clear that the threat would shortly be carried into
effect if nothing was done. Vancouver at once wrote to Lord Grenville,
whose advice had been wise and impartial, despite his close relationship
to Camelford. Vancouver and Grenville met next day. In the face of
Camelford's persistence, Grenville reluctantly agreed that Vancouver had
no choice but to invoke the protection of the law. Grenville wrote to
inform Camelford of this: upon which the young man, touched by his
distinguished brother-in-law's continuing concern for him, replied that
he looked upon 'the whole of the affair to be now concluded, at least
for the present'. This asseveration did not appear altogether conclusive,
and Vancouver duly applied to the courts for protection against assault.
There were legal complications in the case of peers, and on 20 September
counsel recommended that the matter be laid before the Lord Chancellor.

Next morning the two Vancouver brothers crossed Bond Street from
the captain's house at number 142, and began walking up Conduit Street
on their way to the Lord Chancellor's house in Bedford Square. By ill-
chance Lord Camelford was standing on the opposite side of the road,
talking with two companions. He caught sight of his enemy, dashed
across the street and aimed several blows at the captain with his stick.
Charles Vancouver managed to seize Camelford by the throat and struck
him in turn a series of violent blows on the arm and shoulder. Their
assailant turned from the captain and attacked his brother, who was,
however, hauled off by some passers-by. Camelford turned on George
Vancouver again, and belaboured him violently with a series of blows
which the other attempted to ward off with his own stick. His purpose
accomplished, Lord Camelford swore to do the same again to George
Vancouver whenever he met him, and issued a hasty challenge at the
same time to Charles.

The brothers managed at last to break away, and continued on their
way to the Lord Chancellor, Lord Loughborough. That evening Lord
Camelford received a note requesting his attendance next morning at the
Lord Chancellor's private house. At ten o'clock on 22 September Lord
Camelford appeared at Bedford Square, still trembling with agitation and
anger after the previous day's encounter. So wild was his appearance that

33

Lady Loughborough persuaded a friend to remain outside the door to come if necessary to her husband's aid. The Lord Chancellor's tact, however, soon calmed the young man; a few kindly words were generally enough to dissolve his fiercest rage. Loughborough informed the other that he must find two sureties to enter into a recognizance for his keeping the peace. Camelford agreed, and he, Lord Grenville and a friend were held to forfeit a total of £10,000 if any further violence took place.

There the affair might have rested, but for an unfortunate newspaper article that appeared on the Saturday following. Charles Vancouver, stung by a report of the Caning in Conduit Street, inserted a long refutation in the *Morning Chronicle*. This gave great offence to Lord Camelford for a number of reasons. It alluded to Camelford's 'misconduct' when on board the *Discovery* and described his consequent punishment as 'indispensibly necessary'; it also hinted in clear terms that Lord Grenville approved of Vancouver's conduct. Above all, as Camelford pointed out in a note to the Lord Chancellor, such an attack should not have been published now that he, Camelford, had given surety for good behaviour. He requested permission to issue a public defence of his conduct, a measure which Lord Loughborough held to be fully justified in the circumstances.

So far the affair had received only passing notice in the press. Over the next few weeks a series of accounts and malicious squibs, clearly inspired by Lord Camelford's friends, began to appear in the newspapers. There were suggestions that Vancouver, following his chastisement, should change his name to *Rear-cover*. Worse puns were to follow with telling effect; for example, in the *True Briton* on 24 and 26 October 1796:

'Captain VANCOUVER says that Lord CAMELFORD cannot *write*. He must, however, acknowledge, that the young Nobleman can *make his mark*.'

'Lord CAMELFORD can boast of a power which rivals that of the First Lord of the Admiralty – He has made Captain COUVER *a yellow rear*.' (This pun was an allusion to the rank of Yellow Admiral: the next promotion to which Vancouver might aspire.)

On 1 October a grinning crowd was drawn to Mrs Humphrey's famous print-shop, situated by an unfortunate chance opposite Captain Vancouver's house in Bond Street. Prominent in the window display was a sketch depicting 'The CANEING in Conduit Street', sarcastically dedicated 'to the Flag Officers of the British Navy'. James Gillray, the immensely popular caricaturist, had drawn a portly Vancouver, gesticulating with fear before Lord Camelford's attack. The captain is ludicrously dressed in a feathered ceremonial cape, given him by the King of Hawaii as a present for King George, and here inscribed 'forgot to be delivered'. On the ground nearby lies a heap of shackles labelled 'For the NAVY', while from Vancouver's pocket protrudes a long document detailing his misdeeds when in command of the *Discovery*. He shrieks fearfully for the Lord Chancellor's protection, while his brother Charles vainly endeavours to hold back the indignant young peer.

Gillray's ludicrous representation was the talk of London. In Portsmouth gales of laughter echoed round the wardrooms of men-of-war. George Vancouver requested Lord Grenville's approval for a defence of his actions he proposed publishing in the *Morning Herald*. His Lordship declined to offer any support, and Vancouver was obliged to abandon the project. He believed an official public enquiry would vindicate his conduct, but none was forthcoming. Within two years he was dead, possibly of the hyperthyroid condition that had troubled him for years. Like Lord Camelford, ironically, he believed himself to the last to have been a deeply injured man.[52]

It may appear that Lord Camelford had had the best of this tempestuous encounter, but that was certainly not his view. It is true that many naval officers familiar with the case felt that he had indeed been ill-used by Vancouver: Captain Pakenham, Thomas Manby (late master of the *Discovery*'s consort, the *Chatham*), and Joseph Whidbey (late master of the *Discovery*) all testified to what they regarded as Camelford's exemplary record in the service.[53] His old mess-mate Robert Barrie, with whom he had had a difference before their last parting at Hawaii, wrote to his mother, telling her of Vancouver's

> cruel treatment of Lord C. indeed he was very ill us'd by Capt. V. and *some* of his officers, and only served Vancouver as I should have served him ... Tho: I am not on terms with Lord C. I well know him to have a good heart and his true character is very different to that the world gives him he has only one fault and that a very common one he is a wild young man and tho: he sometimes might act imprudently his conduct never merited the ignominious punishment he receiv'd.[54]

It was true, too, that his mother felt equal sympathy for Thomas's sufferings under 'the unexampled species of tyranny and cruel oppression, exercised during several years by my son's wretched commander'.[55]

D

However, Lord Grenville had declined to discuss his ordeal on board the *Discovery*.[56] True, he had provided advice and assistance of great value; but throughout he made it clear he considered this sort of public squabble undignified and harmful to all concerned. In short, Camelford had not accomplished the vengeance he had sworn to inflict and, as Barrie's letter implied, 'the world' seemed to share Vancouver's hostile opinion of him.

Camelford's other burning desire had been to achieve promotion. It will be recalled that he had been appointed to the post of acting lieutenant, promotion confirmed by the commander of the Indian squadron on 26 October 1795. Arriving in Europe, he begged his mother to ensure that this was confirmed so that he might be made a post-captain without delay. But there had been changes at the Admiralty. The First Lord was no longer his easy-going cousin, Lord Chatham, but the stern and high-minded Lord Spencer. Lord Grenville, following Pakenham's enthusiastic reports, had approached Spencer already. On 11 January 1796, however, he had received a depressing reply. Lord Spencer had heard from Admiral Rainier in the Bay of Bengal of Camelford's appointment as acting lieutenant, 'but unfortunately on an irregular Vacancy, which will make it impossible for us to confirm it ... without breaking an invariable Rule of the Service'. True, he could still receive a fresh commission, but there would be 'the necessary Examination', which would cause regrettable but unavoidable delay.[57]

So Lord Camelford had arrived in England to find himself, not a post-captain, but a mere midshipman again, posted to the sloop *Tisiphone*. This appointment lasted only a fortnight, however, and he may well never have set foot on board the vessel, which was moored off Deptford Yard at the time.[58]

The day after the celebrated Caning in Conduit Street, Lord Camelford was reassigned to the 74-gun *London* at Portsmouth. At the great naval base he met several old friends from the *Discovery*. Joseph Whidbey had been awaiting his arrival eagerly. With two other former *Discovery* men he had been on ill terms, but now they were reconciled. Camelford came on board registered as a midshipman, and it must have been galling to find his old shipmate Robert Barrie now a lieutenant. But on 3 November Barrie could report that 'the disagreement between Lord Camelford and myself is *settled*, and we are as good friends as ever'.

Lieutenant Thomas Manby had been associated in Camelford's mind with the tyrannical oppression of Vancouver. But this difference, too, was resolved. To Lord Grenville Manby wrote with satisfaction: 'By chance I met Lord C. some Weeks since, on board HMS. London. a long conversation ensued and concluded by his offering me his hand. Hands met, & friendship is restored.'

But all was far from well. 'Before we parted, Lord Camelford opened his mind to me. With real sorrow, I left him much depressed by his situation, the displeasure of his Friends, talk of the Public and loss of Promotion Are now preying on his Spirits with every appearance of heartfelt misery.'[59]

III

Blood on the Quayside

Lord Camelford was entered on to the roll of the *London* on 22 September 1796, but it was not until a month later that he came on board. The ship was cruising in the Channel, and Thomas managed to obtain a passage on a frigate joining the squadron.[1] A week later he wrote to his sister Anne, bubbling over with enthusiasm:

> I send you a few lines to thank you for the kind congratulations I know you would offer me where I present upon the event of a Spanish war. we have just learnt it [Spain declared war on Britain on 5 October] and are all in high spirits on the occasion: promotion prize money, fame and the Devil knows what is flying about at a glorious rate and the only officer in the ship I believe who does not expect to reap by it is myself but I will not wish myself into the Blue Devils, we have got a new Admiral. Colpoys came a few days ago to supersede Admiral Thomson ... Admiral Colpoys has not behaved with any great attention to me ...

The *London* was Sir John Colpoys's flagship. Fortunately Lord Camelford's first impression of the new commander was swiftly revised:

> I have not spoken enough in favour of Admiral Colpoys; indeed too much cannot be said of him he is a most worthy good man. He detained me the other day as I was going to leave his Cabin and told me if there was at any time any part of my situation which I could wish alter'd he hoped I would mention it to him ...

The liking was mutual, and Lord Grenville was gratified to learn of the admiral's high regard for his brother-in-law.[2]

38

Lord Camelford's desire for promotion was now more avid than ever. He was obsessed with the idea that his advancement was being deliberately frustrated: firstly by Vancouver's ill reports of his conduct on board the *Discovery* and, secondly, as a result of scandal following the challenge to his former oppressor. On 26 October he was appointed acting lieutenant on board the *London*, but this was after all the position he believed he had gained exactly a year previously on board the *Resistance*. In January 1797 his mother wrote to Lord Grenville that her son was now more composed, and justified his impatience: 'There can be no stronger proof of his un-abated attachment to his profession than the extreme degree of des-pondency with which his mind was overwhelmed when he thought himself thrown out ... '

Still, under Admiral Colpoys's favourable regard there now seemed to be hope of fair treatment. In February Robert Barrie noted: 'One of my old messmates in the *Discovery* was made a captain the other day his name is Manby. Lord Camelford will pass next month – and then soon get made a captain.' It was not in fact until April that Camelford, having served the necessary six years and passed his examination, was com-missioned as a lieutenant.[3] He had already on 20 February, a day after his twenty-second birthday, taken his seat in the House of Lords.[4] It is a measure of his overriding desire for personal recognition that this occasion of hereditary splendour was as nothing to him in comparison with gaining the first rank of earned promotion. Yet Horatio Nelson had been obliged to fight the battle of the Nile in order to gain the coronet so lightly prized by Lord Camelford.

On 7 December Camelford had written an affectionate note to his friend Barrie, referring to Admiral Colpoys as 'a good fellow', and urging Barrie to keep out of scrapes.[5] The admonition might better have been applied to himself. On Tuesday 14 March 1797 Lord Camelford was up in town. Strolling into Mr Ramsden's, the optician in Piccadilly, he happened to glance through an open door into the back premises. Sitting in the room was Charles Vancouver, the brother of his old enemy! Camelford at once became highly agitated, and began pacing up and down the shop. The wild scene in Conduit Street came flooding back to his mind. But for this fellow, Captain Vancouver might have received the chastisement he merited; moreover he had, in consequence of the blows Charles Vancouver had delivered on that occasion, sent him a challenge to a duel. To this he had received no reply.

39

He strode into the back room and abruptly suggested that they step outside into the street for a moment. Vancouver declined, saying he had pressing business with Mr Ramsden, but would readily listen where they stood to anything His Lordship had to say. Camelford shut the door behind him, and in a voice shaking with rage asked if Vancouver had received a letter from him after the Conduit Street fracas. Vancouver admitted he had received the challenge, but had felt it improper to reply, since 'Your Lordship had pledged your honour to the Lord Chancellor not to take any further steps in the business'. Camelford retorted angrily that he might at least have had the courtesy to reply. His failure to do so could well bear an unfortunate interpretation.

'But the question now is,' Camelford went on, 'will you or will you not provide me with just satisfaction, when the time for which I am bound over to keep the peace expires? You consented to this unequivocally when we met in Conduit Street!'

Vancouver replied that he would not commit himself at present. Anything might happen between now and September, when the year's recognizance should be up; if Lord Camelford were to approach him *then*, he would reply in appropriate fashion.

Baulked, Lord Camelford swore that he would have his revenge by some means or other. 'You gave me a damned hiding in Conduit Street — my arm and shoulder are still black and blue. You and your brother have reduced me to a state of mind which has deprived me of all the enjoyments of life, and nothing short of the satisfaction to which I am entitled as a man of honour and a gentleman can appease or quiet the torture of mind under which I exist!' Vancouver began to justify his conduct, but the nobleman interrupted angrily, accusing Vancouver of abdicating all right to be regarded as a man of honour. 'If you are concerned about the danger,' he went on contemptuously, 'or conceive I have some advantage over you, you may have two shots to my one!'

But Vancouver again declined, giving the same reasons. Lord Camelford, furious, flung open the door and marched out of the shop, swearing as he went that he would be revenged on the pair of them.

Lord Camelford's slur was unjustified. Though Charles Vancouver would make no prior commitment, on 28 September 1797 (the exact day of the expiry of the recognizance) he wrote to Lord Camelford, accepting the challenge if Camelford remained obdurate. Vancouver had been in America in the interval, and wrote his letter from Holland on his return. As a result he was unaware that his adversary was by then in the West Indies. When the letter arrived at Camelford House in London, it was inadvertently opened by Lady Camelford. Greatly alarmed, she sent it at Lord Grenville's suggestion to the Lord Chancellor, imploring him to intervene once again. This time it was Charles Vancouver who was required to provide sureties for his keeping the peace, and the feud between Lord Camelford and the Vancouvers came to rest.[6]

Lord Camelford's posting to the Leeward Islands station had been notified in the spring of 1797. In April he was undergoing a course of medicine, but the physician felt that he was strong enough to complete the treatment while on board.[7] Though he had left the *London* in February, he was still quartered at Portsmouth, and so was witness to the great mutiny of the Channel Fleet at Spithead in April. The sailors resented the fact that the army and militia had received pay increases not extended to the Royal Navy. Astonishingly, the ringleaders were able to concert their preparations unknown to the officers, who were all abruptly deposed and replaced by the leaders of the mutineers.

The Board of Admiralty, headed by Lord Spencer, arrived at Portsmouth on 17 April to negotiate with the ringleaders, who were assembled on board the *Royal Charlotte*. Lord Spencer wished to go on board and attempt by personal intervention to bring the sailors to reason. The rest of the board successfully objected to this bold suggestion. They may well have been influenced by a letter received from Lord Camelford, who on 20 April informed Lord Spencer 'that I have just learnt by mere accident of an intention to detain the Board of Admiralty in case they should venture on board any of the ships now in a state of mutiny'.[8]

The board left Portsmouth next day, recommending that the seamen's demands, which were eminently reasonable, should be met. Unfortunately a delay ensued as a motion for a supply to increase the wages of seamen was put through parliament. During this interval the board issued a tactless disciplinary order, which aroused the sailors' suspicions and caused a renewal of the mutiny on 7 May. On board the *London* Admiral Colpoys took preparatory measures to resist the mutiny by force. A man who continued to resist orders was shot by one of his lieutenants, whose life was only saved from a bloody reprisal by Colpoys's personal intercession. Ultimately the mutiny was pacified by Admiral Lord Howe. The sailors' increase in pay was confirmed, and the government conceded that Colpoys and other officers who had made themselves

41

particularly obnoxious to the men on this occasion should be transferred to other commands.[9]

All this must have made a deep impression on Lord Camelford. True, the mutiny had in the main been orderly, and conducted with restraint and good sense. But there had been the bloody and dangerous episode on his old ship, and all of the participants were personally known to him. He had learned, too, of a more violent undercurrent of feeling existing among certain sailors. Admiral Colpoys, whom he admired, had been successfully ousted from his command under what was something of a cloud. Finally, the relatively pacific mutiny at Spithead was followed by a far more violent one at the Nore, where the sailors' action became tinged with dangerously revolutionary overtones.

Officers at sea for some time after this occasionally glanced down nervously from their quarterdecks on to the men padding the decks below. A ship could be at sea for months or even years. During that time half-a-dozen officers had to keep iron control over scores of men, all trained in arms, powerful and fearless, and mostly drawn from a background of ignorance and violence. Discipline, Lord Camelford perceived, was a dangerously precarious structure. Possibly that thought was the cause of much that happened in the next few months.

The summer of 1797 saw Lord Camelford once again sailing for palm-fringed islands in the tropics, to take up his post at the Leeward Islands station. To his sister Anne he wrote hurriedly on 6 June: 'The signal for weighing is out and we are at last on the wing, when I see you next I hope to have my shoulders kept warm with an Epalet ... ' – an epaulette on the left shoulder denoting the rank of master and commander.[10] On 2 August he joined the *Vengeance*, a 74-gun ship commanded by Captain Thomas Macnamara Russell, senior officer of the squadron based at St Kitts. The task of the squadron was to harry the French trade with their possessions in the Leeward Islands and, where possible, combine with the military in seizing French and Spanish Caribbean islands. Already Trinidad and St Lucia had been captured, and the Leeward Islands station offered tempting prospects for a young officer desiring promotion and prize-money.

Captain Russell was soon won over by Thomas's single-minded determination to excel. Afterwards he was to write that 'I know his Lordship's Head, and Heart, better than most Men; and I Consequently, and of Necessity Love Him as if he were my Son.'[11]

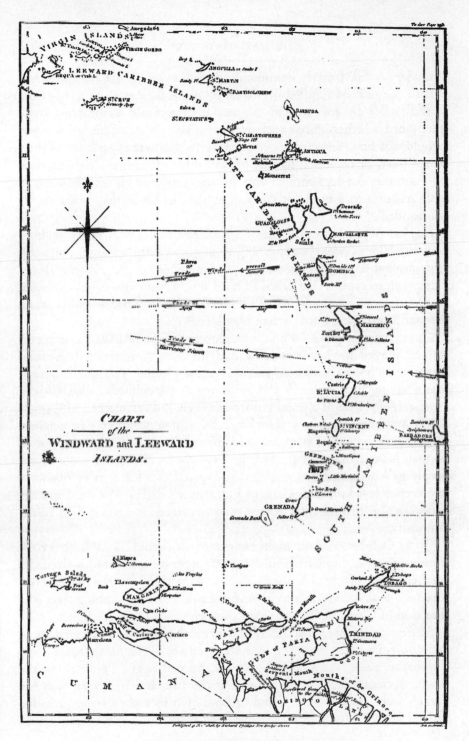

The Windward and Leeward Islands from Sir William Young,
West India Commonplace Book, 1807

Under tactful, fatherly commanders such as Pakenham, Colpoys and Russell, Camelford fulfilled his duties to more than average satisfaction. It seems fair to concur with an early anonymous biographer, who questioned whether officers such as Vancouver, aware of his hot temper, 'would not have reflected more honour to themselves to have slightly passed over, or neglected to take notice of his momentary passion, than by a contrary conduct compel him, in vindication of his own honour, to have recourse to a mode of conduct which, in his cooler moments, he condemned'.[12]

But just when it seemed that Camelford's career was really making progress, things went wrong. It all began, oddly enough, with his appointment as acting master and commander of the *Favorite* sloop. Her previous captain had fallen ill, and on 16 September Rear-Admiral Harvey, commander-in-chief of the fleet at the Leeward Islands station, directed Lord Camelford to take his place.[13]

Camelford was piped on board his ship at St Kitts. At last the moment he had prayed for had come: he had his own command! There was someone on board, however, who was not so pleased. The first lieutenant was a young man of much the same age as Camelford, called Charles Peterson. He came of a good family at Nevis and resented Lord Camelford's appointment, as he was senior to the young peer on the lieutenants' list. He was somewhat arrogant in his manner and inclined to toping; so he may have let something of his feelings appear. If so, this would have deeply galled Camelford, who was convinced that his own commission had been delayed through Captain Vancouver's malice. For the moment, however, the two irascible young men managed to contain their mutal animosity.

On 25 October, at about eight o'clock in the evening, a messenger rode hurriedly to Government House at St Georges on the island of Grenada, southernmost of the Leeward Islands. Governor Charles Green was informed that sounds of heavy gunfire could be heard coming from the direction of Charlotte Town, some thirteen miles away.

At first he assumed that British and French ships were engaged in an action off the coast, but then a fresh report brought news that a large ship had appeared off Charlotte Town and had begun bombarding the town. A coastal battery was returning the fire, and it seemed that the French were attacking the island. About two in the morning, a canoe arrived at St Georges, bearing a message from the commanding officer at Charlotte Town. The nationality of the hostile ship was still unknown, apparently the mysterious vessel had approached the battery at dusk, bearing no lights. She had been hailed from the battery, but without eliciting a reply. A gun was fired to bring her to, and when that was ignored it was followed by another. The ship fired back, the battery fired again, the ship returned a broadside, and then sailed off.

Governor Green was reading this report on the beach at St Georges when a ship was sighted approaching through the darkness. The garrison had already been turned out, and every gun was hastily made ready. Matters were in this alarming state, when a cutter appeared out of the gloom and grounded on the shingle. A British naval officer sprang out, saluted the governor, and presented him with a letter. To Green's astonishment he read that it was a *British* vessel that had caused all the disturbance, a vessel commanded by Lord Camelford.

Green at once sent for the battery commander to find out the cause of this extraordinary affair. But before that officer could arrive, Lord Camelford himself appeared, in a state of high indignation. He declared that the Royal Navy had been insulted by an unprovoked attack on one of His Majesty's ships, and he berated the governor soundly. Green replied with dignity, and Camelford then moderated his attitude towards the representative of civil power.

The governor despatched a full account of these 'extraordinary and unprecedented' proceedings to Admiral Harvey at Martinique. Harvey replied, assuring the governor that he would take measures to ensure that there was no recurrence of such an event, and in particular that Lord Camelford would be strictly instructed to 'avoid approaching the Forts of the Islands in the Night, without shewing a Light, as is always customary, or sending a Boat to make known the Ship to the Commanding Officer of the Fort'. With this Governor Green was satisfied, as no lasting damage had been done. Lord Camelford himself maintained that he 'did not consider it as a regular Fort but as a Shore Battery, perhaps not manned', and that therefore it was not requisite to display colours or lights.[14]

A report from the West Indies at this time represented Lord Camelford as a highly eccentric character, though it is impossible to tell how accurately:

Lord Camelford appears to be a new character in his class. His

45

person is not altogether unlike the late Lord George Gordon, when he was the same age; their whimism is somewhat similar. Lord Camelford provides a table of plenty of good fresh meat every day for the men who are sick in his ship. He is very severe in carrying on duty: seldom ties up a man but he gets six or seven dozen lashes, which is a more severe punishment, in this country, than what's produced by giving the same number in a northern climate. Although his lordship is a master and commander, he does not set an expensive example, by wearing extravagant clothes. He makes use of no swabs [gold shoulder knots], but still appears in a lieutenant's uniform. His dress is, indeed, extremely remarkable: all the hair is shaved off his head, on which he wears a monstrous large gold laced cocked hat, which, by its appearance, one would think had seen service with sir Walter Raleigh. He is dressed in a lieutenant's plain coat, the buttons of which are as green with verdegrease as the ship's bottom; and with this all the rest of his dress corresponds.[15]

Certainly Lord Camelford acted at this time in a violent and eccentric manner more appropriate to the Spanish Main a century earlier. Soon after assuming command of the *Favorite* he found the sloop to be seriously undermanned. There was at that period only one effective method of remedying the deficiency: the press-gang. Camelford decided to slip across to Barbados, where he might hope to take his pick from among the crews of merchantmen at anchor. There would, however, be no chance of success unless he acted with secrecy. The sight of a man-of-war off Bridgetown would send every sailor in the port running for refuge to the deeply wooded ravines of the interior.

On the morning of 6 November the *Favorite* was off the coast of Barbados, beating up to windward of Speightstown. It was still night-time when three of the sloop's boats were cautiously lowered, each with an armed party of sailors on board. With only an occasional splash of oars, they glided stealthily along the coast towards the entrance of Carlisle Bay. In the half-light they passed under a small battery, which had a Union Jack hanging limply from the pole above. Before them lay the port, above which low hills were silhouetted by a faintly brightening sky. On the beach a continuous screen of coconut palms concealed all but the taller buildings of Bridgetown. The only sound was the shrill stridulation of myriads of grasshoppers.

Two merchantmen lay moored snugly at anchor within a cable's length of each other: here there could be fat pickings for the press-gang. There was no time to be lost; it was already half-past five and dawn was breaking with tropical suddenness. The names of the ships could be clearly picked out: the *Harriett* and the *Kitty*. Lieutenant Peterson, who commanded the party, directed two of the *Favorite*'s boats to go alongside the *Kitty*, while Lieutenant Parsons with the remaining boat boarded the *Harriett*.

Lying in his bed in the stern cabin of the *Harriett*, Captain Matthew May was astonished to see the boatload of armed men gliding past. The next moment he heard them scrambling on board at the gangway on the larboard side. He sent the cabin boy to find out what was happening, but a moment later came up himself on deck in his nightshirt. Before him was a body of a dozen sailors, armed with muskets, pistols, cutlasses and boarding pikes. Lieutenant Parsons followed his commander's lead in eccentricity of dress: he was clad in a uniform coat with blue trousers, and no distinguishing mark of rank or service beyond the anchors on his buttons.

'Are you an Englishman or a Frenchman? Have you come to plunder or what?' blurted out Captain May nervously.

'You must know very well who I am,' growled Parsons, 'and if you don't, you soon will.'

He followed by ordering all the *Harriett*'s men to come on deck, and after a while some sleepy-looking hands appeared. Suspicious of the small number, Lieutenant Parsons ordered his men to 'fire into the buggers' still hiding below. The few remaining hastily clambered from their bunks and ran on deck.

There were ugly expressions on the faces of many of the crew, and Parsons quickly ordered a marine in his party to stand guard over the *Harriett*'s arms chest, where it lay on the deck. At once the men of the *Harriett* sprang into action. Crying out 'damn my eyes, are we all going to be taken?', a seaman named Conolly grabbed a gunner's handspike and knocked the marine on to the deck. There was a flurry of bare feet as his shipmates rushed for the chest and armed themselves. Outnumbered, the boarding party backed to the ship's side. The scene looked very ugly, and Lieutenant Parsons shouted out unconvincingly that it was only volunteers they intended to take.

'The Devil thank you!' bawled Conolly sarcastically, 'but you shan't!'

He and his fellows grabbed four- and six-pound cannon-balls from the shot lockers and hurled them at the retreating press-gang. The boarding party escaped, but the lieutenant was limping from a badly bruised leg. The *Harriett*'s men then imprisoned Captain May in his own cabin (it is hard not to believe with his own connivance), and prepared to defend themselves from any further attack.

Meanwhile the *Kitty* had fallen into the hands of the much larger boarding party commanded by Lieutenant Peterson. The *Kitty*'s captain, Alexander Anderson, had spent the night ashore. On hearing what had happened he came aboard, to be informed by Lord Camelford's officers that the ship was temporarily under the command of the Royal Navy. Parsons and his men, unexpectedly expelled from the *Harriett*, had rowed hastily over to the *Kitty* to report on the failure of their attempt. Lieutenant Peterson became very angry when he heard the news.

Captain Anderson could only watch impotently as the men of the *Favorite* now began charging the ship's guns with grape and canister shot up to the muzzles. Lieutenant Peterson hailed the *Harriett*, threatening to sink any boat the crew attempted to take to the shore. He and Parsons were beside themselves with rage. The *Harriett*'s men had expelled them ignominiously, while on board the *Kitty* were only discharged man-of-war's men and apprentices, categories exempt from pressing. Captain Anderson had taken the precaution of landing the remainder of his crew at Speightstown before coming into Carlisle Bay.

A yell from the *Harriett* informed Peterson that the crew was determined to escape to the shore whatever happened. Shortly afterwards the *Harriett*'s men scrambled into a boat and made for the beach. Peterson ordered the guns of the *Kitty* to fire on the fugitives, but the angle was too low and a hail of shot whizzed harmlessly overhead. Loud jeers arose from the small boat, and the exultant *Harriett* men thrust their backsides towards the *Kitty*, slapping them 'in an insulting manner'. Next moment came a more alarming riposte, as a gun roared from the *Harriett*; the ball smashed through one of the *Kitty*'s gunports and wounded a man.

But there was no more firing, and the *Favorite*'s officers went below with Captain Anderson to have breakfast. Conversation was friendly enough; Anderson and his men had after all made no attempt to obstruct Peterson's force. But when the party emerged on deck, matters flared up dangerously once more. Two of the *Kitty*'s apprentices had disappeared, apparently in the captain's tender, and one of the *Favorite*'s men was also nowhere to be found. Peterson, suspecting that Captain Anderson's men had assisted the desertion, promptly seized ten of the *Kitty*'s seamen, together with two apprentices. In answer to Anderson's protests, he replied curtly that he would return the apprentices if the captain could lay hands on the deserter. Anderson promptly went ashore, found a constable who tracked down the missing seaman, had him lodged in Bridgetown gaol, and reported his success to the lieutenant.

Matters rested thus until the following morning, when, at about nine o'clock, H.M.S. *Favorite* herself sailed into Carlisle Bay. Four boats, crammed with armed sailors, put out from her and moored alongside the *Harriett*. Her captain, Matthew May, had been released from the captivity in which his men had placed him the day before. Lord Camelford himself now headed the boarding party, and demanded to know who was the man who had fired the gun that damaged the *Kitty*. Captain May pointed him out; the unfortunate sailor was rowed away to the *Favorite* and 'returned in the course of three or four Hours, his Back having the appearance of a very severe Flogging, insomuch so, that Captain May who had seen many Men flogged on board Men of War, never saw one worse except where Men were flogged round the Fleet'.

Lord Camelford was clearly in a towering rage at the unexpected failure of his press-gang's attempt the day before. The men of the *Harriett* had outwitted his sailors and were still at large on the island. That afternoon he was standing on the wharf, with Lieutenant Peterson, when Captain Anderson came up to him. In polite but firm tones, Anderson requested the return of the two apprentices whom the *Favorite*'s men had illegally pressed. He pointed out that Peterson had promised to return them if he recaptured the deserter, and that this had been done. As this elicited no response, Anderson declared he would have to apply to Governor Ricketts.

At this Lord Camelford lost control of his temper. He told Captain Anderson to be damned, and apply wherever he chose: he would not get back the apprentices. 'Begone, you scoundrel!' he shouted, and he 'squared his Arms and Elbows to Fight and actually struck Capt. A. a violent Blow upon the left eye and afterwards upon the right ear ... ' When Anderson attempted to resist, he was threatened by Camelford's two lieutenants, who drew their swords in threatening manner. A Captain

Cox coming to Anderson's assistance was railed at as 'a damned suspicious looking rascal' and carried off by the press-gang into their boat.

This violent scene attracted an increasing number of hostile Barbadians, and a cry went up from someone of 'Let us have Captain Cox out of the boat!' A scuffle broke out, the accounts of which vary greatly. The bell of St Michael's Church had begun ringing, and Lord Camelford believed that the inhabitants were mustering to rescue the pressed men. There was an ugly scene: one of Cox's men was shot in the chest by a sailor from the *Favorite*; a moment later Lord Camelford had stabbed the shot man through the body with his sword, and as the dying man turned and fell to the ground, he drove his sword again deep between his buttocks. Another man was badly wounded and knocked off the wharf. Above the medley of yelling, shots and groans pealed the insistent clang of the alarm bell, followed soon after by an ominous roll of drums beating to arms somewhere in the town.

By now it was dark, and Lord Camelford and his party pushed off hastily in their boats. They were none too swift, for shortly afterwards the Barbadian militia came marching to the water's edge. A strong guard remained until the *Favorite*'s departure, prepared to resist any further attempts to press men in the town. Lord Camelford succeeded in seizing half-a-dozen more men from the *Harriett* and then sailed away.

Indignation ran very high in Barbados for several weeks following. On the Saturday following the *Favorite*'s departure the *Barbados Mercury* advertised a sale of goods newly arrived on board the *Kitty* and the *Harriett*. After noting the further sale of 'eight valuable negro and mulatto slaves, as workers, seamstresses, a butler and groom, and a taylor lad about 17 years old', the *Mercury* went on to an editorial, fiercely denouncing 'this unpardonable outrage', and demanding that justice be visited on the perpetrators. A later issue reminded its readers of the fate of Lord Ferrers, hanged in 1760 for the murder of his steward. Steps were taken by indignant relatives of the dead man and other sympathisers to bring a prosecution for murder against the absent commander of the *Favorite*.

In England, when accounts of this episode became known, Camelford's mother and sister, Lord Grenville and other relatives and friends were greatly alarmed. Lord Grenville's solicitors prepared to brief counsel, witnesses were interviewed, and Lord Camelford was advised to insist – if it came to such a point – on his legal right of trial by the peers at Westminster. But the affair slowly subsided, and by April of the following year the governor of Barbados reported that 'the affair of Lord Camelford seems to be quite forgotten'.

This incident shows Camelford in an ugly light. The violence seems to have been greatly exacerbated by his truculent behaviour and by that of his lieutenants. However, it must be borne in mind that the accounts given above are based on the testimony of Captains May and Anderson and other witnesses strongly hostile to Lord Camelford. Both captains were indeed described by a solicitor acting for Lord Grenville as 'very clever sensible prudent Men', a verdict there is no reason to doubt. But on the crucial point, the killing on the wharf, the attestations of witnesses were wildly at variance. Captain Anderson stated that the dead man was a carpenter named Howard, and that he was first stabbed by Lord Camelford where he stood, and a moment later shot by one of the *Favorite's* seamen. Yet another witness, a sailor named Adamson, referred to the victim as 'John Thomson', said that he saw Thomson flee up a street from the wharf, *where he met Lord Camelford's party coming down towards the wharf*; and that Thomson was shot first and *then* stabbed by Lord Camelford.

This may support Lord Camelford's contention that the death of Thomson (or Howard) was not a coldly inflicted murder, but resulted from the confusion of an increasingly wild mêlée. Lord Camelford told the prize agent at Antigua that he had been obstructed in his attempt to press men at Barbados, 'a scuffle ensued, and a Life was lost'. This is not an entirely satisfactory explanation, but neither is it to be altogether rejected.

It is undeniable that, on this and many other occasions, Lord Camelford proved himself to be excessively overbearing and hot-tempered. He believed that violent action was generally the most efficacious way of checking a mutinous or rebellious affray.[16] But he cannot be held personally responsible for the iniquities of the impressment system, which at all times aroused the fiercest opposition from its potential victims.[17]

At Barbados Lord Camelford was faced with a difficult situation. He had Admiral Harvey's instructions to impress men, and Governor Ricketts's warrant to do so at Barbados. Captain Anderson's concealment of the pressable seamen of the *Kitty* was a legitimate, if frustrating, measure. But the violent resistance of the *Harriett*, extending to assaulting a King's officer and firing on what was at the time a King's ship, amounted to an act of rebellion against the Crown. Under these circumstances any naval officer would have felt himself bound to resort to any

E

measures – however warlike – to achieve his object.[18] The whole community of Bridgetown, understandably enough, favoured those resisting, even to the extent of the militia's marching out to oppose the *Favorite*'s landing-party *before* the news of the death on the wharf became known.[19] It should be noted, finally, 'that two Seamen, named Jno. McQuin and Henry Shea, belonging to His Majesty's Ship Favourite ... had the misfortune to be maimed in impressing Men and in defending the Person of Lord C ... at Barbadoes (where he was assailed by an armed Multitude),' as the surgeon at the Naval Hospital at Martinique reported on 23 June 1798; a circumstance mentioned by none of the hostile witnesses.[20]

Highly indignant at his reception at Barbados, Lord Camelford sailed off in the *Favorite*. Determined to seek out and harass the enemy, he made northwards for the French island of Guadeloupe. In the harbour of Pointe-à-Pitre lay a 40-gun frigate, *La Pensée*. Lord Camelford led his ship's boats into the bay in a cutting-out expedition, which, if successful, would have been one of the most striking in the naval annals of the period. The frigate's armament proved too heavy, however, and the boats were driven off, Lord Camelford being wounded in the thigh. Despite this misfortune, Camelford's raiders were able to bring back with them three privateers, who would prey no longer on British merchant shipping. The *Favorite* sailed first to Martinique, perhaps to deliver the captured ships to Admiral Harvey, and then put about for Antigua, where Camelford went ashore to recover from his wound. He lay in hospital for nearly a fortnight, chafing at the boredom of his enforced confinement. Through the windows came the shouts of sailors and distant singing of slaves working in the sugar plantations. In the evenings he heard sometimes the jaunty music of banjos and tambourines, as the negroes danced away the memory of their harsh day's toil. But what he longed for was a speedy return to active service.

As soon as he could walk, Lord Camelford returned to his ship, which was moored in English Harbour on the south side of the island. He had left Lieutenant Peterson in command, but was furious to find that Peterson had left signals supposed to be secret lying where all who passed might read them. This was the last straw: Camelford had found his subordinate's manner supercilious and insolent to a degree that maddened him. He seized the opportunity offered by Peterson's laxity to require him to leave the ship. Peterson departed and was accepted on board another sloop in the harbour, the 20-gun *Perdrix*, as first lieutenant.

Shortly afterwards Captain Fahie of the *Perdrix* departed on leave to his home on St Kitts, and Peterson took over command of the ship. By ill chance, Fahie's departure was followed on 12 January 1798 by that of H.M.S. *Babet*, the only other ship of war in the harbour. The ill chance lay in the fact that the *Babet*'s captain, Jemmett Mainwaring, had been the senior officer in the port. Now he was gone, the command devolved on to one of the two young men who so cordially detested each other. Mainwaring appears to have presumed that the senior must be Lord Camelford, an acting master and commander, and to have deposited the port orders with him.[21]

That day Camelford was restless and tense. He had had no contact with Peterson for two or three weeks, since Peterson's transfer to the *Perdrix*. Now he would have to issue orders to a man he intensely disliked, and who scarcely troubled to conceal the contempt he felt for the *Favorite*'s commander. How would Peterson, temporarily master of his own ship, accept the position? Would he obey with that cool sneering manner which implied so much, or might he even refuse? But to refuse would be mutiny. Mutiny seemed to be in the air. News had recently reached the Leeward Islands station of the uprising in September on board H.M.S. *Hermione*, whose crew had brutally murdered Captain Pigot with most of his officers, and sailed the ship into a Spanish port.

Indeed, this very day one of the *Favorite*'s seamen had been overheard growling that 'if he was at Spithead he would throw the irons overboard and somebody else along with them'. He had been awarded a technically illegal but not infrequent seven dozen lashes for the threat.[22] Mutiny was an ever-present possibility. However, the strongest potential threat to Camelford's command was not the sullen sailors, but the supercilious Peterson.

For the remainder of that day and night there was no contact between the rival officers. It was soon after breakfast on the next morning that the quiet of the little harbour was broken by the muffled echoes of a gun-shot resounding from the hills around. A wisp of smoke above Fort Shirley on the ridge indicated that an alarm signal had been given. Lord Camelford despatched a petty officer up the hill, who returned with news that ships had been sighted firing out to sea, and that enemy men-of-war might be approaching the coast.

By the time the message arrived, Lord Camelford was on the point of being rowed across the harbour from his quarters in the dockyard to the east quay, where the *Favorite* lay moored. He turned to Lieutenant Parsons, and ordered him to send Acting Lieutenant Milward to Peterson to instruct him to hold the ship's company of the *Perdrix* in readiness to act in concert with the military upon the shortest notice. Camelford was then rowed off in his boat, and Milward, following instructions, went to Peterson's mess in the capstan-house on the wharf. Peterson curtly declined to accept the order, and Milward returned to Lieutenant Parsons.

It was about three o'clock in the afternoon by then, and Parsons decided not to inform Lord Camelford of this rebuff. As nothing more had been heard of the alarm since that morning, he may have hoped that the struggle for precedence between the two headstrong young men might blow over. Some hours later, however, Lord Camelford returned from the *Favorite* and ascended to his mess-room, which was in another capstan-house, separated by a yard from that occupied by the officers and men of the *Perdrix*. Learning that nothing had come of his previous order, he made out a written one. This confirmed the earlier oral command, that Peterson was, with a slight modification, to put into effect the departed Captain Mainwaring's commands regarding a guard to be rowed at the harbour entrance. But clearly the main purpose of this move was to establish which of them commanded the naval forces in English Harbour, and a rider to the order demanded that Peterson should 'acknowledge the receipt of the enclosed letter on service'.

William Granger, master's mate of the *Favorite*, took this letter across to Peterson, who replied scornfully that 'they were very presumptuous in writing to him in that manner'. This was reported to Parsons, who in turn informed Lord Camelford. This was enough; Camelford ordered Peterson's second-in-command, the master of the *Perdrix*, to be told 'he [the master of the *Perdrix*] should confine Lieutenant Peterson to his cabin, and take upon him the temporary command of the ship'. Master's mate Granger was again entrusted with the mission, and was shown up once more to Peterson's mess-room in the capstan-house. He delivered the message to the *Perdrix*'s master, Crawford, who made no answer, but merely looked across to his captain. Peterson directed the message to be taken down in writing, making Granger sign it. He then repeated several times his indignation at Lord Camelford's presumption. Granger returned to the *Favorite*'s capstan-house and reported on the failure of his mission.

Meanwhile, Peterson decided he would take the initiative. About a quarter-past eight he entrusted Crawford with a letter which was a virtual duplicate of the one he had received from Camelford earlier; only this time it was Lord Camelford who was ordered to prepare his men in case of an enemy attack. At the same time, anticipating an attempt by the *Favorite*'s men to arrest him by force, he took some preliminary precautions. The single sentry armed with a cutlass stationed at the door to the mess-room stairs was replaced by two, armed with loaded muskets and fixed bayonets. The armourer was instructed to give every man of the *Perdrix* a musket, bayonet, cartouche-box and cutlass. Drawn up in ranks, they were inspected by Peterson, who checked every musket carefully. He then dismissed them, telling them to keep their arms by them 'ready at a minute's warning'. That done, Peterson returned to his mess-room.

He had correctly divined Lord Camelford's probable reaction to his defiance. The young commander of the *Favorite* regarded Peterson's letter as 'throughout … highly mutinous and refractory (inasmuch as it … set me at defiance, and usurped my authority as senior officer of the port …)' Camelford ordered Parsons to go over to Milward on the *Favorite*; Milward was to be instructed to return with a party of marines and place Peterson under arrest. If he resisted, Peterson was to be taken 'dead or alive' and brought over by boat to the eastern capstan-house. Parsons, who evidently felt strong misgivings about the whole affair, again modified his order; he told Milward indeed to attempt to arrest Peterson, 'but if he [Peterson] made any resistance, not to commit bloodshed, but to apply to Lord C. for further orders'. As Parsons had been serving only the year before on the *Perdrix*, he may well have been disturbed at the prospect of provoking bloody conflict with his old shipmates. He was, in addition, a very sick man, and was obliged not long afterwards to leave the service and return to England.

Milward at once assembled his marines, and was rowed across the harbour to the dockyard. The little party marched to the mess-room door of Peterson's capstan-house, where they encountered the two armed sentinels posted by Peterson earlier. Evening was coming on, and Milward called out to the shadowy figures:

'Who is that?'

'Sentry!' came the reply.

'Can I go up here?'

'No. Not without an order from the commanding officer.'

A boy was despatched upstairs, who returned with the requisite permission.

Leaving his marines below, Milward went up and entered Peterson's mess-room. The lieutenant was sitting at a table, with the master and purser of his ship. According to some accounts, he appeared to be 'in liquor'. But whether that was true or not, he seemed to know what he was about. He listened without interruption to Milward's declaration that he must consider himself under arrest.

'I will not go,' he replied emphatically. He rose to his feet, strode to a table at the far end of the room, and returned with a pair of brass-bound pistols and a drawn sword. He laid the pistols on the mess-table. Milward at once shouted for his marines to come upstairs. A clattering on the steps told him they were coming; as they burst into the room, headed by a sergeant, Lieutenant Peterson roared at Milward to take himself off. As Milward showed no inclination to do so, Peterson thrust at him with the sword. Milward had hastily drawn his own weapon and parried the lunge, crying out to his men at the same time to seize the mutinous lieutenant. It looked for a moment as if a murderous scrimmage would break out in the crowded room. The *Perdrix*'s master, Crawford, snatched up one of the pistols on the mess-table and started shoving Milward's sergeant back towards the door with his free hand.

'Don't shove me!' threatened the sergeant, 'I have my commanding officer here and will cut your head off directly!'

Meanwhile Peterson sprang back, rapped on the wall with the pommel of his sword and shouted through to the next room for his gunner and boatswain to turn out and arm the crew. He then rushed to the window, yelling out to his sailors in the room below and in the yard:

'*Perdrix*'s, *Perdrix*'s, arm yourselves! Mr Maddocks, get the people under arms!' A moment later, and there might have been a savage scene of bloodshed. All at once Milward heard an insistent bellow from the foot of the stairs.

'Mr Milward!'

It was Lord Camelford, who had heard the noise of the *Perdrix*'s men assembling in the yard, and had run down to see what was happening.

'Here, sir!' cried Milward, with some relief.

'Desist, desist!' shouted Camelford. 'Come downstairs!'

Down they trooped, and were ordered to form up in a rank outside. A few yards opposite, the bewildered men of the *Perdrix* were piling out of their quarters, muskets in their hands, but in a state of some confusion. Many thought that the enemy attack, signalled that morning, was about to take place.

Lord Camelford attempted to order them to disperse, but in the confusion no one paid any attention. Realising the futility of any further attempt in this direction, Camelford ran to the quayside and yelled across the narrow neck of water in the harbour to Lieutenant Parsons to hurry the rest of the *Favorite*'s ship's company over at once. Camelford and Milward then walked up and down the wharf. It was past nine o'clock in the evening, dusk was drawing on, and under the shadow of the capstan-house it was difficult to distinguish what was happening in all the bustle. But the crowd of *Perdrix*'s men had increased to thirty or forty, and the position of Camelford, Milward and their half-dozen marines was becoming precarious.

Peterson himself next appeared through the doorway, calling out, '*Perdrix*'s, *Perdrix*'s! Are you all ready?'

'No, sir,' came several shouts. Only about ten men were drawn up in rank, and the rest were still milling about in confusion.

'Load with ball cartridge, and fix bayonets!' came the next command. The swaying throng began to assume a more uniform appearance, and there was a rattle of ramrods in the shadows. Faint pinpoints of light were beginning to glimmer in the sky and from the dark encircling hills. The *Perdrix* lay, a silent silhouette, off the wharf, while cries, shouts and sounds of hasty movement echoed across the water from the *Favorite*. Lanterns were moving on deck and a boat was being lowered from the side.

'Are you ready?' again called out Peterson.

Lord Camelford, glancing across, turned back to Milward at these ominous words.

'Are you armed?' he asked Milward.

'I am, sir.'

'Have you pistols?'

'Yes, sir.'

Camelford ordered Mr Milward to give him one, checking that it was loaded.

He swung round and took a few steps towards the men of the *Perdrix*. 'Where is Mr Peterson?' he demanded.

'Here he is,' came an answering shout.

Not being able to distinguish his rival among the shadowy figures before him, Lord Camelford repeated his question. Peterson was still standing near the entrance to the capstan-house, a drawn sword in his left hand. Placing his hands on his hips, he rose upon his toes and sank back upon his heels, answering contemptuously,

'I am here, sir, damme.'

Lord Camelford walked up close, cocked his pistol, and presented it to Peterson's chest.

'Do you still persist in refusing to obey my orders?' he demanded.

'I do, sir,' came the haughty reply.

That was enough. Camelford squeezed the trigger of his pistol. There followed a muffled report and a stab of flame, and Charles Peterson reeled back, shot through the heart. Lord Camelford sprang back from the corpse, shouting to his marines to support him. Milward, expecting the worst, came forward, proffering his commander a spare cartridge for the pistol. But no answering volley came from the larger body of *Perdrix*'s men. They were at a loss to know what to do next. Several still did not know what they had been summoned for in the first place. Realising this, Lord Camelford came forward, announcing that he had been obliged to shoot Lieutenant Peterson for mutiny, and ordering Crawford, as the *Perdrix*'s master and next in command to dismiss his men. Crawford complied sulkily, and Camelford returned by boat to the *Favorite*.

The next day, Sunday, a coroner's inquest was held, and came to the highly unsatisfactory verdict that the victim's death had come about as the result of a mutiny, '*but on which side* such mutiny did exist, they cannot pretend to say ... ' This was not a matter that could be allowed to blow over like the affray at Barbados. That night there arrived at English Harbour Captain Henry Mitford, of the *Matilda* man-of-war. Two days later he wrote to Admiral Harvey that:

As the circumstances attending this unhappy affair appeared to me of a very extraordinary nature, and related in a most confused stile, I could but consider it my duty, as senior officer on the island, to go over with all despatch, and make myself acquainted with the facts, as related by both men personally, and from the evidences which have been given, the coroner's inquest seem undetermined as to the name to be given to the crime; but in my own dispassionate opinion, formed on many leading proofs, the whole has arisen from a vast deal of bad blood, long existing between the two parties.

Captain Mitford accordingly arrested Lord Camelford, and had him despatched in a sloop to stand court-martial at Martinique. The trial was held in Captain William Cayley's spacious cabin on board the 74-gun H.M.S. *Invincible* and began a week after Peterson's death, on 20 January 1798. Fourteen participants were called as witnesses, eight from the *Favorite* and six from the *Perdrix*. Lord Camelford arranged his own defence, which he conducted on the premise that Lieutenant Peterson had been guilty of mutiny in refusing to obey a superior officer, and that he had armed his ship's company to further that mutiny. 'Under these trying circumstances, there appeared to me but one measure left, and that was, by cutting off the ring-leader, to destroy the source of contention.'

Captain Mitford's letter had been read out on the first day of the court-martial, and Lord Camelford was therefore at great pains to establish the falsity of any charge 'that my motives for slaying Lieutenant Peterson were only those of private pique and resentment; and that in order to cloak my own diabolical designs, I availed myself of a difference on service to perpetrate my detestable revenge'.

After all, he pointed out:

I walked unarmed, my usual side-arms excepted ... to the scene of action; but before I had arrived there, I turned short round, and hastened back to Lieutenant Milward, of whom I borrowed a pistol, with which I returned; and after a very short explanation with the deceased, (during which time I held my pistol openly to his breast) shot him. The whole of this does not look very much like prepensed malice. I am strongly afraid that the heart which charges me, is more acquainted with the turnings and winding of that passion than I am: on the contrary, I should suppose, that the short turning, the borrowing of a weapon, with which I was unprovided before, the quick use I made of it, and the open manner in which I held it, inferred that some sudden change of things and circumstances had taken place, which on the instant altered my mode of action. Indeed the thing is brought very close, when we find from all evidence (but one) that my turning and acting as above mentioned, immediately followed the order of the deceased to load with ball cartridge, and fix bayonets ... the danger at that time was apparent to all parties ...

However, Mitford had not on the face of it necessarily suggested that the killing was planned; it was quite possible to believe that it had resulted from personal animosities, without suggesting it was premeditated.

On the fifth day of the trial, after all the evidence had been heard and Lord Camelford had delivered a lengthy summary of his case, the court was cleared. It reassembled, to 'adjudge that the Right Honourable Lord Camelford be *honourably acquitted*, and he is hereby *unanimously* and *honourably acquitted* accordingly'. The grounds for this verdict were that Lieutenant Peterson had indeed mutinied against an officer who was proved to have been his senior.

During the trial Captain Russell's order appointing Camelford acting master and commander had been read out, together with Admiral Harvey's confirmation of the same. Evidence was heard that Peterson, as first lieutenant of the *Favorite* at the time, had been present at the reading of those orders, and was therefore aware of Lord Camelford's superior, even though provisional, rank. Moreover, one of the captains sitting on the court-martial was that Jemmett Mainwaring who had been senior officer at English Harbour until his departure twenty-four hours before Peterson's death. As the court was unanimous in acquitting Camelford, Mainwaring by implication acquiesced in his claim that he had been left as port officer.[23]

It has also been suggested that a major factor influencing the court was the fear aroused by the recent dangerous mutinies at Spithead, the Nore, and on board the *Hermione*. Sir John Laughton, in his article on Lord Camelford in the *Dictionary of National Biography*, believed that 'the court was panic-stricken at the very name of mutiny'. Certainly, after the Spithead Mutiny (which Lord Camelford had witnessed), the Admiralty had issued rigorous instructions requiring ships' commanders to apply the most vigorous measures in suppressing mutiny, and to bring the ringleaders to judgment. A lieutenant who had shot and killed a mutineer preparing to fire on superior officers was upheld in his action by Camelford's former commander, Admiral Colpoys.[24]

However, an impartial assessment of the evidence must take other factors into account. The consulting captains were probably sincere in believing that Lord Camelford, as an acting commander, was senior to Lieutenant Peterson. But Peterson was senior on the lieutenants' list, and was in addition acting in place of Captain Fahie who, if present, would have been the port officer.[25] Above all, evidence presented at the trial suggests convincingly that Peterson genuinely believed himself to be the senior of the two. He noted that Admiral Harvey addressed his orders to 'Lieutenant the Lord Camelford'; eyewitnesses agreed that Camelford never appeared in a commander's uniform coat. Peterson's attitude may have been the result of error, and not of a conscious usurpation of office.

The argument that the verdict was justified in view of the need to stamp out mutiny is weak. By the testimony of all present — including Lord Camelford himself — the sailors of the *Perdrix* did not display the sort of insubordination that had so shaken the fleet in recent months. They obeyed Peterson's command to arm, many not knowing for what purpose. When Peterson was dead, they meekly obeyed Lord Camelford's order to dismiss.

What Peterson's own intentions were remains unclear, but it appears that his arming and parading the men of the *Perdrix* was a defensive measure, intended to avoid the arrest with which Camelford had threatened him. His continued defiance of his rival, even with a pistol pointing at his breast, suggests he did not believe matters would come to bloodshed. Perhaps, though, he did not see the pistol in the half-light, and did not appreciate the sudden danger until it was too late.

The most reasonable explanation seems to be that the tragedy did indeed result from 'a vast deal of bad blood, long existing between the two parties', as Captain Mitford's enquiries on the spot had suggested. The shooting on the wharf was not the outcome of premeditation on Lord Camelford's part, but of the rivalry of two hot-headed young men, long-standing enemies with a crucial point of precedence suddenly thrust upon them. Perhaps some blame should light upon Captain Mainwaring for his failure to clarify the issue of seniority beyond doubt before his departure. The quarrel, with its fatal sequel, can be regarded almost in the nature of a duel; indeed, the distinguished naval historian Admiral P. W. Brock has termed it such.[26]

How precisely the blame should be apportioned for the violence of the quarrel is impossible to assess today. Was Lord Camelford so obsessed with maintaining his freshly won command that he virtually forced Peterson to resort to arms? Or had Peterson's cool insolence and undisguised air of contempt goaded Camelford beyond endurance? Something of both clearly entered into it, but in what proportions cannot be assessed.

The one certain thing is that Lord Camelford's conduct cannot be justified on the grounds that he was suppressing an individual mutiny by

Peterson. The resort to arms was entirely the result of Camelford's intemperance. Once he realised that Peterson did not accept his claim to seniority and would not submit voluntarily to arrest, Lord Camelford could have taken measures to establish the perpetration of the offence – a very serious one if proved. That very evening two superior officers, to whom he could have appealed for judgment, arrived in the harbour (though this was not necessarily predictable). The apprehension aroused by the morning's alarm had long passed off, and what was clearly a sincere difference of opinion could have been deferred for authoritative judgment. That this was perhaps Peterson's view of the matter is in-dicated by his insistence that Camelford's order for his arrest be recorded in writing. On the other hand, the arming of the *Perdrix*'s men un-doubtedly provoked the fatal clash; a dignified submission under protest would have been only temporary, and have earned Camelford a rebuke if unjustified.

All this must have been apparent to the officers sitting on the court-martial. They must have appreciated that they were not dealing with a case of conscious mutiny before a known superior; several witnesses testified that Peterson had repeatedly expressed his conviction that he was the senior officer.

What then influenced the verdict? Were the five distinguished officers who presided simply overawed by Camelford's rank and connexions? Those may well have borne weight, but can surely not have outweighed all considerations of justice and maintenance of discipline. The most likely explanation seems to be that the court felt it had no alternative to granting an acquittal. The case appeared to be without precedent[27] and, besides, what other course was there? Lord Camelford's action was mis-taken, ill-advised and probably unnecessary. On the other hand, Peterson appeared really to have been the junior, to have disobeyed orders, and to have behaved in an equally irresponsible manner. If Camelford's action was not justified, then what construction should be placed on it? There would surely be no alternative to a verdict of murder or man-slaughter, according to the interpretation placed on Lord Camelford's motives. In fact, however, not even this distinction could be made. As an authoritative writer has explained: 'Naval Courts Martial of the eighteenth century appear, as far as I can discover, rarely to have under-stood that killing which falls short of murder may yet be manslaughter, and deserving of punishment. They at least acted as if they had no choice between condemning for murder and acquitting.'[28] It may have been an awareness of this anomaly that made Lord Camelford rest his defence so largely on the fact that he had acted without premeditation. Faced with such a choice, the court reasonably concluded it could only acquit. It was thoroughly unsatisfactory, but pragmatic. As stated earlier, we can never know what lay behind the verdict, but the above seems the most likely conclusion.[29]

Finally, the verdict illustrates another important consideration. 'If men knew that they would be acquitted for killing unless it could be shown that they had slain maliciously and deliberately with intent to despatch a particular person, they would assuredly be the less likely to take care.'[30] This does not justify Lord Camelford in all his actions, but does set them in fairer perspective.

Though Camelford had been legally exonerated, public opinion in the Leeward Islands was predominantly hostile. He had already acquired a bad name for the death inflicted during the impressment at Barbados, and now a furious outcry arose. Immediately after the shooting of Peterson a crowd had assembled in St John's, in the north of Antigua, intending to march the twelve miles to English Harbour and lynch the culprit. They desisted, presumably when they learned that Captain Mitford had already placed Lord Camelford under arrest. Peterson's parents were old, but his two brothers arrived in Antigua from Nevis 'for the purpose of seeing what can be done against Lord Camelford in a civil court of justice'.[31]

From the French island of Guadeloupe, where Lord Camelford had attempted to capture the frigate *La Pensée*, Victor Hugues published a broadside which denounced the crime of the English 'milor', and suggested that the officers conducting the court-martial had been inspired by venal motives. As Hugues had organised a reign of terror among whites and negroes under his rule, Lord Camelford was particularly irritated at criticism from such a source, and swore one day to be revenged on the Jacobin chieftain.[32]

However, Victor Hugues's strictures were shared for once by much of English public opinion, at home and abroad.[33] Harassed on every side by what he regarded as wholly unjust condemnation, he now began to grow wild. Had not a Barbadian court failed to find any case for him to answer over the affray at Bridgetown? And had not an impartial court-martial upheld his actions at Antigua? Let those who traduced him beware: he could protect his own honour. A friendly prize agent at St John's on

63

Antigua wrote anxiously to Lord Grenville in March, warning him that his brother-in-law had been led 'into a variety of unpleasant altercations not only with his Superior Officers, but also with the Officers of the Dock Yard'. And Lady Camelford was warned 'that Lord Camelford is justified in all that has hitherto passed, but ... his having challenged a superior officer, will ... deprive the service of an able officer ... Your Ladyship will too much foresee as I do, the consequence of his returning degraded in his favourite pursuit & having no employment at home — I dread it'.[34]

Who these officers were and what was the outcome is unclear, though there exists an unsubstantiated allegation that Camelford had 'killed Lieut. Rich. Stiles Tremlett, R.N. in a duel at Martinique'.[35]

One further scandalous incident remained to outrage West Indian public opinion. After his court-martial, Camelford returned to Antigua to resume command of the *Favorite*. Determined to prove his critics unjust, he made elaborate preparations for distinguishing himself in the service. As Mr Colquhoun, the prize agent, reported: 'Since his arrival he he has incurred many heavy Expenses, in, additional Guns, Gun Carriages for his Ship; his Tender he purchased at a very high price; he has coppered her, armed her, made many expensive alterations and repairs on her. He has built two Gun Boats for the purpose of cutting out Vessells from under Batteries.'

Unfortunately his zeal made him excessively intolerant of any obstacles or delays to his project. The naval officer and storekeeper at English Harbour was a Mr George Kittoe. Lord Camelford, conceiving that Kittoe was deliberately obstructing the work (for which Camelford was paying liberally from his own pocket), lost his temper and ordered a servant, James Brown, to horsewhip Kittoe on the wharf. Mr Kittoe was highly respected on the island, which Lord Camelford was *not*, and an indictment for assault was issued by the Court of King's Bench at St John's.

The Chief Justice summoned Camelford to come before the senior magistrates in the court house. They declared their intention of demanding a very large sum as recognizance for him to appear for trial at the next sessions. At this announcement, Camelford rushed out of the court house, sprang on his horse and galloped off at breakneck speed on the dusty road to English Harbour. Behind him galloped the town posse, a motley crew of constables and amateur enthusiasts who had been lounging outside the court house. The flying peer was captured midway on his journey, on the hills above Body Ponds, and brought back in ignominious disarray by an exultant mob.

The case was resumed at the point where it left off, and Lord Camelford was bound over to find the sum of £5,000 bail to ensure his appearance at the forthcoming trial. This he was obliged to do. But he had no intention of submitting to the indignity and danger of a public trial. Rather, he would forfeit his recognizance and leave the island. He sailed from English Harbour for Martinique on 14 March[36] in his specially constructed tender, on his way managing to recapture a brig seized by the adherents of the officious Victor Hugues off Guadeloupe.[37] It was clear that Admiral Harvey could no longer permit the *Favorite*'s commander to commit any more assaults on British islands, ships, officers or private citizens. The news of his definitive promotion to commander the previous December having come through (ironically, a month before the killing of Peterson), Lord Camelford was tactfully given command of the *Terror* bomb-vessel on 4 May 1798. The *Terror* departed for England, a comfortable 4,000 miles away.[38]

IV

✿✿✿✿✿✿✿✿✿✿✿✿✿✿✿✿✿✿✿✿✿✿✿✿✿✿✿✿✿✿✿✿✿✿✿✿✿

A Secret Expedition

By July, when Lord Camelford arrived back in London, the furore over his misdeeds had given way to a new topic of public interest: a remarkable exploit by his cousin, another naval officer.

Two years previously Captain Sir Sidney Smith had fallen into French hands while conducting operations off the Channel coast. He was at once taken to Paris and lodged in the gloomy prison of the Temple. His aunt, Lady Camelford, and other relatives and friends (including Camelford, then recently returned from the East) made vain efforts to induce the Republican government to release him;[1] but an English post-captain was far too rare a prize to be surrendered lightly. Camelford, who had never met his cousin,[2] at once set to work to organise his escape. Money was supplied to an agent who had arrived from France, and who was then smuggled back again. Camelford then had to depart for the Leeward Islands, but not before matters were well in train.

The scheme did not come to fruition until May 1798, but when it did, it went off perfectly. It had all the circumstances of a dramatic scenario: a pretty gaoler's wife with a *tendresse* for the handsome captain; forged documents; friends disguised as guards; asylum provided by faithful royalists on the way; a small fishing vessel lying concealed in a creek … Small wonder that, when Sidney Smith arrived in London on 8 May 1798, he was the lion of the hour.[3]

Lord Camelford, arriving home from the Leeward Islands a few weeks later, must have found it hard not to envy his brilliant cousin. But as they soon met and became close friends, it seems that Camelford found Sidney Smith a character to emulate rather than envy. Both men were alike in their courage, love of adventure, and impatience with authority. For the moment, however, the contrast between the receptions they received stimulated yet further Camelford's desire to win public acclaim by some dashing exploit.

The difficulty was to gain a suitable posting. He was now a master and commander, but bore an ill reputation among his fellow officers. Past scandals would not lie down. On 13 July he had to attend the Lord Chancellor to provide assurances that he would not pursue his old quarrel with Charles Vancouver, and on 31 July Lord Grenville suggested tactfully that a posting in the Mediterranean might keep him safely out of the way if the Barbadian court continued to press charges from across the Atlantic.[4]

By September nothing hopeful had materialised, and Lady Camelford learned of her son's intention 'of engaging in *foreign service* upon the idea of seeing that it is hopeless for him to look for promotion at home'. Perhaps he had gained this idea from Sidney Smith, who had first acquired fame when serving the King of Sweden; 'the project of the moment however is ... that of cruizing in his own schooner ... under a letter of marque made out to some of his crew.' In pursuance of this adventure, he advertised for a captain. A plausible-seeming gentleman styled George Conway Montagu, 'son of a gentleman of £6000 per annum', presented himself to the young peer. The two went shooting together near Bath; meanwhile Lady Camelford discovered to her alarm that 'Montagu' was almost certainly a swindler. The faithful Lord Grenville was called upon once again to intervene. He was hesitant about doing so: Lord Camelford, he noted shrewdly, might 'consider me only in the light of an importunate censor of his actions, instead of a sincere and warm friend: and ... I might ultimately make his sister's house irksome & disagreeable to him, instead of accustoming him to look at it as one of his own homes'. But Camelford's scheme was more than usually hare-brained. Another peer, Lord Hawke, had recently maintained a privateer in the Channel, and had entered in consequence into a serious altercation with the Board of Admiralty.[5] Lord Grenville supplied his young brother-in-law with a few wise recommendations when he was next at Dropmore, and 'Mr Montagu' and the privateering scheme were dropped.[6]

Lady Camelford's great hope was that her son would get a posting in a ship under Lord St Vincent's command in the Mediterranean. She was accordingly overjoyed when, on 27 September, Lord Grenville informed her he had prevailed on the First Lord of the Admiralty to provide Lord

Camelford with a command. 'My unfortunate and ill-judging Son stood on the perilous edge of ruin from which I had rather owe his rescue to you than to any other being,' she replied the next day.[7] Lord Camelford did indeed owe much to his distinguished brother-in-law and adoring sister. Lord Grenville was at the time a month off his fortieth birthday. To the outside world the Grenvilles seemed an oddly paired couple. 'Lord Grenville ... looks like a fool,' wrote a sharp observer, 'but his conversation immediately destroys that first impression and is most remarkably sensible. Lady Grenville is very pretty, at least more Tournure [graceful] than anybody I ever saw and the nicest little round head and small features. She looks like his grand-daughter, but I hear she is the best wife in the world and that he has the highest opinion of her understanding and judgment.'[8]

Lord Camelford's appointment was to the 44-gun sloop *Charon*, until then commanded by Captain Thomas Manby, an old friend and companion from *Discovery* days. The *Charon* was being fitted out at Woolwich, and would not be ready for service before Christmas. None the less, Lord Camelford at once began energetic measures to equip her for the splendid exploits he had so long anticipated. He could scarcely have selected a more propitious moment. In May Napoleon had sailed from Toulon with a fleet of 400 transports, escorted by thirteen ships of the line, and carrying 35,000 troops. Evading the watchful Nelson, the French seized Malta on 12 June. The next month the expeditionary force had landed in Egypt, routed the Mamelukes at the Battle of the Pyramids on 21 July, and entered Cairo in triumph three days later.

Napoleon was now master of Egypt. His fleet was destroyed by Nelson at the Battle of the Nile on 1 August, but the French army, under its invincible commander, remained a potent threat to British India. However, on 9 September the Sultan of Turkey, nominal suzerain of Egypt, declared war on the French. It was now British policy to blockade Napoleon's force by sea, and to lend every aid to the Turks' war effort on land. Sir Sidney Smith was required in this connexion to proceed on a special mission to Constantinople. He had on an earlier occasion been despatched by Lord Grenville on a secret mission to the Sultan, and his brother Spencer was at this time British envoy in Constantinople.

With such contacts and experience allied to his exceptional qualities of daring and resource, Sidney Smith was clearly the ideal man for the post.

He was ordered to take up command of the 80-gun ship of the line *Tigre* at Spithead, and await further orders.

Sidney Smith did not forget his wealthy young cousin in all this excitement. Lord Camelford and his mother had done much to comfort and aid him during his two years' incarceration, and now was his chance to repay them. A few days after receiving his new command, he invited Lord Camelford to dine at his home in London. Also present were some Swiss gentlemen, whom Camelford had known as a schoolboy at Neuchâtel. He was able to reminisce over days by the lakes with his neighbour, a certain Charles Philippe de Bosset. Bosset was a lieutenant in the Count de Meuron's regiment, brought into British service by Professor Cleghorn in Ceylon.

Soon after this dinner Sir Sidney travelled down to his ship at Spithead. To celebrate his new command, he invited a number of friends to dine with him on board the *Tigre*; they included Camelford and Bosset. It seems likely that it was at this gathering that Smith disclosed his plans for including Lord Camelford in the glory and adventure that must undoubtedly be awaiting them in the eastern Mediterranean.

He proposed to have gunboats constructed by the Turks, man them with British sailors, and then harass French shipping in the mouth of the Nile. For these boats good guns would be required, and Smith proposed to his cousin that he should bring the *Charon* to Constantinople with a cargo of cannon. Smith and Camelford would then sail south to wreak havoc on the vessels of 'that arch-fiend', Bonaparte.[9]

Camelford accepted eagerly. It was not until midnight that he, Bosset and another Swiss returned to land. All three were in high spirits, and immediately set off for London. As they rattled along the turnpike road, Lord Camelford described his adventures in the East. He revealed something too of the ideas which were forming in his mind for inflicting some unexpected and personal blow on the French. Bosset shared his enthusiasm, declaring that though he could no longer serve his own country, he would like to accomplish something under the British flag. When they arrived in London, Camelford pressed the Swiss to lunch with him to discuss matters further.

They met as arranged, and after the meal strolled out into Oxford Street.[10] Lord Camelford began to confide to his companion that he had a scheme in view that would require the assistance of a bold and reliable agent, one who was well versed in military science. He had seen the results achieved by a secret agent in Ceylon, and he was convinced that there were occasions when such an agent could, by some *coup de main*, achieve what might otherwise require the setting in motion of whole fleets and armies. Hints of what sort of service was intended followed. Bosset declared himself willing, only requesting time to settle his affairs. Lord Camelford suggested they resume the discussion that evening over dinner.

The two met in the fashionable Prince of Wales Coffee House in Conduit Street, where dangerous plots could be hatched more safely than under the eyes of an anxious mother at Camelford House. In a snug box, dimly lit by a single candle on the table, Lord Camelford unfolded his plan in detail. During his voyage in the *Discovery*, he had seen something of the coast and ports of New Spain and other Spanish Pacific colonies. Having witnessed the success of Professor Cleghorn's secret mission to Ceylon, he was now seized with the idea that something similar, but on a far vaster scale, might be achieved in Spain's American dependencies. The scheme sounded fantastic, but Lord Camelford had devoted careful thought to the project.

Firstly, however, it was necessary for a trusted agent to cross the Atlantic and draw up a full intelligence report. Would Monsieur Bosset consider that hazardous role? The Swiss responded with enthusiasm. He was impressed by the quickness and clarity of Lord Camelford's mind, his grasp of the underlying principles of strategy, and his capacity for innovation and improvisation – qualities reflecting the spirit of his great-uncle, Lord Chatham. Moreover, Bosset had also witnessed the astonishing *volte face* achieved by secret diplomacy in Ceylon.

A few days later Lord Camelford provided Bosset with a detailed account of what he required. Bosset was to establish himself at first in a provincial town, taking two or three months to learn the language, passing himself off as a huntsman and naturalist. He would then set out to draw up a detailed account of Spain's military preparations, fortresses, ports, fleets and trade.

Bosset was to note in particular potential sources of rebellion or mutiny: what were the numbers and political views of the Irish in Spanish service? Were there divisions between the established inhabitants and the viceregal governments? Subject of course to the results of Bosset's survey, Camelford's preliminary plan appears to have been much as follows. A small squadron should be despatched to the Pacific, there to establish a base on the islands of Juan Fernández. From this lonely ocean outpost ships could be sent to strike at any point along the coasts of Chile and Peru. A small force of sloops or gunboats could be detached and sent north. In the Gulf of Panama were many thickly wooded and uninhabited islands, in whose creeks small ships could lie concealed. This raiding force could co-operate with British garrisons and the Royal Navy across the Isthmus in the Caribbean.

Meanwhile, Bosset's survey would have revealed the weak points at which to strike. The cities of Acapulco, Panama and Lima were the priorities, but anywhere that Bosset noticed a weakly guarded fortress, port, arsenal or powder-magazine could be menaced by an expeditionary force of, say, 1,000 or 1,500 men. Naturally, these raids would be in themselves only pinpricks; but they could be made to coincide with a massive uprising of dissident elements of the population in Chile and elsewhere. These would be supplied with small arms and artillery from the base at Juan Fernández.

This scheme, grandiose though it was, need not be ridiculed. In the spring of 1795, after Camelford had left the ship, the *Discovery* had put in at Valparaíso, after sighting Juan Fernández.[11] There can be little doubt, therefore, that Lord Camelford had already obtained a first-hand appreciation of the political and military situation in Chile from his friends Manby and Barrie.

The plan being agreed, Lord Camelford broached the question of expenses. So long and elaborate a reconnaissance would require extensive funds. Brushing aside Bosset's protestations that he was not concerned with money but wished only to aid the country under whose flag he now served, Lord Camelford took the young Swiss with him on 8 December to Drummond's Bank at Charing Cross. There he arranged for Bosset to be provided with a draft of £3,000, payable at a bank in Hamburg.

The pair met regularly to discuss the grand project, and a few days later Camelford announced over lunch that he now found it necessary to modify their plans a little. The *Charon* was sailing shortly for the Mediterranean, and under Sir Sidney Smith's command Lord Camelford would have many opportunities of attacking enemy ports and shipping. He had had special boats constructed for cutting-out expeditions, and Bosset, without abandoning Camelford's private project against Spain, might well be able to gain intelligence that would be of use to the official naval operations in the Mediterranean.

Bosset's instructions now were: to proceed via Hamburg to Switzerland, where he needed to settle some family affairs. From there he would post to Paris, where he would find contacts who could arrange his subsequent journey to Madrid and then South America. Before doing that, however, he would travel south to conduct a secret survey of the great naval base at Toulon and other French and Italian ports. Lord Camelford meanwhile proceeding by sea to the Mediterranean, a rendezvous would be arranged at Leghorn, where Bosset could report on the results of his mission.

Camelford then suggested that they should both travel to Paris. The precise purpose of this expedition was not explained, but Lord Camelford asserted that he could easily disguise himself by assuming the appearance of an American captain. Bosset felt distinctly apprehensive at the obvious dangers of such an adventure. Taken by Lord Camelford to view the *Charon* at Woolwich, he expressed his reservations over lunch. Matters had gone no further than this when public opinion was suddenly startled by yet another of those colourful exploits of Lord Camelford's, which regularly punctuated his career.

Just outside London, on the Dover road, lay the prosperous little town of Dartford. About four-thirty one chill January afternoon a post-chaise drew up before the Granby's Head Inn. A singular-looking passenger descended and entered the taproom. He was tall and athletic, but presented a shabby appearance with his close-cropped hair, old round hat, dirty coat, white waistcoat, fustian breeches, and boots splashed with mud. He had neither servant nor luggage. The landlord, John Lillybourn, eyed his visitor a little askance, but nevertheless bustled off to prepare the meal ordered by the stranger.

Meanwhile the visitor stretched himself in a chair by the fire and requested pen, ink and paper. When these arrived, he began writing in a book he produced Every now and again he glanced about him furtively. The landlord returned to his kitchen, declaring his conviction to Mrs Lillybourn that the new arrival was maybe a little soft in the head. His meal finished, the stranger asked Lillybourn what coaches were leaving that day for Dover. The landlord replied that none could be expected before ten o'clock. The visitor — it was, of course, Lord Camelford — asked for a bed, stressing that he wished to be woken at half-past eight.

Lillybourn lighted him upstairs, promising to have a place reserved in the coach if available, and went below. The stranger's behaviour seemed odder than ever, for he threw himself down between the blankets without even troubling to remove his filthy boots. At ten o'clock promptly the mail coach clattered into the sleeping town and drew up at the Bull further up the street. There was a vacant space, and Lord Camelford strode across from the Granby's Head and sprang in.

Eventually there came the familiar cry of 'All ready, Gem'men!' as the coachman clambered up to his seat. Passengers reluctantly emerged from the warmth of the Bull's blazing fireside, and the mail coach trundled on towards Northfleet and Gad's Hill. Lord Camelford leaned back and attempted to sleep—no easy matter, with the jolt and sway of the vehicle, the sudden lurches and starts of his tightly packed companions, and the occasional bray of the guard's horn. Twice they came to a halt and drove into inn yards. Ostlers and tapsters shouted, sleepy passengers dismounted, and then they rattled off again along the cobblestoned streets and out on to the windswept turnpike road.

It was half-past four in the morning as they passed under the Westgate and into the mediaeval walled city of Canterbury. All the passengers but two departed, leaving Lord Camelford with a single companion for the remainder of his journey. The other man had been asleep hitherto, but now a conversation struck up. Lord Camelford's new acquaintance was a Frenchman, and had soon confided his history to the friendly, if shabby, fellow passenger.

His name was Désiré de Maistral, and he was a captain in the navy of the French republic. He had commanded the 74-gun ship *Hoche*, flagship of a fleet which had sailed from Brest in the previous October. Their destination had been Ireland; they escorted transports bearing weapons and troops for the rebels then in arms against King George, and on board the *Hoche* itself had been the Irish patriot Wolfe Tone. But on 11 October the French fleet had been attacked by a powerful British fleet commanded by Sir John Borlase Warren. A ferocious battle ensued, which was fought with conspicuous gallantry on both sides, but resulted in the customary British victory. The *Hoche* herself was reduced virtually to a hulk, with five feet of water in her hold, when Captain Maistral was obliged to strike his colours to the British 74-gun *Robust*. Maistral became a prisoner, but at the end of the year an agreement was arranged between the British and French governments, settling terms for an exchange of prisoners.[12] It was in accordance with this civilised arrangement that

73

Captain Maistral was travelling to Dover, and then on to Calais and his homeland.

Lord Camelford listened to this distinguished officer's story with interest. Then he began to tell his own history in the fluent French that was a heritage of his schooling at Neuchâtel ten years previously. He explained that he too was a convinced republican, one who was burning to strike a blow at the tyrant George Rex, and who had long desired to perform some signal service for that noble Republic, One and Indivisible, that was so unselfishly attempting to bring to all mankind the Rights of Man and blessings of Liberty, Equality and Fraternity. He was, in effect, in a position to perform a particular service of a nature too secret to divulge, but which if successful could advance the cause of liberty. Maistral was impressed by his companion's fervour: here clearly was a man of exceptional intelligence, strength and daring. He agreed willingly to supply this fervent republican with a document ensuring him an audience with one of the three Directors who ruled France.

All this conversation had taken place in the darkness of the coach. It was still dark when they clattered through the streets of Dover and drew up in the yard of the City of London Inn. The French officer and his Jacobin companion were soon able to find a private corner where they could complete their business. Pen and ink were brought and Maistral wrote a letter addressed to 'La Municipalité de Calais à Calais', in which he explained that the citizen who would present it was one of the most ardent friends of the French republic; that he had occasion to confer with one of the Directors — Citizen Barras — and that he (Maistral) expected the municipality to forward him immediately to the Directors *pour le salut de la République*. The letter was signed, sanded and sealed, and Lord Camelford put it safely in his breeches pocket.

The two men agreed to travel together on the ship provided for prisoners returning under cartel. It would be some time, however, before she sailed, and after breakfast Camelford left the inn and walked down to the harbour. By the wooden pier-head he saw a fisherman standing on the beach. Lord Camelford jumped down and asked the man if he could procure him a boat to go to Deal. Another fisherman joined them and offered to convey the gentleman there for a guinea. Camelford now adopted a confidential air, and explained that he wished to go further than Deal ... in fact, he had a load of muslin he wished to land in France. How much would they charge to take him over and land him on a

9   The wreck of the *Guardian*. A mezzotint published by Carington Bowles in 1790

10   The escape of some of the crew in boats. An aquatint after Dodd

11 Matavai Bay, Tahiti, scene of Lord Camelford's first flogging aboard the *Discovery*

12 The *Discovery* on the rocks in Queen Charlotte's Sound, 1792. An engraving from Captain Vancouver's own account of the voyage

13   Captain George Vancouver   14   Captain Robert Barrie

15   The Caning in Conduit Street

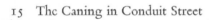

16　An early woodcut of the shooting of Lieutenant Peterson

17　English Harbour, Antigua

secluded beach? There was some bargaining, and a compromise sum of twelve guineas was agreed on. The boatman, Edmund Adams, suggested that they embark at dusk that evening and cross over under cover of darkness.

Lord Camelford agreed, and returned to wait in his inn until the time came to depart. Adams and his friend, John Gillett, stood for a while conferring on the freezing beach. Their customer appeared a very rum cove indeed. His speech had been liberally interlarded with expressions indicating a familiarity with ships and the sea. He had remarked in passing that James Turnbull, a soldier recently captured after robbing the Mint of 2,000 guineas, had been a bungler, and might easily have made his escape had he known his business. The fishermen decided the gentleman might not be all he purported to be, and went to the house of the collector of customs, Peter Newport.

Newport listened attentively to their tale, and then told them to continue with their arrangement as if nothing had occurred to interrupt it. At six that evening, therefore, Adams arrived at the City of London Inn to conduct the stranger to the boat. Night was falling, and an icy wind was coming off a grey and unwelcoming sea. Camelford accepted Adams's offer of a voluminous greatcoat, and came on board heavily wrapped up. The fisherman at once began pushing the boat off the shingle into the sea, when Mr Newport and his clerk leaped on board and seized the disguised peer. Hampered by Adams's greatcoat, Camelford could not resist. The clerk, Rutley, gripped hold of his hands, while Newport seized his arm. As the boatmen were clearly privy to the collector's action, Camelford realised it was useless to resist and accompanied his captors to the Customs House.

There he was searched, and on him were found Maistral's letter, some money, a pair of pistols, ball, powder, flints, and a short two-edged curved dagger. He had no other luggage or possessions. At the sight of the incriminating letter, Mr Newport at once declared that 'this is sufficient to authorise me to detain him'. Lord Camelford at first claimed his name was Johnson, and that he had picked up the paper in the necessary (lavatory). Next moment, however, he admitted he was Lord Camelford, a peer of the realm.

As neither story appeared convincing, Newport held him in custody under guard, and then took him before a magistrate. The prisoner was ordered to be taken to London. The same evening Camelford was conveyed to town in a post-chaise, still accompanied by the watchful Newport and Rutley. At eleven next morning the party arrived at the office of the Home Secretary, the Duke of Portland, who of course was acquainted with Lord Camelford and decided that the incident must be investigated at the highest level. While various witnesses were being examined, a special session of the Privy Council was summoned to meet at six o'clock. A source of embarrassment lay in the fact that several of the councillors were close relatives of the prisoner. The Prime Minister (Mr Pitt), the Foreign Secretary (Lord Grenville) and the President of the Council (Lord Chatham) accordingly took the tactful step of voluntarily absenting themselves.

Sessions were held over the next few days, during which a number of witnesses as to Lord Camelford's character and likely intentions in wishing to cross to France were examined. They included Monsieur Bosset and Captain Manby, Camelford's predecessor in command of the *Charon* and companion on the voyage of the *Discovery*. All attested to Lord Camelford's loyalty, his detestation of the French, and his desire to perform some signal exploit against them. Lord Camelford himself explained that his motive lay solely in the desire to visit Paris as a tourist and view the changes that had taken place there since his last visit before the Revolution. His meeting with the captain of the *Hoche* had been entirely accidental, though he had seized the opportunity of taking advantage of it.

Unfortunately, an act had been recently passed by parliament declaring it to be a capital offence for any man to attempt to travel to France, *whatever his motives*, and a man named Langley had actually been hanged for infringing the act not long since. The question of Lord Camelford's motives and intentions was therefore irrelevant in law; it was merely necessary to prove – as had been done – that Camelford had been embarking for France. But this was a legal absurdity, as the Lord Chancellor and law officers tacitly acknowledged, since Lord Camelford could put up no defence to the indictment. It was eventually decided that the only way round the problem would be the granting of a royal pardon. Camelford was clearly guilty under the act, but equally clearly was not guilty of any treasonable deed or intention.

On 17 January the Privy Council recommended to King George 'to grant Lord Camelford a free pardon'; they added also a rider that they 'submit to his Majesty that it is not advisable that Lord Camelford should be intrusted with the command of any ship or vessel in his Majesty's service'. The pardon was granted and the prisoner set free.

The newspapers made great play with the incident, providing readers with detailed accounts of the whole transaction. The opinion held by most was that 'little doubt is entertained of his Lordship's intellects being in a deranged state' (the *London Chronicle*); to *The Times* it was clear that he was 'insane, and indeed this is the best apology that can be made for his conduct in many instances'. Most public opinion shared this view: Lord Granville Leveson Gower thought the culprit's conduct 'the consequence of insanity', and Lord Minto declared flatly, 'He is certainly mad.'

Lord Camelford's friends and relatives did not publicly challenge this interpretation. A young Swiss officer, a friend of Bosset, wrote to Lord Grenville during the Privy Council hearing to ask whether it would 'be necessary to accredit the rumour that Lord Camelford suffered under a mental derangement?' The Swiss knew him to be 'the very reverse', but was ready to assist with contrary testimony if it would help. John Lillybourn, the host of the Granby's Head, was summoned a second time, in order to testify to Lord Camelford's eccentric behaviour at his inn. (His going to bed in his boots was certainly odd, but quite possibly represented Camelford's idea of the social habits of the type of radical politician he was impersonating.) Lord Camelford himself referred to 'the kind Idea that I was *insane*': an idea he clearly did not share.

For if Lord Camelford's adventure had *not* resulted from some mental aberration, awkward questions might be asked as to the real motive that took him to Dover on 12 January. Just what *was* he up to? Firstly, Lord Camelford's own version must surely be dismissed at once. He claimed he was travelling purely as a tourist. That is to say, in order to gaze upon the Tuileries and Notre-Dame, he set out with no other luggage than a pair of pistols and a sharpened dagger. To get there he was to travel disguised as a smuggler, landing at night on a deserted piece of coastline. And what was the purpose of the ingeniously gained introductory letter to Citizen Barras?

Lord Camelford claimed at his examination that it was the purest chance that he had encountered Captain Maistral in the night mail. This too is open to doubt. His friend Captain Manby testified before the Duke of Portland on 15 January that:

Lord Camelford has frequently expressed his opinion of the facility with which information might be procured from the French Prisoners in this country and that about a fortnight since this Deponent [Manby] having mentioned that he had travelled with three French Prisoners from Lynn in the Stage Coach to London his Lordship observed that he would have given fifty Pounds or some such sum of money to have had the same opportunity for that by assuming a Republican language he could have obtained from them much information ... Lord Camelford speaks French fluently and gave this as a reason why he might have procured more information than another person.

Within a fortnight of this conversation Camelford was travelling on the same coach as one of those very French prisoners. He took care not to be seen entering the mail with Maistral at its setting out from the Angel Inn in the Strand, but drove fourteen miles out of London to pick it up at Dartford. There again he took care not to put up at the Bull, where the mail was known to stop. Having deceived the Frenchman into providing him with the introductory letter, he then made arrangements to cross the Channel independently. From his instructions to the Dover boatman it seems clear he had no intention of presenting his credentials to the municipality of Calais, to whom they were addressed. Probably he wished to avoid the searching enquiry he might expect there, and instead to produce the document in Paris, where it might carry the implication that he had already been accorded official permission to enter the country.

What then was his ultimate purpose? The pistols, the dagger (specially made at the very time of his conversation with Manby about the French prisoners!) and the letter to Barras surely tell their own story. A writer in the *London Chronicle* conjectured that His Lordship had 'been prompted by a too ardent desire to perform some feat of desperation, by which, he thought, the cause of Europe might be essentially served'. This does indeed appear the most likely explanation. Everything we know of Lord Camelford's character suggests that he would not have scrupled, if offered the chance, to rid the world of England's greatest enemy. Sidney Smith may well have told his cousin from personal knowledge of the barbarities perpetrated by the Director at the recapture of Toulon in 1793, and his friends amongst the French *émigrés* had tales to tell of the brutal suppression of the royalist uprising of 13 Vendémiaire.

The attempt, whatever it was, had failed, owing to the vigilance of the Dover fishermen.[13] Camelford was once again in disgrace, and this time the damage to his career was beyond repair. To the royal pardon had been added the proviso that Lord Camelford should never again hold command in a King's ship. On 21 January Lord Spencer wrote to Lord Grenville, confirming the irrevocable nature of this decision. When Lord Camelford learned of this he wrote angrily to the Board of Admiralty, offering to resign his commission. The board accepted with alacrity, and Lord Camelford's naval career thus came to an abrupt end.[14]

What was he to do next? He spent £30 on a couple of lottery tickets,[15] and reflected on his situation. Everything he had set his heart on, and to which he had devoted his burning energy, was lost. The expedition to France had failed as miserably as previous ventures, and no longer could he look forward to gaining glory in the Mediterranean under the inspiring and tolerant leadership of his cousin, Sidney Smith. Not only was his naval career now over. So, too, was the project against Spain, which would have required naval support. But could a man of his ambitions and physical energy be content to reside on his estate at Boconnoc and support his brother-in-law's interest in the House of Lords?

For a while he dabbled in politics, employing his political influence to have a friend, Sir George Yonge, brought into parliament and appointed governer of the Cape of Good Hope. But this use of his patronage brought further unfavourable public comment. Sir George, despite a background of honourable lineage and distinguished public service, had fallen on ill times. He was hopelessly insolvent and two years after his appointment at the Cape was superseded in his office as a result of various complaints.[16]

It was probably inevitable that Camelford's frustration should result in yet further indiscretions. His friend Robert Barrie wrote to his mother on 7 April that 'Poor Lord Camelford has got himself into another scrape but he is not in fault there is a fatality attends us unfortunate Discovery's'.[17]

What had happened was this. Five days before, on Tuesday 2 April, the popular farce of *The Devil to Pay* was being performed at the Theatre Royal in Drury Lane. The performance had begun, while outside in the box lobby was gathered the crowd that nightly attended the theatre for purposes other than that of viewing dramatic representations. Attractive *fancy pieces* (courtesans) strolled up and down under the watchful gaze of *coves of cases* (proprietors of houses of ill-fame), throwing out alluring glances to prospective *rich friends. Well-breeched swells* and *sprigs of fancy*

79

(gentlemen of fashion) walked in to meet acquaintances, *quiz* the assembled multitude, or make enquiries of Catherine Brown, the fruit-woman at the refreshment bar, concerning fancy pieces on or off the stage.[18]

All at once a violent commotion broke out. A number of young gentlemen, led by the Hon. Richard King, had arrived after dining too well, and proceeded to set about breaking the windows looking into the boxes. So great was the noise made by this high-spirited band, that the performance on stage came to an abrupt halt, and numbers of the audience hastily withdrew from their boxes. Having stormed the boxes, King and his friends were preparing an assault on the chandeliers, when a strong body of constables burst in and overpowered them. The joyful Richard King was borne down by numbers and carried off to St Martin's watch-house.

It so happened that Camelford had been present in the lobby. He had played no part in the riot, uncharacteristically, but had come in search of some friends. He went up to a box and peered through the window; unfortunately another young man chose the same moment to look in. A jostling ensued: Lord Camelford lost his temper, turned round and knocked the man down a flight of steps. The injured person – he was called Humphries – got up and asked what was the cause of this assault? Lord Camelford's fist flew out again; Humphries shot back and cannoned into a Quaker coming up behind him. Recovering, he asked Lord Camelford why he insulted him so, and what was his name?

Lord Camelford disdained a reply and turned to go, when Humphries boldly called him 'a scoundrel'. The peer sprang forward and delivered a number of steam-hammer blows at poor Humphries' head, which left him with a black eye, a bleeding gash on his forehead, and several painful bruises. Lord Camelford turned on his heel and strode off. Disgusted bystanders at once sent for a constable, who soon found the peer in one of the upper boxes.

Lord Camelford was taken to the watch-house, but as the constable of the night recognised him as an old acquaintance, he was released for the night upon condition of appearing before a magistrate next morning. As two witnesses testified to the brutality of the assault, and as Mr Humphries understandably declined to accept an apology, Lord Camelford was bound over upon bail to appear at the Westminster Sessions.

The case was heard before Chief Justice Kenyon and a special jury on 16 May. Witnesses for the prosecution told a consistent and unpleasant story: Lord Camelford, on minimal or no provocation, had committed a savage assault on a peaceful citizen who made no attempt to defend himself. Perhaps the worst aspect of the encounter was the disparity in strength between the two men. The box-keeper of the theatre testified that 'the defendant was a tall, powerful man, near six feet high, and the plaintiff a short man, and comparatively weak'.

Lord Camelford's defence was so unconvincing as to be derisory, and Lord Kenyon's summing-up to the jury was stern. The jury had no hesitation in finding Lord Camelford guilty, and recommended very high damages of £500. Lord Kenyon expressed strong approval of this verdict, observing that 'young men of high rank and hasty tempers ought to have such a lesson read to them'.[19]

Lord Camelford had indeed behaved badly; in this ugly incident he appears as nothing better than an arrogant bully. The most that may be said for him — not much — is that three months of kicking his heels in London had left him frustrated and embittered beyond control. At all events, whether shame, boredom or ambition was the spur, he made his will[20] and abruptly left the country ten days after the trial. The *London Chronicle* reported in its issue of 8–11 June 1799 that: 'Lord Camelford arrived on the 27th inst. with a companion and two servants at Cuxhaven; as soon as his carriages were put together, his Lordship set off for the interior of Germany ... '[21]

Before doing so, he had startled a German baron he met by requesting him 'to procure him Girls'.[22]

On the Continent the war between the French republic and the Allies was still raging. Though opposed by a coalition of Russia, Austria, Britain, Turkey, Portugal, Naples and the Pope, and with Bonaparte's army still blockaded in Egypt by Sidney Smith, the armies of the directorate had begun the campaign of 1799 with a series of victories. Naples was defeated, and on the Rhine and in Switzerland the forces of the Revolution were pressing eastwards. By the time of Lord Camelford's arrival, however, the tide had begun to turn. The brilliant Russian general Suvorov took command of the Austrian and Russian forces in North Italy and routed the French at the battle of the Trebbia. As a consequence of this victory, the French general Masséna's forces were driven from their advanced posts in the Tyrol, back into central Switzerland.

On 7 June the Austrian commander, the Archduke Charles, established his headquarters in Zürich, Masséna having hastily evacuated the city the day before. In North Italy Suvorov was driving the French before him, and it was hoped that the Russians and Austrians could effect a junction of their armies and drive the French from Switzerland. It was therefore at a propitious moment that Lord Camelford arrived at Zürich to offer his services to the Archduke Charles. Unfortunately the Archduke was unable to offer him a command, and Lord Camelford, who while in Zürich lived and entertained in grand style, was compelled to think of some other plan.

He struck up a friendship with a French royalist officer named de la Brunerie. De la Brunerie had set up his quarters in an inn at Augsburg, and from there he directed a number of lengthy epistles to his new friend. Unfortunately Lord Camelford's replies have not survived, but from de la Brunerie's letters (carefully preserved by Camelford) it can be seen that Camelford became deeply interested in the progress of the war and the state of politics in France. He made some study of the principles underlying the French Revolution. There is evidence in this correspondence of Camelford's continuing penchant for espionage: de la Brunerie suggested writing with lemon juice that could only be read when warmed before a fire; he also sent a detailed report on the hazards involved in engineering entry into France under the guise of an *émigré*.

Lord Camelford also came to know a number of British officers serving in the Austrian army. One man in particular greatly impressed him: a Colonel Williams, who led a flotilla of gunboats threatening French communications on the banks of Lake Zürich. Failing to obtain a command himself, Camelford toyed for a while with the notion of recruiting a regiment of dragoons in England, and then obtaining the Emperor's commission as their colonel. Perhaps he wished to emulate Sidney Smith's achievement when he served the King of Sweden. This scheme failed — it is not known why — and Lord Camelford travelled into Italy to visit Marshal Suvorov. That flamboyant character might have found in the rash English milord a kindred spirit, but Camelford returned soon after via Switzerland and Germany.

He left Monsieur de la Brunerie with the declaration that he intended to enlist in the Duke of York's army, which had sailed to Holland in August. This too came to nothing, and on 14 October 1799 Camelford obtained a passage from Cuxhaven in the frigate *Iris*, and returned to England. On arrival at Harwich, the captain of the *Iris* wrote to the Lords of the Admiralty, reporting his arrival and describing a little adventure that took place on the voyage:

I have also to add that His Maj[s]. Ship which I have the Honor to command—having miss'd Sluys—grounded on a sand call'd the Cutler a little to the L[d]. of Orford Ness—but was got off without Damage—having been on shore nearly 3 hours. I am much Indebted to Lord Camelford—for his Assistance in going in the Boats to sound round the Ship—as well as Ordering one of his Maj[s]. Tenders—(the Helena of Shields) to anchor near us—so that by making our Stream Cable fast to Her—we very shortly hove the Ship off—I must say His Lordship show'd as much Anxiety—& us'd equal Exertions as tho' he was one of the Officers & I shall ever gratefully feel His Assistance ...

Lord Camelford had not, as he had hoped, taken part in the fighting on the Continent; but he had made valuable friends and had learned much of the armies, politics and revolutionary doctrines of the French Republic.[20] This knowledge and experience was to prove invaluable to him in the hectic period of his life now opening.

V

❧❧❧ ❧❧❧❧❧❧❧❧❧❧❧❧❧❧❧❧❧❧❧❧❧❧❧❧❧❧❧❧❧❧❧❧❧❧❧❧❧❧❧

The Lion Tamed:
Lord Camelford in Love

Lord Camelford appears to have returned home a temporarily chastened character. His mother still resided at Camelford House, so he set up bachelor quarters at 64 Baker Street.[1] In November 1799 he was present on the melancholy occasion of the funeral of one of his old *Discovery* shipmates at Kensington parish church; the deceased was the twentieth to have died (most of them in action) since the voyage had ended three years previously.[2]

But if some old friends were passing, Camelford found himself, now he was settled in London, renewing acquaintance with other valued friends and gaining some interesting new ones. Robert Barrie was present at the Kensington funeral, and the two were henceforth inseparable comrades. Monsieur de la Brunerie wrote regularly with detailed accounts of the campaign in Switzerland, now going badly for the Allies. The crazy Tsar Paul had ordered Suvorov to withdraw the Russian contingent, and Masséna was once again advancing through Switzerland.

Lord Camelford continued to follow events on the Continent with studious interest, possibly for a time with an intention of returning and making a further attempt to play a role in the stirring events taking place. But before long his interests became centred on matters at home and, to everyone's surprise, he became active in the politics of the day.

He had taken his seat in the House of Lords in 1797, but did not participate in debate during his brief sojourns in England. His opinions were strongly in support of the Government, which was headed by his close relatives. His father, at the time of his sister Anne's marriage, had urged Tom henceforth to look to Lord Grenville for guidance.[3] This advice he had consistently followed, and there is a record of Grenville

84

confidently applying to him for his proxy vote on a crucial issue just before Camelford left for the Continent in the previous May.[4]

It was not merely family loyalty that led Camelford to support Mr Pitt's ministry. He was a strong — even violent — believer in the necessity of continuing the war against France. He despised what he regarded as revolutionary humbug, and had spent more time than most in studying the principles and sources of Jacobin doctrines. As a child he had exulted in the family triumphs over Fox, the great Opposition leader, and his views had been strengthened by his experiences. But, suddenly, in the early months of 1800 it seemed that Camelford had made a political somersault. Before examining the episode in detail it is necessary to explain briefly the political background.

In October 1799, Bonaparte had eluded Sidney Smith's blockade, and returned from Egypt to France. There followed shortly after the *coup d'état* of 18 Brumaire, as a result of which he became First Consul and absolute master of France's destinies. On Christmas Day he wrote personally to King George III, offering peace negotiations. These were a blind, designed to mask his preparations for an attack on the Austrians in North Italy, and to satisfy French public opinion. Pitt and Grenville had no faith in the proffered negotiations, and they were rejected in a letter despatched by Lord Grenville to his French counterpart, Monsieur de Talleyrand.

In parliament a small section of the Opposition was incensed at what they considered an unjustified rebuff to a sincere overture. When the Houses reassembled shortly after the Christmas recess, Bonaparte's peace offer and Lord Grenville's reply were the subject of hot debate. On 28 January an address was moved in the House of Lords to express approval of the Government's action. Lord Grenville himself moved the address, which was opposed by only a handful of peers. The majority in favour of the address was overwhelming: 92 to 6. This was predictable; but what was not was *the presence of Lord Camelford amongst those six*. Amusement or embarrassment were the reactions of all present, and it was presumed that the eccentric young peer had mistakenly voted in the wrong lobby.

Lady Camelford was greatly upset at this inexplicable behaviour on her son's part, but Lord Grenville appears to have accepted it with equanimity. The affair was not ended, however. The debate on Bonaparte's offer continued in both Houses, and a few days later Lord Stanhope, who had not been seen in the House of Lords for five years, appeared to deliver an impassioned speech. He moved 'upon his knees' that the House put an end to the calamities of this cruel war by declaring at once for peace with France. The peers listened politely but without enthusiasm, and then divided. Lord Stanhope found only one other peer prepared to enter the Opposition lobby with him — Lord Camelford.

Lord Stanhope was an eccentric radical peer who had displayed strong support for the French Revolution and openly expressed Republican sympathies. In 1792 he 'renounced' his title, removed the coronets from the iron gates leading to his estate at Chevening in Kent, and styled himself Citizen Stanhope. As the crimes committed by the Jacobins in France grew ever more atrocious, Lord Stanhope's views became less and less acceptable in England. He retired to his estate, where he busied himself with various experiments. He built a toy steamboat that he launched on the lake at Chevening, invented new types of printing press and lightning conductor, and developed a fireproof house. He induced some friends to enter this edifice, set fire to it, and watched with deep satisfaction the flames roaring some ninety feet into the air. The friends emerged, shaken but unscathed.

Stanhope's greatest triumph, in his own eyes, was the construction of a reasoning machine capable of exposing the sophistry of false logic. Like many other advocates of social egalitarianism he maintained a despotic attitude to those placed under his authority, whether servants or family.

He prided himself on his independence, and did not appear to mind that few respectable people shared his political views. Indeed, he seemed to rejoice in his isolation and was quite annoyed with Lord Camelford for detracting from the singularity of his vote. 'Why,' he exclaimed afterwards, 'you spoiled that division!'[5]

The morning after the vote Lord Grenville received a hasty note from his brother-in-law, which explained the whole *contretemps* as a pure misunderstanding.

There must appear something so brutal in the manner in which I divided last night upon the question of a call of the house that I can not be at rest with myself till I have assured you that at the time I gave my vote I was totally deceived as to the ultimate object of the motion in question which I was led to believe as well from the little I could collect in the cource of a part of the debate as from something that dropt from a person sitting bye me was 'for the house to resolve itself into a Committee to consider the state of the nation &' and it was upon this general question that I conceived myself voting and not any other which so nearly attatched to yourself. This short explanation I owed to myself as nothing would give me greater pain than for you to Imagine that any difference of opinion upon general political topics could so far make me forget the laws of nature and gratitude as to join in any measure which would directly aim a blow at your character and my sisters happiness.

Lord Grenville was relieved to receive confirmation that it was all a mistake and forwarded the letter to Lady Camelford.[6]

Others placed a less charitable construction on the affair, and continued to be mystified by Camelford's conduct. The Hon. William Lamb (afterwards, as Lord Melbourne, Queen Victoria's first prime minister) declared that Camelford was 'a madman'. 'What has made Lord Camelford,' he wrote, 'who was so eager to assassinate Barras, wheel about? He had better not attempt to go to France now. He will not find the King's pardon easy to be obtained. I understand that the first time he divided in the minority, it was so little expected that the Chancellor sent to him to assure him that he had made a mistake. He is a noble accession to the Opposition Lords, and I think he, Stanhope, King, and Holland may challenge Europe to produce equal oddities.'[7]

It seemed inconceivable to many that absent-mindedness alone could account for Lord Camelford's having voted *twice* in so short a space of time so markedly against his own principles and family interest. The gossiping Bobus Smith reported a rumour that Camelford 'had, for some offence, challenged a German officer who refused to fight him till *after* the war, and he therefore felt himself bound, in spite of his political opinions, to vote for peace'.

In private Lord Camelford continued to express strong contempt for democrats and levellers of all kinds. There was a coffee house named Tom's where radicals used to assemble at night to discuss various schemes for introducing perfection into the body politic. Treasonable toasts, songs and sentiments were uttered freely, and the established order was threatened with imminent destruction. One evening Lord Camelford entered this hotbed of sedition. He was accompanied by a blind street-corner fiddler, whom he placed in a corner and ordered to play 'God

Save the King'. The offending strains began to sound through the republican sanctum, and an enraged company turned to see who had
dared to confront them in so insolent a fashion. There sat Lord Camelford, lounging in a chair beside the fiddler, a heavy blackthorn cudgel
leaning against his knee and a very peculiar expression in his fierce blue
eyes. The loyal anthem was not interrupted.[8]

There is, in fact, an explanation for Lord Camelford's political conduct
which is a great deal more probable than suggestions of absent-mindedness, madness, or anxiety to fight German officers. The clue very possibly
lies in another 'scandalous' incident which, at first sight, appears to have
no connexion with the politics of the day.

In the summer of 1798 Sir Sidney Smith had introduced to his cousin
a young gentleman named Peter Abbott. Camelford and he soon became
close friends, and had planned to travel together on the *Charon* to Constantinople. Some time after Camelford returned from the Continent in
October 1799, he invited Abbott to take up quarters with him at 64
Baker Street. Abbott agreed, and the two shared the premises until the
end of February. An incident then took place, which was described in a
magazine article shortly afterwards under the heading:

DANGEROUS ECCENTRICITY.

A circumstance occurred on Friday the 28th of February, which, if
it applied to any other than the person to whom it does, would be
considered as most extraordinary indeed.

Lord Camelford having invited Mr. Peter Abbott to dine with
him at his house in Baker-street on the above day, the conversation
turned after dinner on a subject of gallantry, in the course of which
something dropped from Mr. Abbott, which appears to have given
great offence to the Noble Lord. Nothing, however, passed at the
time to give room to suppose that he was offended. He offered to
take Mr. Abbott ... [for a drive] in his carriage, which was accepted.
His Lordship had, previous to getting into it, desired his servant to
drive out of town on the Acton road, and he had procured a couple
of swords, and a brace of pistols, to be put into the carriage.

When they had got a little distance from town, Mr. Abbott expressed some uneasiness at seeing no lamps, and frequently enquired
whither his Lordship was taking him. No direct answer was received;
but when the carriage reached Acton Green, Lord Camelford told

Mr. Abbott, that some expressions he had used after dinner conveyed such a reflection on his character, that he could not suffer them to pass unnoticed; he had accordingly provided himself with swords and pistols, and he insisted on Mr. Abbott's fighting him. There was some struggle between them; but the latter having disengaged himself, and got out of the carriage, ran to a farm-house at some little distance from the road, where he perceived a light. Lord Camelford followed him into the house, and some violence ensued. Mr. Abbott however got back to town safe, and having consulted with his friends on the steps necessary to be taken, Townsend, the Bow-street officer, was sent with a warrant to apprehend Lord Camelford, at his house in Baker-street ...

Lord Grenville and his nephew Lord Temple put up large sums for bail to ensure Camelford's appearance before the courts on a charge of assault, as it seemed he would be prosecuted on this serious charge. However, Peter Abbott was eventually persuaded to withdraw the case, and a legal adviser reported to Lord Grenville

the most satisfactory intelligence ... the assurance that Mr. Abbott's Affair will never bring his Lordship under the sentence of the Court, as the whole is referred to the decision of 5 gentlemen of high character & weight in the world; who will, & who alone can, fully clear his Lordship according to his own feelings, before the whole world from the consequences of the *nature of the insult he imagines himself to have received.*

The matter was thus apparently settled to the satisfaction of both parties; at least, no more was heard of it.[9]

There are strong reasons for believing that Lord Camelford's unaccountable behaviour in the House of Lords and his quarrel with Peter Abbott sprang from the same cause. A novel circumstance had arisen in his life, which had imposed an overpowering effect on his feelings and actions.

The wild Lord Camelford had been unexpectedly tamed; in short ... he was in love. And the object of his passion was the daughter of that Lord Stanhope whose politics Camelford had so inexplicably espoused. Thus the mystery appears resolved. That Peter Abbott had tactlessly referred to this *amour* is less certain, but likely. Lord Camelford could not, as his solicitor had pointed out, defend himself in a court of law, as he could not honourably reveal to the public the nature of the affront. The lady's name was sacrosanct.

Lady Hester Stanhope was aged twenty-three, a year younger than Lord Camelford. She was his cousin, being the grand-daughter of the great Earl of Chatham, Camelford's great-uncle. Despite this, it seems that the cousins did not meet until Lord Camelford's return from Germany in October 1799. A mutual attraction at once sprang up.

Lord Camelford was just under six feet two inches in height, with curly brown hair, bold blue eyes, and a lithe and muscular figure. He radiated physical strength and mental energy. Lady Hester, too, was exceptionally tall, with a finely rounded figure, and grace and elegance extolled by Beau Brummell himself. Her beautiful complexion, white teeth, rosy lips and flashing blue-grey eyes were remarked upon by all. Her uncle, Prime Minister William Pitt, turned to her once in admiration, and asked: 'Hester, what sort of a being are you? We shall see, some day, wings spring out of your shoulders; for there are moments when you hardly seem to walk the earth.' Another who knew her well observed of her:

> Her mien was majestic; her address eminently graceful; in her conversation, when she pleased, she was enchanting; when she meant it, dignified; at all times eloquent. She was excellent at mimickry, and upon all ranks of life. She had more wit and repartee, perhaps, than falls to the lot of most women. Her knowledge of human nature was most profound, and she could turn that knowledge to account to its utmost extent, and in the minutest trifles.

And, like her handsome cousin, 'She was courageous, morally and physically so; undaunted, and proud as Lucifer.'[10]

The resemblance in the cousins' characters was marked. Despite her father's views, she was no radical. 'I am an aristocrat,' she declared, 'and I make a boast of it. We shall see what will come of people's conundrums about equality. I hate a pack of dirty Jacobins, that only want to get people out of a good place to get into it themselves.' She would undoubtedly have approved of Camelford's actions in Tom's Coffee House. 'Had I been ... a man, I should have fought more duels with Radicals than my cousin, Lord Camelford. Every flower that grows upon his tomb is a greater hero than they are — for the chief cause of all their masquerading is *fear* ... ' she asserted years later.[11] She was alluding to wealthy Whigs who voiced radical opinions in order to allay or deflect the envy of those less fortunate.

Despite the political chasm between father and daughter, it was necessary for Thomas to cultivate the revolutionary peer in order to be on close terms with his beautiful cousin. Lord Stanhope was, for all his advanced views, a harsh parent. Hester's mother had died when she was four; within six months Lord Stanhope had married again. The step-mother was 'stiff and frigid, with a chilling, conventional manner'; the children saw so little of her that Hester's sister Lucy declared that, had she met her in the streets, she would not have known who she was. Lord Stanhope himself ignored his daughters, remaining locked in his library with his logical machine.

As a result, Hester's childhood had been as lonely and neglected as Thomas's. She was, like him too, largely self-taught. Her Swiss and French governesses were unable to control the high spirited girl, and her father's belief in the moral superiority of manual labour (for others) led him to send her out regularly to guard turkeys on a common. When she grew into a young woman, her freedom was still greatly curtailed.[12] To gain acceptance at Chevening, the evidence suggests, Thomas had to dissociate himself from the politics of their mutual relatives Pitt and Grenville.

Though Stanhope claimed not to have approved of Camelford's support for his House of Lords address, the ruse seems to have proved remarkably successful. Within a short time Stanhope's daughter was permitted to conduct her friendship with cousin Thomas with unusual freedom, strikingly in contrast to the conventions of the age and to her father's former principles. Many years later Hester told her doctor that she 'admired Lord C.'s character, and, in some things, imitated him'.

Lord Camelford was not such a man as you would have supposed. He was tall and bony – rather pale – with his head hanging generally a little on one side – so. What a fright people were in wherever he came. I recollect his taking me one evening to a party, and it was quite a scene to notice how the men shuffled away, and the women stared at him. At last there was a countess, then a little *passée*, with a ten years' reputation for fashionable intrigues, who came and sat down by him on the sofa, and began talking to him. She was a woman who had seen a great deal of the world, and knew, as well as anybody, the true characteristics of men of high breeding and fashion. He went away before supper; and then how she broke out about him! she could talk of nothing else but Lord Camelford. Such delightful manners, such fascinating conversation! He was quite charming, irresistible; so well-bred, such a *ton* about him!—and so she ran on, in a perfect ectsasy of admiration ...

Mr. Pitt liked him personally as much as I did; but considerations of propriety, arising out of his position, obliged him to keep him at a distance. How frightened Lady Chatham was for fear he should marry me! Lord Chatham thought to have the Bowcourt estate (or some such name) [Boconnoc], but he was prettily taken in; for Lord Camelford paid £50,000 to cut off the entail, and left it to his sister. Mr. Pitt took little or no notice of him, out of absolute fear of the scrapes he was constantly getting into. He was greatly perplexed about him when he shot the lieutenant [Peterson]: but Lord Camelford did it from a quick perception of what was right to be done, which was a sort of instinct with him. He saw that the ship's crew was ready to mutiny, and he stopped it at once by his resolute conduct. Everybody at home was open-mouthed against him, until the news came of Captain Pigot, of the Hermione, being thrown overboard, and then all the lords and ladies began to tremble for their sons and nephews. Then nothing was too good for Lord Camelford, and the next mutiny which took place in our ships showed how well he had foreseen what would happen.

This account of the Peterson affair is, of course, exceedingly inaccurate, but is of interest as being presumably the version Thomas himself provided. Lady Hester Stanhope concluded her account with a characteristic anecdote:

I recollect once he was driving me out in his curricle, when, at a turnpike-gate, I saw him pay the man himself, and take some halfpence in exchange. He turned them over two or three times in his hand without a glove. Well, thought I, if you like to handle dirty copper, it is a strange taste. 'Take the reins a moment,' said he, giving them to me, and out he jumped; and before I could form the least suspicion of what he was going to do, he rushed upon the turnpike-man, and seized him by the throat. Of course, there was a mob collected in a moment, and the high-spirited horses grew so restive that I expected nothing less than that they would start off with me. In the midst of it all a coach and four came to the gate. 'Ask what's the matter,' said a simpering sort of gentleman, putting his head with an air out of the coach-window, to the footman behind. – 'It's my Lord Camelford,' replied the footman. – 'You may drive on,' was the instant ejaculation of the master, frightened out of his senses at the bare apprehension lest his Lordship should turn to him.

The row was soon over, and Lord C. resumed his seat. 'I dare say you thought,' he said, very quietly, 'that I was going to put myself in a passion. But, the fact is, these rascals have barrels of bad half-pence, and they pass them in change to the people who go through the gate. Some poor carter perhaps has nothing but this change to pay for his supper; and, when he gets to his journey's end, finds he can't get his bread and cheese. The law, 'tis true, will fine them; but how is a poor devil to go to law? – where can he find time? To you and me it would not signify, but to the poor it does; and I merely wanted to teach these blackguards a lesson, by way of showing them that they cannot always play such tricks with impunity.'

Doctor, you should have seen, when we came back again, how humble and cringing the turnpike-man was. Lord C. was a true Pitt, and, like me, his blood fired at a fraud or a bad action.[10]

This account is of great interest, not only for the vivid impression it provides of Camelford's appearance and personality, but also for what it unwittingly reveals of the relationship between the cousins. Careless of convention, the young couple went to parties unchaperoned, and even drove alone together in the countryside. From their observation of the relations between them, Hester's uncle and aunt, the Chathams, concluded that a marriage was in the offing. Clearly the friendship was a close one. Abundant evidence testifies to the warmth of Lady Hester's affection for the much-abused Thomas; how deeply he felt is less fully attested.

What Hester admired in her new beau was his reckless disregard for the opinions of others, his love of adventure, and his contempt for humbug and hypocrisy.[14] His blunt manner and disinclination to waste time on idle compliments and fripperies found a responsive echo in her own forthright nature. At times her language echoed his almost to the very expressions. She declared later:

'As for what people in England say or have said about me, I don't care that for them,' (snapping her fingers); 'and whatever vulgar-minded people say or think of me has no more effect than if they were to spit at the sun. It only falls on their own nose, and all the harm they do is to themselves. They may spit at a marble wall as they may at me, but it will not hang. They are like the flies upon an artillery-horse's tail—there they ride, and ride, and buz about, and then there comes a great explosion; bom! and off they fly. I hate affectation of all kinds. I never could bear those ridiculous women who cannot step over a straw without expecting the man who is walking with them to offer his hand. I always said to the men, when they offered me their hand, "No, no; I have got legs of my own, don't trouble yourselves." Nobody pays so little attention to what are called punctilios as I do; but if any one piques me on my rank, and what is due to me, that's another thing: I can then show them who I am.'[15]

The distaste with which Lady Hester Stanhope regarded all forms of cant led her to coin a word, *primosity*, by which she implied prudery and social affectation. She was not backward in expressing her dislike of primosity wherever she encountered it. Thomas shared her principles, and on occasion quizzed people he took to be bores and prigs in an alarming manner.

One Saturday in March 1800, a number of respectable citizens were travelling north from town on the Barnet stage. At the Black Bull in Highgate a young man sprang in, glanced jauntily about, and began to volunteer his life history. One of the stolid burgesses recognised their companion as Lord Camelford. Mr Thomas Harding was on his way to visit a clergyman near Barnet, and listened with mounting horror to the appalling scheme that was disclosed.

Lord Camelford explained that he was a lieutenant in the Royal Navy, and hoped in three or four weeks' time to have his own command. If for any reason he did not receive it, he added casually, 'he would as sure pistol Mr. Pitt, as he had a head upon his shoulders; meaning that he would destroy him'. The passengers sat mute and horror-struck; Mr Harding then ventured in calming tones that he would surely not be allowed to see the Prime Minister, and even if he did, 'he would meet with certain death'.

Lord Camelford replied breezily 'that he would go to the House of Commons, or some other place; that he knew how to get at him, and when he did he would be sure to put a pistol to his head'. As for meeting with certain death, 'he did not care a rush about being hanged. These assertions were accompanied by such solemn protestations and oaths, as to shock all who heard them; and were repeated over and over again'.

Mr Harding had a vision of a leaderless Britain, consols falling, the country abandoned by her allies, invaded by the French ... When he reached his friend, the Reverend Mr Heathfield, he recounted the whole horrid plot. The clergyman agreed that the Government must be informed of this impending danger without delay. As soon as he returned home, Mr Harding despatched a full account to the authorities. Mr Pitt, who knew his wild cousin, was probably amused by this prank; his niece, Lady Hester, must certainly have been so.[16]

There was another side of Thomas's nature with which she was familiar. Hester was prone to ridicule pretentious people, especially of her own class. On the other hand, as she herself declared, 'I have a *particular* passion for people who have met with misfortunes.'[17] She was strongly sympathetic to the sufferings of the improverished masses. 'Show me where the poor and needy are, and let the rich shift for themselves!'[18] she would declare.

Thomas felt if anything an even stronger sympathy for those forgotten millions who suffered appalling deprivation in the fetid alleys of the city. Both he and Hester had experienced exceptional loneliness and neglect in their childhood, so it is perhaps not surprising that, despite their aristocratic birth, they could feel personal involvement with the plight of people the world seemed to have abandoned. Thomas, too, possessed much first-hand knowledge of the lives led by the submerged masses. In the confined quarters of the *Guardian* and the *Discovery* he had lived for years alongside the common seamen, and in London he kept up this experience through his acquaintance with prize-fighters, jockeys and other companions of his energetic pleasures. He frequently returned from some revel in the early hours, and saw there in the streets or the watch-house the ragged flotsam of humanity in all its squalor and suffering.

We should not forget, as Lord Camelford and Lady Hester Stanhope did not, that beyond the gilded salons of the West End lay a warren of pestilential slums. Between Camelford's return to London in October 1799 and June of the next year no fewer than one in four of the poor had died of typhus in the crowded courts about Temple Bar, Clare Market and St Giles's.[19] This mortality was largely the result of hideously insanitary living conditions, without any effective sewage or water supply. Destitute families huddled in verminous rooms, whose windows remained sealed in the hottest weather. There is not space here to survey effectively so important a subject, but two examples from contemporary charity reports may suffice to convey an impression of the suffering involved.

> At No. 2 Crown-court, Bell-alley, Goswell-street, William Spicer, his wife, and four children, sleep in a room *less than nine feet square*, in which, as there is *no fire-place*, and as they were always accustomed to sleep with the door and window closed, the air was always wholly confined during the night. Every individual of this family was affected by fever *in the course of one week*, about Christmas last [1800], and all of them did not recover their health for more than four months afterwards.

Also very far from the sylvan grandeur of Chevening or Boconnoc was No. 5 George Street in Whitechapel.

> A fever commenced in the family . . . early in July [1801], with the illness of one of the children; and was communicated successively to three other children, the mother, a fifth child, and lastly, to the father. The room which this family occupied, was sufficiently large and airy, having two good windows; but this advantage was more than counterbalanced by their having only one bedstead for the whole family. The bedding was miserably bad; it consisting only of some straw mats, one sheet, a few linen rags, and a rug. The poor woman had lain in just before the fever appeared among them, and was attacked by it while in the state of debility incidental to that situation; five of the children died of the fever . . .[20]

Small wonder that so many of the city poor sought consolation in cheap gin, or *blue ruin* as they expressively termed it. Perhaps one eighth of the total of poor people dying above the age of twenty resulted from excessive drinking of spirits.[21]

The plight of these wretches deeply distressed Lord Camelford. No one could suggest a practical method of removing the scourge of poverty, but something, he felt, could and should be done to alleviate the suffering of the more helpless. Some of those who condemned Camelford's escapades would have been astonished had they learned about the other side of his life. Late at night he would regularly leave 'a crowded and brilliant assembly, to dress himself in an old brown coat and slouched hat, in order to visit some poor family in the crowded courts between Drury Lane and Charing Cross'.[22]

He dispensed thousands of pounds a year in this way, the only condition imposed on the recipients being that of secrecy. He did not wish the world to know of his benevolence, probably fearing misinterpretation of his motives, and ridicule. Primosity was one vice he eschewed. One of the very few who remembered the other Lord Camelford was a close friend and legal adviser, who probably knew better than his client just how much money was distributed amongst the destitute of Seven Dials or Wapping. His Lordship's 'liberal benevolence', wrote Mr Cowper years later, 'I can bear testimony, was ever ready to fall, as the dews of Heaven, when wanted.'[23]

Thomas confided in one whom he knew to be loyal to himself, and a true sympathiser with his actions. To Hester he related anecdotes of the adventures that befell him. As she reflected later to Doctor Meryon:

> People were very much mistaken about him. His generosity, and the good he did in secret, passes all belief. He used to give £5,000 a-year to his lawyer to distribute among distressed persons. 'The only condition I enjoin,' he used to say, 'is not to let them know who it comes from.' He would sometimes dress himself in a jacket and trowsers, like a sailor, and go to some tavern or alehouse; and if he fell in with a poor-looking person, who had an air of trouble or poverty, he would contrive to enter into conversation with him, and find out all about him. 'Come,' he would say, 'tell me your story, and I will tell you mine.' He was endowed with great penetration, and, if he saw that the man's story was true, he would slip fifty or a hundred pounds into his hand, with this admonitory warning – 'Recollect, you are not to speak of this; if you do, you will have to answer for it in a way you don't like.'[24]

Small wonder that as early as August 1800, Lord Camelford was obliged to take out a mortgage on one of his estates.[25]

Hester was enchanted: her newly discovered cousin was as unconventional, reckless and lacking in primosity as she could desire; at the same time, behind all the bravado lay a warm heart, concealed by unexpected modesty and shyness. She had doubtless heard of his boyish bravery on board the *Guardian* when she was a young girl at Chevening, either from her uncle, Lord Chatham, or from Captain Riou, on board whose ship she had once romped.[26] His schemes for entering France in disguise must have appealed to her love of the romantic. She was fascinated by tales of spies and disguises, and even planned in 1811 to emulate Lord Camelford's feats by travelling to Paris in wartime to see Napoleon with her own eyes.[27]

Apart from the fracas with Peter Abbott, which most likely resulted from a too free reference to Lady Hester, the first year of Lord Camelford's attachment to his cousin seems to have been one of exceptional happiness. It was, at any rate, a very peaceful one, leaving the newspapers free to concentrate on Bonaparte's new conquests rather than the vagaries of a notorious young nobleman.

It may have been in that summer, or the following one of 1801, that the handsome young Pitt cousins knew idyllic moments in the wooded combes and uplands of Cornwall. A chance reference in one of Lady Hester's later letters – written after Camelford's death – contains a tantalising hint that she may have accompanied Thomas on a visit to his estate at Boconnoc. After referring scathingly to the gardens of Stowe and Dropmore, she turned suddenly to Boconnoc, asserting that 'it was made for its late owner [Lord Camelford], and for a great mind'.[28] It sounds a little as if she had seen the late owner in this setting.

VI

⚜⚜⚜⚜⚜⚜⚜⚜⚜⚜⚜⚜⚜⚜⚜⚜⚜⚜⚜⚜⚜⚜⚜⚜⚜⚜⚜⚜⚜⚜⚜⚜

Politics and Prize-fighters

Though Lord Camelford's superabundant energies landed him in occasional scrapes, he appears to have been in a relatively sunny and peaceful mood during his early courtship of Lady Hester Stanhope. He was beloved and admired by his small circle of intimate friends.[1] Among them he laid aside all claims of rank, insisting he was plain 'Tom'; 'he is too fond of ... the people to *lord* it over his bottle, or larking companions.'[2] His reputation had greatly suffered as a result of episodes such as the ill-treatment of Mr Kittoe on Antigua and Mr Humphries at the Theatre Royal. But now his courage, which no one had doubted, became tempered with chivalry. He had, after all, a lady to account to; one, moreover, of lofty pride and principles.

True, an early historian of duelling claimed that Lord Camelford was still a murderous ruffian, who 'sought for quarrels on every occasion'. It was alleged that he went out of his way to dress eccentrically, and even cruelly ill-used his horses, in order to provoke bystanders into providing pretexts for duels.[3] This account was based exclusively on the claims of an Irish adventurer named Felix MacCarthy. MacCarthy used to describe how he witnessed Lord Camelford's ill-treatment of his horse in St James's Park. MacCarthy, according to his own account, at once intervened, threatening to 'bate' Camelford, who responded angrily. The two retired 'into a shop' (near St James's Park!) where they exchanged cards. Mysteriously, no duel ensued; doubtless MacCarthy reflected that there would have to be some explanation as to why both survived unscathed, and why the incident remained totally unnoticed by contemporaries.[4]

But the story, fictional though it must be, is of interest in that it shows how Lord Camelford's reputation attracted challenges from men anxious to prove themselves. If Lord Camelford's conduct was sometimes provocative, he must often have suffered provocation.

Not all his actions were regarded with censure, however. Early in 1800 London suffered a visitation from a tribe of men whom many regarded as more dangerous than the French. Their activities, or lack of them, were confined to a very small area of the fashionable West End; despite this their presence made life well-nigh intolerable for elderly admirals and gouty baronets making their way north from the clubs of St James's Street. The invaders were recognisable from their appearance and speech, but there seemed to be little that could be done to check the menace.

The Bond-Street Loungers, as they were termed, were fashionable young men with little to do but appear dressed in the peak of eccentric fashion, stroll about and yawn the day away. So exhausted were they by the expenditure of even this amount of energy that they spoke in a sort of listless, drawling jargon all their own.

'Sa, we va ga see ya,' would drawl a trio of exquisites, their arms linked for support; in other words, 'Sir, we are very glad to see you.' 'Gea, I va ma bidge to ya, vaa ma inde,' yawns their *cater cousin* (close friend), as they meet outside Owen's fruit shop in Bond Street. ('Gentlemen, I am very much obliged to you! very much indeed!')

What sort of lives did these exotic creatures live? Heavily ironic instructions to the uninitiated appeared in the press:

… be on the fashionable pavements … about two o'clock, before there will be *no fun*, as ladies of fashion are rarely out sooner … You may start either in St. James's-street, Pall-Mall, or Bond-street, which ever is most convenient to your lodgings — get *four of you abreast, close locked* arm in arm, three deep, to support each other … As to female passengers, you have *nothing to dread*; keep firm, and be sure keep the wall — the lady will most likely have her drapery and stockings splashed — look her full in the face, which will naturally create confusion on her part, and join in a loud laugh … If there are any ladies of character near, let your conversation be as *loud and indecent* as possible, alluding, in the *broadest manner*, to the fictitious gallantries and debaucheries of the last night. Should you observe at a distance any gentleman who you take not to be *one of yourselves*, instantly commence a conversation about him, talk loud enough to be heard, and endeavour to laugh him out of countenance.

On 6 February 1800, the *Morning Post* went on to suggest to the Loungers among its readership:

At the breaking up of the parade, stroll, as it were, accidentally into the Prince of Wales's Coffee house, in Conduit Street, walk up with the greatest ease, and consummate confidence to every box in rotation: look at everybody with an inexplicable *hauteur*, bordering upon contempt; for, although it is most likely you will know *little* or *nothing* of *them*, the great object is, that they should have a *perfect knowledge* of *you*. Having repeatedly, and vociferously, called the waiter when he is most *engaged*, and, at each time asked him various questions equally frivolous and insignificant, seem to skim the surface of the *Morning Post* (if disengaged), humming the *March in Blue Beard*, to show the *versatility* of your genius ...[5]

One unfortunate Bond-Street Lounger appears to have taken these instructions quite literally. One evening a haughty-looking young blood stalked into the Prince of Wales Coffee House. In a nearby box a mild-looking young man in a shabby coat sat reading his newspaper. The fop threw himself down in the seat opposite, yawned, stretched, and called out in a loud, affected tone: 'Waiter! bring a pint of Madeira and a couple of wax candles, and put them into the next box!'

He then drew the stranger's candle across the table to himself, and looked languidly through his pocket-book. The other glanced up in momentary irritation, but returned to his newspaper. A moment later the waiter reappeared, bowing obsequiously, to announce that he had fulfilled the gentleman's order. The exquisite lounged off into the next box.

His neighbour finished his paragraph, and then called out in mincing tones uncommonly similar to those of the Bond-Street Lounger: 'Waiter! Bring me a pair of snuffers!' The waiter quickly obliged; the gentleman slowly folded his newspaper, walked round to the neighbouring box, snuffed out the Lounger's candles, and returned to his seat.

White with fury, the beau shrieked out, 'Waiter! Waiter! Who the devil is this fellow, that dares thus to insult a gentleman? Who is he? What is he? What do they call him?'

'Lord Camelford, sir,' replied the terrified waiter.

'Who? Lord Camelford?' gasped the beau, the hair beginning to rise on his head and the sweat to trickle down his back.

'Lord Camelford! ! !' he repeated in shaking tones. 'W-what have I to pay?' With trembling fingers that could scarcely untie his purse, he placed the money on the table and fled to the safety of Conduit Street.[6]

Not long after this encounter, however, Lord Camelford himself began to appear in the pink of fashion. Sir Anthony Carlisle, a fashionable surgeon, recalled that 'he desired to be at the head ... to Have the best Horses – in points of dress, and in other things to be first'.[7] He was one of the first to wear the newly fashionable Jean de Bry coats, with padded shoulders, low-backed collar and tight waist; the front was cut high, to reveal a section of vertically striped waistcoat. The brim of his hat was tilted up rakishly at the sides, and he even, according to a crude contemporary engraving, sported a quizzing-glass. The same engraving suggests too that it was he who made fashionable the celebrated 'Belcher' neck-cloth, named after the great prize-fighter, whose first patron was Lord Camelford. In short, he was *all the rage* and *quite the tippy*.[8]

Camelford's appearance as a beau (he was 'a well looking man, but with rather a *slang manner*'[9]) seems to have coincided with the beginning of his relationship with Lady Hester Stanhope. She had at last found life with her father at Chevening impossible (he had taken to threatening her, with a knife at her throat; he was also attempting to deprive his son of his inheritance), and took refuge with her grandmother, Lady Chatham, widow of the great statesman. Lady Chatham's home was the beautiful house and park of Burton Pynsent, near Langport in Somerset.[10] As she was also Lord Camelford's great-aunt, it was a home to which he had ready access.

Despite this break with the eccentric tyrant of Chevening, Camelford found himself once again adopting a course that posed questions about his political allegiance. On 21 January 1801 Gillray published one of his most ferocious caricatures, portraying an imagined gathering of the Opposition leaders. At 'The Union Club' all is debauchery and dissipation. The Prince of Wales, Sheridan, Fox and other Whig luminaries are suffering in varying degrees of drunken abandon; bottles, chairs and chamber-pots hurtle through the air; while the remainder of the participants sings, shouts, fights and vomits in careless abandon. The drawing is one of Gillray's most brilliant. Among those present is Lord Stanhope, depicted as a foolish dotard lying unconscious beneath the table with a bottle held to his lips. Near by sits Lord Camelford, a glass in one hand and a cane in the other, his lithe, athletic figure apparently unaffected by dissipation. The perceptive Gillray appears to be indicating Camelford's equivocal position in this rake-hell society. He sits aloof, away from the revelling crowd; his back is to the viewer, so that an impression is given that Camelford, though present at the debauch, is an observer and outsider, rather than a participant.

A month later a companion engraving was published, this time an inferior one by Isaac Cruikshank. Here the company is emerging from the portals of the Union Club into Pall Mall. Stanhope is stooping to vomit in the gutter, while Camelford stands, again with his back to the viewer, watching with a professional eye two fellow members who have stripped to the waist to box it out.[11]

Clearly Lord Camelford was still associated in the public mind with the opposition Whigs, who were widely regarded as obstructive and anti-patriotic. He was soon to provide alarming confirmation that this was indeed the case. Camelford's estates included land in Wiltshire on which was situated the decayed hamlet of Old Sarum, which had the privilege of returning a member to parliament. In the unreformed parliament of the eighteenth century, Old Sarum was notorious as the rottenest of all rotten boroughs. Two centuries earlier, in 1624, King James I had urged the disfranchisement of the borough, which did not even contain a permanent building in which a returning officer could register the poll.[12] Now, at a time when neither Manchester nor Birmingham returned a single M.P., six electors at Old Sarum solemnly cast their votes to send their representative to Westminster. (It was widely believed at the time that Lord Camelford's butler and steward were the sole electors, but in fact the electorate was three times as large.)

Old Governor Pitt, founder of the dynasty, had bought the borough in 1691 and with it the right to nominate the member. Lord Camelford's father had installed his rich father-in-law, Pinckney Wilkinson, as member; though (as a supporter of parliamentary reform) not without pangs of conscience.[13] Now young Lord Camelford himself was to bring the embarrassing anomaly of the Old Sarum franchise to public attention in remarkable fashion.

John Horne Tooke was a 64-year-old parson, politician and author, with a long history of opposition to the establishment. He had been an advocate of 'Wilkes and Liberty', had supported the American colonists in their struggle for independence, and – most notorious of all – had been prosecuted for high treason in 1794. He had been acquitted, but few had forgotten his fervid support for the French Revolution. 'Citizen' Stanhope and he had joined in congratulating the new rulers of France on the anniversary of the fall of the Bastille.[14] But if Horne Tooke was a radical demagogue, he was also a genuine lover of liberty, a learned antiquary, and a man of great personal charm.

He was anxious to obtain a seat in parliament, and had in 1790, and again in 1796, unsuccessfully contested elections at Westminister – a seat with a relatively popular franchise. Now, to his intense surprise, he was approached on behalf of Lord Camelford at his home in Wimbledon with the proposition that he should sit for Old Sarum. There was something ludicrously paradoxical in the idea of the arch-opponent of 'borough-mongers' thus being put up for the most notorious of rotten boroughs. But Horne Tooke had a warm sense of humour, and may well have felt too that, provided he could obtain a platform for the propagation of his views, he need not be over fastidious about the means of getting there.

For all that he nurtured scruples. Would he be obliged to follow an unacceptable political line laid down by his patron? He agreed to meet Lord Camelford, without prior commitment. The two sat up for three days and nights, their talk ranging over many subjects. By the end of this conference, Lord Camelford declared 'that he had reaped more instruction, as well as more pleasure, from his conversation, than from that of any other person whom he had seen, during the whole course of his life'. Horne Tooke was equally delighted with the young peer: the arrangement was confirmed, and the two became firm friends.

Lord Camelford's frightening reputation, coupled with his own sense of severance from his fellow men, had left him strangely isolated from the society of his equals. Now his new friend insisted on introducing the peer to that circle to which his own charm and intelligence had already admitted him.

The Earl and Countess of Oxford had a house at Ealing, to which Horne Tooke and Lord Camelford were invited one evening. The former Lord Chancellor, the old Lord Thurlow, was also present at the dinner table. He had expressed a desire to meet Tooke, whom he had once prosecuted for libel in a case conducted with great bitterness. Also at the dinner were Sheridan, the playwright, and Sir Francis Burdett, a rich radical politician.

Lord Camelford found the new company much to his taste. They were not 'proud', and responded readily to his diffident charm and far-reaching knowledge of many subjects. He, Tooke, and Burdett in particular became very friendly. They found they had much in common. One day they were dining together, when Tooke expressed regret that he had not profited more by his schooldays; indeed, he had run away from Eton. Surprised, Camelford confessed that he too repented having run away from Charterhouse.

'Well, then,' interposed Burdett, 'I may as well tell you that *I* ran away from Westminster!'

Many wondered why Lord Camelford had put up so unpopular a candidate. Lord Minto heard that it was further contrariness: 'I understand Lord Camelford asked him [Tooke] what he could do that would annoy Government most, and he said, "Bring me into Parliament." ' Camelford seemed to be repeating his erratic behaviour of a year before when he had voted in the Lords with Lord Stanhope against Lord Grenville. He could scarcely have chosen a more unseasonable moment to do so. The Prime Minister, William Pitt, was on the point of resigning office in consequence of his inability to persuade the King to accept Catholic emancipation in Ireland; the fall of the ministry would also see the retirement from office of Camelford's two other relatives in the Government, Lords Grenville and Chatham. Yet Lord Camelford chose this time to place in parliament an opponent of the ministry so inveterate that he was widely regarded as a traitor and French agent.[15]

'You never heard any thing to equal poor Lord Camelford's conduct ... — surely quite insane,' lamented Lady Stafford; while Lord Malmesbury declared that 'Lord Camelford should be confined for this act of madness and wickedness'. Curiously, one person who was not offended by Camelford's patronage of the radical orator was Pitt's chief supporter and Foreign Secretary, Lord Grenville.

'I am much obliged to you for your very kind letter,' he wrote to Camelford on 11 February 1801. 'I beg you to be persuaded, that convinced as I am of your regard & affection for your Sister and myself, I never allow myself to think that any part of your political conduct is actuated by motives inconsistent with those feelings.'[16]

Probably only Grenville and his wife, Camelford's sister Anne, were aware of the young peer's unacknowledged true motive. Despite his personal respect and liking for Horne Tooke, Camelford's political beliefs were in strong opposition to those of the Wimbledon thinker. Before offering Tooke a parliamentary seat he had not even been acquainted with him. It seems that once again the beautiful and strong-minded Hester Stanhope had brought her influence to bear on Thomas. She was an old friend of both Horne Tooke and Sir Francis Burdett, despite her disagreement with their beliefs. She declared:

> I always said Sir Francis was no democrat. He threw himself into the hands of the people merely that he might have an excuse of business to be out or by himself. All the democrats that I have known were nothing but aristocrats at heart — ay, and worse than others. Even Horne Tooke was not a democrat — that I am sure of, by the court he always paid me, and by his constantly making so many civil speeches to me and of me — . . . Horne Tooke always liked me, with all my aristocratical principles, because he said he knew what I meant.

The feeling was reciprocated, and when it had been feared, seven years earlier, that Tooke might be convicted of high treason, Hester (though only eighteen) had begged her father to adopt his two daughters.[17]

Lord Camelford indicated his wishes to the electorate of Old Sarum, who duly registered a unanimous vote in favour of the candidate. On Monday, 16 February 1801, Horne Tooke took his seat at Westminster. There was an embarrassing moment when he went through the customary ritual of shaking hands with the Speaker, Sir John Mitford. It was Mitford who, as solicitor-general, had laboured so hard to bring Tooke to the gallows for high treason in 1794. Though this opening ceremony passed off with dignity and good humour, opposition was already arising among indignant members.

The movement, first to prevent Horne Tooke's adoption as a member and then to eject him from the House, was led by Lord Temple, M.P. for Buckinghamshire. Temple, though only a year younger than Lord Camelford, was his sister's nephew, being the son of Lord Grenville's elder brother, Lord Buckingham. Lord Temple urged that priests were ineligible by virtue of their office to sit in parliament, and submitted that in consequence a motion should be passed removing the newcomer from his seat. Lord Camelford was very indignant and, 'it is said, told Lord Grenville that if the [clerical] black coat were rejected he would send a black *man*, referring to a negro servant of his, born in England, whom he would qualify to take a seat'.

But the *dingey Christian*, a boxer named Mungo, was not to become Britain's first negro M.P. Every denunciation of Tooke from Lord

Temple brought defiance from Lord Camelford. On 15 March Gillray published another amusing satire, entitled 'Political Amusements for Young Gentlemen'. Temple and Camelford are represented as playing at shuttlecock, the shuttlecock itself being the head of Horne Tooke. Temple stands before the House of Commons, and Camelford before a dilapidated alehouse in Old Sarum. Back and forth goes poor Tooke, Temple threatening to return him 'Twenty Thousand times before such a high flying Jacobin Shuttlecock shall preach it here in his Clerical band'. Camelford, a muscular, active figure in Jean de Bry coat and striped sailor's trousers, replies in characteristic phraseology: 'There's a stroke for you, Messmate! and if you kick him back, I'll return him again, dam'me! – if I should be sent on a cruise to Moorfields for it!' – the latter an unkind allusion to the Bethlehem Hospital for lunatics.

The battle continued for two months, the reforming opposition Whigs being placed in the curious position of defending a specimen of the very 'borough-mongering' they were normally in the habit of denouncing. Sheridan, who must surely have found the situation not far removed from one of his own comedies, urged that Tooke 'had a right to sit after being returned by a certain portion of the people of England'. On 8 May Temple's motion that Tooke be excluded on the grounds of his being a clergyman was rejected. This was, however, only because Pitt's successor as prime minister, Addington, felt it necessary to pass a new act of parliament, excluding all clergymen from sitting in the House. This was passed, and to this day clergymen are as a result debarred from becoming members of parliament.[18]

Lord Camelford was disgusted with the outcome. He sold the borough of Old Sarum for nearly £40,000 soon afterwards, and also (in return for a similarly large sum) brought in a rich nabob, Josias Dupre Porcher, as M.P. for another of his private boroughs, Old Bodmin. But he remained friends with Horne Tooke for the remainder of his life.[19]

Lord Camelford's activities at this time were not confined to politics. He was a fine amateur boxer, and by 1801 had become renowned amongst the Fancy as the foremost patron of prize-fights. Already in 1800 his lavish patronage of promising fighters had become well known,[20] and by the following summer virtually no *mill* was complete without his appearance at the ringside.

On Monday, 13 July 1801, a huge mob assembled below the windows of Horne Tooke's house on Wimbledon Common to see a battle between

Elias Bitton, a fighting Jew, and the famous Tom 'Paddington' Jones. The crowd swarmed over the open heath below the gibbet where still hung in chains the six-year-old remains of Jerry Abershaw, a popular highwayman. Not a few of the citizenry gathered beneath seemed from their appearance destined for the same elevated situation. Few watches or purses were safe from little groups of *bungnippers* and *files* moving with professional skill through the packed crowd; sharpers with ready dice assured poor Surrey *chawbacons* of the vast sums their skill might win; attractive *flash Mollishers* jostled likely customers; and from every side arose the cries of hucksters, quack-doctors, gingerbread sellers and ballad-mongers, the strains of fiddles and hurdy-gurdys, the neighing of horses and shrieks of children.

One man found little difficulty in making his way through the sea of fellow creatures. 'Joe Bourke,' muttered the knowing ones, hastily pressing back and opening a path before a heavily built ox of a man, who pressed on towards the ring, vaulted over the ropes, and turned to face the expectant crowd. Now everyone recognised the fierce features and muscular frame of Bourke, the prize-fighter, a boxer whose stupendous strength and courage made him feared even by the pink of the Fancy. Bourke roared out a general challenge to anyone who wished to fight him, contemptuously pushing at one or two of the men nearest him.

There was a general movement backwards on the part of the listeners; few among the broken-nosed and swollen-eared fraternity wished to feel the weight of this colossus's fists. Only Jones and Bitton, wrapped in their greatcoats and attended by their seconds and bottle-holders, looked on indifferently. Glaring about him, Bourke called out in jeering tones for Jem Belcher, the Bristolian. A murmur of approval and appre-hension went round, and heads craned for a sight of the intended victim. A moment later the crowd parted and a young man sprang lightly into the ring. Belcher, slimly built, handsome and just twenty years old, had come up from the West Country a year previously to seek his fortune in the prize-ring. It was by now clear that Bourke had been drinking heavily, but Jem enquired politely what he wanted.

In reply, Joe Bourke lashed out with his gigantic fist, knocking Belcher violently backwards. Belcher fetched up against the ropes, and sprang back to the attack. The spectators pressed eagerly forward once again; from the top of his carriage Lord Camelford could watch every blow. For twenty minutes the conflict raged; size and strength were all on the side of Bourke, but Belcher displayed such amazing science and agility that he was able to avoid his opponent's most dangerous blows and dart in some punishing ones of his own. At length Bourke stumbled; Belcher, who never missed an opportunity, sprang in and delivered a lightning *douse in the chops* that toppled his gigantic adversary.

A roar of approval went up from the crowd, and an impassioned argument arose as to the merits of the two pugilists. True, Belcher had levelled Bourke to the ground: the giant was even now being carried off unconscious, blood streaming from a gash in his upper lip. But everyone could see that Bourke's wits and actions had been slowed by his drunken condition. Had he been sober, then some of those terrific blows must have landed home, with disastrous results for young Belcher. The majority opinion was that, when fit, Bourke would make short work of his adversary.

A cheer went up as Lord Camelford ducked the ropes and entered the ring. It was clear that he was about to promote the very contest over which all were wrangling. Belcher, his chest still heaving with exertion, listened deferentially as Camelford offered to put up a large purse for a fight between him and Bourke. Eventually Belcher nodded approval, and there was another cheer as it was realised there would soon take place the greatest fight since Jackson and Mendoza met at Hornchurch back in '95. Bets were placed with eagerness; Bourke had been a Shropshire butcher, and his fellow butchers invested large sums in his anticipated triumph. Lord Camelford, too, believed in Bourke's success, particularly when he learned that Bourke had been by no means so severely hurt as had at first appeared. 'He was accordingly put out to *nurse*; a *teacher* appointed to initiate him into the *mysteries* of the *science*; and it was reported of *Burke* that he was a *promising child*—took his food regularly, minded what his master said to him, and, for the short time that *he* had taken to *study*, great improvement was visible.'[21]

Throughout the summer of 1801, Lord Camelford was apparently absorbed in his patronage of the ring, and in various high-spirited pranks. The great Bourke-Belcher fight was eventually arranged for 12 October, and increasing attention was paid to the training of Bourke. Hitherto the great butcher had gained his victories purely through his unparalleled strength. But the humiliation on Wimbledon Common had not only called in question his invincibility, but caused an unusual amount of bets to be laid against him. Lord Camelford was determined that Bourke should win. The boxer's training became increasingly rigorous: 'Raw eggs to improve his wind, and raw beef to make him savage, were the main ingredients in his regimen of diet; and in all his exercises, he topped their expectation.' Camelford, who was acknowledged to have a deep understanding of the pugilistic art, believed that if Joe Bourke could add science to his strength, he must be invincible. Bourke eschewed alcohol, and practised sparring and exercising without ceasing, under the instruction of the famous boxer Daniel Mendoza.[22]

Before the battle could take place, however, Lord Camelford himself became involved first in a practical joke, and then in some pugilism on his own account. On 2 October he was at the fashionable resort of Margate. He and another young buck, the Honourable Mr Tufton (one of the best cricketers in England), were drinking at an inn. There they entered into a game of cards with a young clerk, who was doubtless taking the week-end off from his counting-house, and an actor named Jackson. Jackson was passing himself off as one of the gentlemen he played on the boards at the Theatre Royal in nearby Hawley Square. Accordingly, when he caught his companion cheating, he demanded satisfaction in a haughty voice.

Lord Camelford promptly offered himself as Jackson's second, while Tufton agreed to assist the sharper. The quarrelsome pair seemed taken a little aback, but managed to sustain their bellicose deportment. When all four men met early next morning on the beach, however, the duellists found their courage draining away. But their seconds were there to see they kept up to the mark, and the reluctant duellists were obliged to take the pistols in their trembling hands.

The signal was given, and both pistols roared. The double report echoed round the little bay, and gulls rose shrieking from bathing machines and fishing-boats. Fortunately, Lord Camelford had seen to it that neither pistol was charged with ball; so no one was hurt. As this slowly dawned on the participants, they regained their courage. The cheat yelled out an oath, while the actor assumed the dramatic posture of a lunging fencer. So great was the restoration of valour that they were persuaded to exchange a second shot. This time the two larking seconds added a little bird-shot to the powder. The combatants fired again, taking care not to aim too straight; unluckily the poor actor was slightly peppered in his beautiful profile, and his adversary felt a stinging pain in his leg. Both fell screaming on to the sand and lay writhing for some time in an apparent death-agony. Some fishermen, hearing the shots, ran up and helped the duellists to their feet. Then all walked back into town to have a hearty breakfast.[23]

Within a day or so Camelford returned to town, to find all London seething with news more remarkable even than the Belcher v. Bourke fight. The war with France, which had raged unremittingly for the past eight years, had come to an end! Pitt's successor as prime minister, Addington, had accepted Bonaparte's overtures for peace, and the preliminaries had been signed on 1 October in London by Monsieur Otto, a French emissary, and the Foreign Secretary, Lord Hawkesbury. Next day the news was announced in London, and began to spread across the country. The stage-coaches set off decorated with laurel leaves and banners inscribed 'Peace with France'. Guns fired, bonfires blazed, crowds cheered and wept.

In London itself people went wild. House after house, from the great mansions of the nobility to the garrets of the poor, began to light up as dusk fell. For days afterwards the streets were ablaze with brilliant displays. Monsieur Otto's house in Portman Square was naturally the *pièce de résistance*. A huge illuminated inscription testified to the French republic's sincere desire for 'Peace and Universal Happiness'. Walls and windows had vanished behind allegorical olive branches, civic crowns and republican red-white-and-blue stars and other geometrical figures. A little shop opposite courteously set up a transparency of Bonaparte, subscribed with the motto, 'Saviour of the Universe'. Along all the great streets of the West End blazed forth 'Peace and Plenty', 'GR', 'May the new friends never become enemies', and interspersed between these slogans were figures of Britannia, the British Lion, olive branches and cornucopiae. Sometimes all these brave emblems appeared together, as on the front of Oakley's furniture shop in Bond Street; a contemporary newspaper report observed: 'Britannia seated on a rock, supported by the British Lion, and the Royal Standard under its feet. Britannia in the attitude of directing Peace to destroy the implements of war; Peace resting her arm on the knee of Britannia.' Read's in Pall Mall rose to the sublimity of a miniature Bonaparte being borne in the arms of a colossal Cupid.

Simpler folk provided less exalted conceptions. At Hammersmith one could read lines composed by a gifted gardener:

> Of roses he is sure the Otto,
> And well deserving of the Grotto,
> Well stock'd with many a flower-pot-o,
> Who kindly gave of Peace the lot-o
> To English, Irishman, and Scot-o.

A glazier in Shoreditch also noted the rhyming propensity of the French emissary's name, and came up with:

> Let's drink their health by way of motto:
> Here's to Lord Hawkesbury and Monsieur Otto!
> As I approve the Peace in toto,
> May he that breaks it first, be shot-o.

Night after night the people of the city gathered in the glittering streets. A horde of 'butcher's swabs' paraded about, howling unceasingly and beating time with marrow-bones and cleavers. This euphonious concert was punctuated by prolonged shrieks of laughter from other bands of workmen, who appeared to have been driven delirious with happiness. The music of the night also included the high, monotonous chants of ballad-singers celebrating the joyous event in rhyming couplets, the sustained grinding of Savoyards' barrel-organs, and a continuous rattle of firing from rusty old muskets and pistols.[24]

There were those, however, who viewed the peace with caution. The King regarded it as a mere truce; Pitt hoped for the best but dreaded the worst; and Grenville wrote from the rural seclusion of Dropmore to Lord Spencer, that the terms 'appear to me so inadequate to any reasonable expectation, and of a nature to leave the country, especially if they are followed by any considerable reduction of our force, in a state of such extreme insecurity, that I do not see how I can easily avoid stating some part of these opinions in public'.[25]

Nor was Lord Grenville's young brother-in-law pleased as he drove slowly through the packed streets back to his lodgings in the West End, after his stay in Margate. The year before, Lord Camelford had voted in the Lords for Lord Stanhope's motion to make peace with France, and only a few months earlier he had befriended the republican sympathiser Horne Tooke. But all that had been to please Hester: what he saw now filled him with disgust. Everyone seemed gulled into believing Bonaparte's peace was genuine, the radicals were triumphant (his old enemies' haunt at Tom's Coffee House was ablaze with festive light), and the millions were parading, rampant and lawless, though the streets. Such a multitude had not been seen swarming in the fashionable parts of town for over twenty years, when the Gordon rioters had sacked and burned large areas of the city.

Lord Camelford had for some time leased rooms at 148 New Bond Street from a firm of tea-dealers, Messrs Bennet and Tolson, who occupied the ground floor. Camelford House he had assigned to his mother and, more recently, for his sister and Lord Grenville's use as their town house.[26] He disliked the ceremony and fuss inevitably attendant on maintaining a great house in London, and no doubt found rooms in Bond Street conveniently near to the Prince of Wales Coffee House and other favourite haunts.

Soon after Lord Camelford had returned home his landlords appeared in a state of agitation. The mob in its nightly visitations was insistent that all should share its joy, and in particular that all houses should be illuminated. Lord Camelford replied abruptly that he disapproved of the peace; indeed, he considered it such a bad one that he would never suffer a candle of his to be lighted on the occasion. Mr Bennet and Mr Tolson pointed out nervously that the people were in no mood to have their will crossed, and if they found the house that evening (it was Wednesday, 7 October) occupied and unlit, there was every likelihood that the windows would be smashed. The house itself might even be attacked and destroyed. But Camelford declined to discuss the matter further: if the police were not doing their duty, he would have to protect the house himself. If any damage occurred, he would stand the cost. Bennet and Tolson, though apprehensive, could not budge him.

Towards evening the tea-merchants closed up their shop, bolted the ground-floor shutters, and departed home. Upstairs, Lord Camelford remained alone and brooding in his drawing-room. The walls were decorated with pictures of racehorses, prize-fighters and fighting-cocks, while on the chairs and floor lay pistols, foils and boxing-gloves. Lord Camelford's gaze fell from time to time upon the ornaments displayed above his fireplace. Two brass hooks supported a long thick bludgeon; above was suspended a lighter weapon of the same kind, and others ascended in a pyramid that culminated near the ceiling in a powerful horsewhip.[27]

As dusk settled on the city, Lord Camelford sat on in his unlighted room. When a servant tapped and enquired whether His Lordship required anything, he was told to be off and await orders. Through the windows came sounds of shouts, and there was the occasional bang of a firework. A distant hum grew slowly louder. The mob, emerging from a warren of uncharted alleys stretching from Seven Dials and St Giles's eastwards, was converging on the festive streets of the West End. Pistols were fired, and a poor woman in Red Lion Square was wounded in the head. The mob moved like a sea, pouring along Oxford Street and Piccadilly, and then flooding out into the network of side-streets, alleys and mews. Already servants and apprentices, who had finished work early, had put tapers to the countless lanterns and flambeaux lighting every building. Their work completed, they too were swallowed up in the advancing wave.

On moved the flood: it lapped the edge of Green Park and poured into the mouths of Old Bond Street and Berkeley Street, engulfing Berkeley Square. Great numbers were already drunk on cheap gin; bottles passed from hand to hand; there were hoarse cries, laughs and ragged choruses of song. Hordes of pickpockets converged like jackals on likely prey. A respectable observer would find himself suddenly jostled up against a wall by the *adam tiler* and the *bulker*; the *bungnipper* swiftly emptied every pocket, passed the booty to the *adam tiler*, and all ran off before a cry could be given.[28]

To protect the great treasure-house of property lying in the mansions of the West End from this ragged army was a force of a few score aged and underpaid watchmen, backed by sixty-seven Bow Street constables.[29] Understandably enough, none of these was to be seen this Wednesday evening. Around the corner, in Bruton Street, Lord Camelford could hear the crash of breaking glass and crockery as the crowd wrecked a china shop. Suddenly came cries from the street below: 'Lights! Lights!'

The shout was repeated and carried along into Bruton Street. There followed the sound of running footsteps; standing back in his darkened room Lord Camelford saw wild-looking individuals yelling back over their shoulders, groups of men with hideous, aimlessly grinning features – and then the great dense throng itself, pressing into Bond Street. A thousand faces stared upwards. Many were cheerful enough, but those gathered in the forefront presented a much more sinister appearance. They were hulking fellows (many of them Irish), coalheavers, porters, draymen, street robbers and criminals of every description. Lord Camelford's reputation as a boxer was widespread, and jeering challenges, punctuated by coarse bursts of laughter, echoed upwards.

His doorknocker was banged insistently, and then came the first of an increasing volley of stones. Youths were crouching in the street, levering up large paving-stones. Slatternly women, clutching babies or pots of porter, screamed encouragement and abuse. Now came showers of stones and bricks, one of which broke a window and struck Lord Camelford on the head. It was then that things began to happen. Lord Camelford was not a patient man, nor one who took kindly to insults and injuries. His eye fell on his favourite bludgeon, resting on its two brass hooks.

There are two accounts of what followed. One appears to be Lord Camelford's own, published two days later in the *Morning Post*. According to this, Lord Camelford was meditating in his drawing-room when the mob arrived. On learning their intentions, he called down mildly that he would have the house illuminated soon. Unplacated, the crowd continued to bombard his windows with stones. Patient and uncomplaining (said the *Morning Post* account), the pacific nobleman wrote a number of letters, requesting his visitors to desist. These he dropped from the window from time to time. It was only when these polite missives were ignored that His Lordship ceased being 'a calm observer of the destruction of his property', went below, and 'attempted to expostulate with the crowd'.

The true version was less peaceful. The front door of the house flew open and Lord Camelford, his bludgeon whirling above his head, leaped down the steps. In a moment he had engaged the foremost ruffians. Drunk and savage, they struck back viciously with their cudgels; as the fight swirled around Camelford, broad-shouldered fellows thrust forward through the crowd to get at their lone assailant; others, less pugnacious, ducked and made their way to where the women howled out execrations. All that could be seen were the bludgeons rising and falling to the accompaniment of grunts, cries and oaths.

In the centre of the throng Lord Camelford was lashing out with such skill and strength that he was soon trampling on the bodies of nearly a dozen men he had felled in fewer minutes. He lost hold of his bludgeon, but swiftly drew a sword and hacked yet another victim across the head. His assailants began to press back; others behind shifted away, and the mob began to retreat. Someone turned, however, and launched a brickbat which struck Camelford on the head and levelled him in the gutter. His remaining assailants sprang forward, kicking viciously at the recumbent

I

body. Lord Camelford desperately strove to rise, but never uttered a groan or plea.

He was saved by a group of his servants (said to have included Bill Richmond, the well-known negro prize-fighter), who took advantage of the mob's temporary withdrawal to drag him back into the house. Howls of triumph filled the air, but the front door of number 148 was securely locked and bolted before the returning attackers could throw themselves against it. Further missiles flew through the few remaining panes of glass. Lord Camelford was upstairs, having his injuries attended to, when he heard this fresh assault begin. Thrusting aside his attendants, he grabbed a loaded pistol and appeared at the open window aiming it at the centre of the throng. But before he could fire, his servants dragged him away.

Next day the house and street outside appeared like a battlefield. The door and walls were scratched and chipped, the windows were all broken, and sticks, brickbats, bottles and hats lay around in the street. A limping but undaunted Lord Camelford began preparations for a second assault that night. Servants were despatched to certain houses and inns known to His Lordship, while others appeared among the clientèle of the badger-baiting ground in Field Lane, Holborn. Later in the afternoon groups of heavily built men were to be seen setting out from these haunts in the direction of 148 New Bond Street. They assembled, to the number of about fifty, in the upper rooms, where they were handed five shillings each and sat down to a good supper. They were for the most part the sparring partners of Bourke and Belcher, fairground bruisers, men with round cropped heads, broken noses, scarred cheeks and swollen ears. Their bulky forms moved surprisingly lightly, all their talk was of 'weaving', 'fibbing', 'straight left-handed facers', 'right-handed luggers', and they illustrated their talk with quick jabs of leathery fists. But there was no battle that evening. The mob, warned by their scouts of the reinforcements, left 148 New Bond Street well alone that Thursday night.

The newspapers gave wide coverage to these events, their verdicts on Lord Camelford's actions varying considerably. The editor of *The Times* commented sourly, 'Is it not very strange that the Public never hear of a certain Lord but in a riot or a duel?'

At the other extreme was an assertion in the *Porcupine* that 'Lord CAMELFORD, in his manly resistance of the lawless mandates of a licentious mob, has displayed a true British spirit, which reflects honour on his rank, character, and profession.' The *Porcupine*'s editor was that epitome of

John Bullism, William Cobbett, who like Camelford mistrusted the peace and had had his windows broken in consequence.

Lord Camelford reimbursed his landlords for the damage to their house. He also prosecuted the local authority, the hundred, which, he held, had not policed the district adequately. *The Times* could not resist the opportunity of suggesting that 'a certain Lord escaped with so little damage for his provocations to the *million*, that it is thought rather severe to bring an action against the *hundred*'.[30]

On the next Monday, Camelford presided over final preparations for the great fight between Bourke and Belcher. Until shortly before the day, he had managed to keep secret the rigorous training to which Bourke had been subjected. The purpose of this was to keep the betting odds in favour of Belcher. Latterly, however, the news had spread abroad that Bourke was in tip-top condition, and the odds turned to 6-4 in his favour.

The fight was due to take place at one o'clock at Enfield Wash, ten miles north of London. It was hoped that this was a sufficiently out-of-the-way spot to prevent interference by the magistrates, should they attempt to enforce the law prohibiting prize-fights. Early in the morning scaffolding was erected to support a twenty-foot-square stage[31] in a field bordered by the river Lea.[32] By dawn a huge crowd was travelling north on the turnpike road. On the previous Saturday a downpour had extinguished London's illuminations and dispersed disappointed revellers to their homes. As a result a great crowd of idlers still had money jingling in their pockets, and were determined to make up for Saturday's loss by seeing what promised to be the greatest fight of the decade. By the time the match was due to begin, it was estimated that an unprecedented 10,000 people were crowding the meadow by the Lea.

At one o'clock the crowd swayed and parted, as Joe Bourke made his way forward and clambered on to the stage. He stripped to the waist and performed feats of agility surprising for one of his bulk. A roar of approval went up from his supporters, and Lord Camelford must have felt his money was safe. To act as Bourke's second, he had secured a man with a greater knowledge of the science than any in England, the gallant old Jew, Dan Mendoza. But where was Belcher? The cry was taken up on all sides.

'Where is he?' echoed Andrew Gamble, a hefty Irish boxer. 'He is at Bow-street, he was grabbed on the road!' A howl of consternation went up, to be repeated when soon afterwards two messengers galloped up to confirm the news. The crowd groaned. For a while it was hoped another fight could be arranged; then people began slowly to move off. Just then a cry arose from one side: 'The soldiers are coming! Don't you see their muskets gleaming in the sun?' A panic began. It seemed the local magistrates must have set the militia in motion. However, when the 'army' came nearer there was laughter, for the 'soldiers' proved to be a body of countrymen returning from work in their smocks, bearing reaping-hooks on their shoulders. A little later still the crowd did scatter – this time with good reason. The Middlesex magistrates had despatched artillery to disperse the nuisance, and the meeting broke up in disorder. A number of carriages driving off at speed were upset in a pond formed by flood water, which afforded at least some innocent pleasure to those who had made so long a journey to no purpose.

Back in London Lord Camelford discovered that Jem Belcher had indeed been arrested the previous night by Townsend, the police officer, in Camelford's own lodgings (the peer himself had spent the night in the Cocoa Tree Club). It is uncertain why Belcher was in Lord Camelford's lodgings. Possibly Camelford hoped in this way to ensure his attendance at the fight. On Monday morning Belcher had appeared before Mr Ford, the Bow Street magistrate, who had obliged him to give his word not to take part in any fight that day. He had been released about the time when the crowd at Enfield Chase was fleeing before the cannon of the militia. Lord Camelford was enraged when he further found out that the police officers had taken this step in order to be revenged on him for the harsh words he had expressed over their failure to appear at the Bond Street fracas the previous Wednesday.[33] He resolved that the match should yet take place. But, by that time, he must already have been setting his thoughts on an infinitely more dangerous struggle.

VII

❀❀❀❀❀❀❀❀❀❀❀❀❀❀❀❀❀❀❀❀❀❀❀❀❀❀❀❀❀❀❀❀❀❀❀❀

Dangers and Disguises

In the second half of October 1801 Lord Camelford suddenly vanished. He was not to be found at Bond Street or Camelford House, nor, so far as anyone knew, was he under the grey skies of a Cornish autumn at Boconnoc. As days and then weeks passed by with no news of the man whose eccentric exploits had so often formed a topic of coversation, gossips began to suspect that he had departed on some new adventure. But where was he? Camelford, with his wealth and his sudden impulses, might be anywhere in England or abroad.

On 29 October Hester Stanhope wrote, as yet without alarm, that 'I have not yet seen Ld C. he was out of town yesterday ... Ld C. certainly does not go to India.'[1]

There were no letters, and no indication of the 26-year-old nobleman's intentions. Lady Camelford learned from her son's bankers, Messrs Hoare in Fleet Street, that from 24 November she and his solicitor had been granted power of attorney to administer his estate.[2] This clearly indicated the likelihood of a prolonged absence, but provided no further clues.

At Christmas, when Hester went to her grandmother's at Burton Pynsent and the Grenvilles to Lord Buckingham's at Stowe, there was still no news of the absent lord. It was not until the New Year of 1802, over two months after his disappearance, that a report reached Lord Grenville. His brother-in-law was said to be confined secretly in a French prison. At once the former foreign secretary remembered Camelford's attempt to across the Channel three years earlier. What wild venture had he undertaken this time?

Lord Grenville sent for Lord Camelford's steward, John Borlinder.

Borlinder was a short, fat, bustling man aged about forty, with dark-brown hair and pock-marked features. Lord Grenville gave him careful instructions: he was to travel to Paris under an assumed name and make discreet enquiries about his master. If he found him free he was to persuade him to return home; in any case he was to keep Lord Grenville informed of every move. Borlinder immediately set to work. His application for a passport was at first turned down, but a quiet word from Lord Grenville to the Foreign Office soon produced the desired result.

Bearing a passport issued in the name of 'Baldwyn', Borlinder set off from London on 29 January. There were further obstructions, but on 14 February a hasty note arrived from 'J. Baldwin' at Boulogne to say that he had obtained the additional requirement of a French passport and was proceeding on his way. Three days later he was in Paris. At a bank where Lord Camelford had arranged to obtain letters of credit, Borlinder learned to his relief that his master was not in Paris. Where he was at present the bank did not know, but they showed Borlinder a letter of Lord Camelford's dated 26 December, addressed from Geneva, stating that he would shortly be returning to Paris. The implication seemed strong that Camelford was not, as had been feared, a prisoner in the French capital.

Next day Borlinder called on the English minister in Paris, Mr Jackson, to have his passport countersigned. As he confessed to Lord Grenville, 'I ... must own I was surprised to hear him say to me that he supposed I was the person come upon Ld C's business, for he has heard such a one was on the roads ... ' Jackson knew more than this, for he was able to inform Borlinder that Camelford had earlier been in Paris for some time. He had used an assumed name, but something had warned him that the French police were on his track, and he had left for Vienna on 12 November.[3]

Borlinder's was not the first enquiry Mr Jackson had received on this subject. He was a long-standing friend of Lady Hester Stanhope, who had written to him ten days before: 'If I may ask a question of you, how is Lord Camelford? I like him better than people do in general, and am anxious about him, after the strange reports I have heard; but do not answer if you do not like it.'[4]

Strange reports were indeed circulating. Lord Grenville received a letter from Admiral Thomas Macnamara Russell, on board whose ship Camelford had served in 1797. Russell, enjoying the peace at his home at

Great Canford, Dorset, had heard that his 'noble Friend ... is, on some pretence, arrested and Detain'd by the French Government'. The admiral was convinced that Camelford's purpose had been to wreak revenge on the notorious Victor Hugues, who had insulted him at the time of the Peterson affair.

But Camelford was not, as far as was known, in France at all. The baffled Borlinder in Paris was, as he confessed to Lord Grenville, 'at a total stand'. He could only wait for a reply to enquiries he had addressed to Vienna, and request His Lordship to supply him with further instructions. Meanwhile, the affair was as mysterious as ever. Where was Lord Camelford? How had he subsisted since his arrival on the Continent without (as Borlinder's visit to the bank had apparently established) drawing any money? Above all, what was the danger that had menaced him in Paris, and what had he done to court it?

It was not only his friends and relations in England who were concerned to know Lord Camelford's whereabouts. Weeks before Lord Grenville despatched John Borlinder on his mission, there were men in Paris who also displayed acute interest in the missing nobleman.

On 8 November 1801, a bare fortnight after Camelford's disappearance from London, General Bonaparte's secretary, Bourrienne, despatched this brief note to the Minister of Police: 'The First Consul, my dear Fouché, having heard that Lord Camelford is here, has obtained information which he requires me to send you. He desires you to make appropriate use of it, and that a great deal of discretion be employed throughout in this business.'

Monsieur Fouché must have been startled to find that this Englishman's entry into France had taken place without his knowledge. Throughout France he maintained a vast network of regular police, spies and informers; everywhere were old-clothes men, hackney coachmen, carmen, pedlars, fruit-sellers, fish-women and prostitutes reporting on anything suspicious. Pawnshops, gambling-houses, lotteries and brothels were employed to draw secrets from the unwary; and everyone was obliged to carry a pass when more than three miles from home, which a traveller must show at the inn where he stayed and to the local commissary of police for interrogation.[5] Never had there been so all-embracing a police system, yet this English aristocrat was said to have entered the country undetected and was now – where? Well, if this madman wished to pit his wits against Joseph Fouché, he would very soon find that he was up against a formidable adversary.

While spies set out to comb the Paris streets, a horseman galloped for the Channel coast. At Boulogne the dusty messenger brought the mayor a despatch ordering him to make the most careful check to see whether Lord Camelford had entered France at that port. A description was swiftly obtained—it is not known how—and everywhere police officials were searching for a tall, well-built man with short hair, wearing a blue coat and round hat, who was reported to 'bear his neck a little low': this recalls Lady Hester Stanhope's 'with his head hanging generally a little on one side'.

The chase was not confined to France. A messenger crossed the Channel to England, not resting until he reached the house of the French Government's representative, Citizen Otto, in Portman Square. Shortly afterwards an unobtrusive-looking fellow slipped out into the street and made his way round the corner to 148 New Bond Street. A maid came to the door.

'Is your master in town?' enquired the stranger.

'No,' replied the girl.

'Will he be back soon?'

'I don't know at all.'

'He's probably staying on one of his estates?'

'No,' ventured the girl at last, 'I think he's been in France for some weeks!'

Checking in Bennet and Tolson's shop below, the visitor received confirmation that His Lordship was absent, and that it was not known when he would be back.

Drawing-room gossip in London salons provided likely confirmation of the maid's guess, and Otto, reporting on all this to Fouché, went on to warn him that Camelford was

notoriously mad—but an extremely dangerous madman, who has already killed two men and who was arrested here some years ago for having wished to get to Paris with the intention of assassinating Citizen Barras ... The madness of this person, his intrepidity and his connexion with the sworn enemies of France are the very worst omens.

Camelford's known hatred of the French regime lends colour to Otto's assertion that the purpose of the earlier attempt to enter France had been to kill Citizen Barras. And now his undetected arrival in France posed an

18   Lady Hester Stanhope

19 Lord Camelford (centre foreground, seated at table) and Lord Stanhope

(left foreground, on floor) at the Union Club. Cartoon by Gillray

20   Camelford House, Oxford Street

21   The Old Sarum Election, by Gillray

even more disturbing possibility. Could it be that Camelford had come on a similar mission? And this time with an even more alarming scheme in mind: nothing less than the assassination of Napoleon himself? Certainly, Lord Camelford's presence in France had seriously agitated Bonaparte, and with good reason. The safety of France rested on the frail security of one man's life, and from every side plots were being directed against the person of the First Consul; from diehard Jacobins on the one hand, and vengeful royalists on the other. On Christmas Eve at the end of the previous year, Bonaparte had been driving along the rue St Nicaise to attend the opera, when an explosive device was discharged which just missed his carriage and blew to pieces several members of his escort. The infernal machine had been concealed in a water cart, and the First Consul at once blamed the Jacobins for the attempt.

But in fact the organiser of the outrage in the rue St Nicaise was a Breton royalist (*Chouan*) named Limoëlan.[6] He was still at large somewhere in France and was accounted to be connected with Lord Camelford, who dispensed a generous bounty to many of the *Chouan* chiefs.

Now Lord Camelford himself was in France, having entered so secretly as to elude the vigilance of all the minister's watchers. He was, as Citizen Otto pointed out, ruthless and dangerous. On 28 November Fouché warned General Duroc, governor of the palace of the Tuileries, advising him: 'In case this person should appear at the Palace of the Consuls, I beg you to give the strictest orders that he be arrested and brought before me.'

The prefect of police was at the same time instructed to track down Lord Camelford: 'If your agents manage to find him, they should follow him with care, finding out where he lives and the places he visits.'

The prefect acted with efficiency. Enquiries along the coast had already revealed that a man whose description answered to that of Lord Camelford had passed through Boulogne on his way to Paris a month previously. Within two days spies established that in Paris he had stayed at a house at 11 rue des Bons Enfants, a street running alongside the Palais Royal, and only a stone's throw from the Tuileries palace. He had entered the city with a false name and under the guise of a respectable banker. His political opinions appeared to be favourable to the Revolution, and there had been no reason to suspect him of ill conduct or intentions. Unfortunately he had left his lodgings a fortnight previously and it was not known where he had gone.

Where then was Lord Camelford? Although the French police had lost track of him, they had been on the right trail. Towards the end of October a smuggler's boat from Rye had put in at Boulogne. A single passenger disembarked and walked into the town. He was tall and active-looking, was dressed in rough sailor's clothes, and had no luggage. At the rue de l'Écu he turned into the Hôtel d'Angleterre, a well-known inn kept by two Englishmen named Knowles and Parker. He explained that he was servant to a Colonel Williams, who would shortly be arriving with a small party, and wished to have rooms prepared for his master.

The landlord showed the stranger a room, and then went off to prepare for Colonel Williams and his party. They would be the first English travellers to arrive since the preliminaries of peace were signed, and he anticipated no doubt a renewal of the steady stream of customers they had known before the war. The Hôtel d'Angleterre was situated in a noisy street, but had comfortable rooms, inviting coal fires, and boasted an excellent champagne.[7] The stranger was not much seen, however, during the first twenty-four hours of his stay. At one point he slipped out to visit a harness-maker from whom he bought a green cabriolet for sixteen guineas in English gold.

Just before lunch on 26 October the police commissary of Boulogne called at the Hôtel d'Angleterre to check on the new arrival, who explained that he was an American sailor. Questioned further, he replied satisfactorily, and the commissary departed. The stranger sat down to eat and was joined at his table by a Captain Brenan, who appears also to have been an American, possibly captain of a merchantman in the harbour. Brenan asked his compatriot which part of the United States he came from. 'New York,' replied the other laconically, and declined to be drawn further. Brenan suspected the man might not be all he claimed, but desisted from further enquiry.

Late that evening Colonel Williams arrived at the inn, accompanied by his wife, two other ladies, and two servants. He possessed a passport issued in London by Citizen Otto which recorded the number of his companions, allowing as an extra servant the young man who had preceded them. Colonel Williams was no invention. He was the officer whom Camelford had met and liked in Switzerland in 1799. Colonel Williams, it will be recalled, was then serving with the Austrian army, and leading a flotilla of gunboats to harass French communications on the banks of Lake Zürich.

DÉPARTEMENT DU PAS-DE-CALAIS.

MUNICIPALITÉ DE BOULOGNE-SUR-MER.

No. du Registre, fol. *112*

No. du Tableau.

Liberté.　　　　　**Egalité.**

SIGNALEMENT.

Agé de *trente ans*

Taille d'un metre *86* centimetres

Cheveux *Bruns*

Sourcils *Idem*

Visage *Rond*

Front *ordinaire*

Yeux *Bleus*

Nez *Épaté*

Bouche *Moyenne*

Menton *Rond*

Signature du Porteur.

Jean Rushworth

Boulogne-sur-mer, le *Sixieme* 'du mois de *Brumaire*

An *dix* de la République Française, une & indivisible

NOUS MAIRE DE LA VILLE DE BOULOGNE-SUR-MER; invitons les Autorités Civiles & Militaires de la République, à laisser passer & librement circuler de Boulogne-sur-mer à *Paris*

Département *de la Seine*

Le Citoyen *Jean Baptiste Rushworth*

Profession *anglaise* 　　　　nati

de *Londres* 　　　　Département

demeurant *à Londres*

& à lui procurer aide & assistance dans toutes les occasions, d'après les formalités requises.

Délivré, *à la charge de se présenter a administration de*

la police générale à son arrivée a paris

Fait à la Mairie de Boulogne-sur-mer, lesdits jour & an.

Le maire

Signé Martin Dubroeuil

Par le Maire :

Signé L'heureux Secrétaire

Délivré pour copie Collationné

Secrétaire-Greffier.

The passport issued to Lord Camelford by the French authorities

The party stayed two nights in Boulogne, and then set off in Camelford's cabriolet for Paris on the 28 October. On the strength of the number of servants provided for on the colonel's passport, an individual passport was obtained for Lord Camelford from the municipality. Issued to a certain 'John Rushworth', it contains a precise account of Camelford's appearance. In the apparent absence of any portrait, this is of great interest, taken as it was from the life. He was 1 metre 866 millimetres tall (6 feet 1½ inches), with brown hair and eyebrows and blue eyes. The passport allowed him to travel to Paris, but obliged him to report to the police there on arrival.

The party set off on the road southwards. As they drove they passed ruins of once-beautiful châteaux and churches, lasting testimony to the appalling destruction wrought by the Revolution.[8] In Paris Colonel Williams (whose assistance was no longer needed) separated with his party from Camelford, who settled, as was previously noted, in the rue des Bons Enfants. On 3 November 'John Rushworth' attended at the prefecture with his passport. He was no longer in his shabby sailor's rig, but wore a smart blue coat, and explained that he had arrived from London to do business with some of the principal Paris banks. The prefect found this reasonable enough, and allowed him a two-month stay. Following customary procedure, an agent was detailed to follow 'Rushworth' and report on his activities. The report was entirely satisfactory: 'Rushworth' clearly was what he purported to be. Indeed, he appeared to be a warm partisan of the French Revolution and government, and declared that he was particularly anxious to witness the celebration of the peace in Paris.

Precisely what Camelford really did in Paris at this time is not known. A police spy reported his presence near the Palais du Tribunat; someone else saw him walking with Colonel Williams in the Tuileries gardens: that is all. Then, abruptly in the second week of November, he and Colonel Williams departed. Fouché's agents discovered too late that they had left for Vienna.

Colonel Williams did indeed go to Vienna, but Lord Camelford did not accompany him there. After the pair had travelled some way eastwards on the main road towards Frankfurt, Camelford bade farewell to his friend at the little town of La Ferté, between Meaux and Château-Thierry.[9] He dined at an inn—he was always dining alone in inns—and continued his journey on the mail coach. Two hours later he was back in

La Ferté and took a room in another inn, the Porcupine. To the landlord
he explained that the coach had broken a wheel a league out of town,
and he would have to stay the night. Next day, 13 November, he prepared to set off again. He was actually stepping into the coach, when
suddenly he slapped his pockets and gave a cry. Where was his passport?
At once servants were set to search everywhere, in the inn and the coach,
but to no avail.

Camelford explained to his host that he had left Paris, where he had
lived for years, with a passport. He was a respectable merchant, bound on
urgent business. Look, the landlord could inspect his letters of credit on
different banks in France. Could nothing be done? By a stroke of luck—
so it seemed—Camelford had chosen a landlord who was also the mayor
of La Ferté. Delighted to be of assistance, he issued 'John Rushworth' with
a new passport, countersigned by a fellow innkeeper—a passport which
did not restrict the holder's movements to Paris.

And so, his new passport safely tucked in his coat pocket, Lord Camelford drove away from La Ferté. His subsequent movements are known.
But the purpose of them is obscure. By swift stages he cast back south-
westwards to Orléans, then south to Bourges, finally, a fortnight later,
he was in Geneva. From there he intended to go to Nice, but something
obliged him to alter his plan. Instead he crossed into Italy by the Simplon
Pass, where thousands of French workmen were toiling to complete the
great military road planned by the First Consul. Lord Camelford came to
Milan, and wintered in North Italy.

Then, in the early spring, while the portly John Borlinder was beginning his enquiries in Paris, and Hester Stanhope was writing anxiously of
her Thomas to Mr Jackson, Camelford himself prepared to return to
France. He had been in Rome, but by 28 February 1802 was at Casal in
Piedmont, then an occupied French province, where he applied to the
prefect for a fresh passport to enter France. A week later he was at Lausanne, having passed over the Great St Bernard, where winter snows still
hung heavy on the surrounding crags. He remained a month in Switzerland, and it would be pleasant to think he visited the lake of Bienne and
the island refuge of his childhood. But he may well have had more
serious business in hand; he had employed Swiss friends in dangerous
work before now, and a month later Fouché was ordering his spies to
watch a certain Mulach from Berne, a constant visitor to Paris and
associate of 'Rushworth'.

Soon Camelford was on the move again. From Basle he travelled north to Strasburg, and then westwards to the capital. In the second half of March he drove once more through the Porte Saint-Antoine, passing an untidy faggot-yard occupying the spot where the eight towers of the Bastille once frowned over Paris. On 24 March he confidently registered his new passport at the prefecture of police – a fact that was speedily notified to Citizen Minister Joseph Fouché. Astonishingly, although Fouché now strongly suspected that 'Rushworth' was Lord Camelford, he apparently did not think of checking at the lodgings where, as his agents had previously established, Camelford had stayed on first arriving in Paris. Perhaps it did not occur to Fouché that even Lord Camelford would take such a risk. And Camelford himself, of course, was unaware of the full extent of the enquiries made about his activities.

The day after registering his passport he encountered, to his surprise, the squat familiar figure of his steward. Borlinder, who had been in Paris for a month now pursuing his investigation, wrote confidently to Lord Grenville: 'I have the satisfaction to inform you that I met my friend here yesterday in good health and I have no other reason to think but that I shall see you in a few days, having given up all thoughts of my journey into Italy.'

But the poor steward's trials were not at an end. Lord Camelford had as yet no intention of returning home, and settled down again at his lodgings in the rue des Bons Enfants. What His Lordship's business in Paris was the steward had no idea. However, there was much to amuse a visitor to Paris in the year 1802.

Without doubt the greatest attraction for the host of English tourists who had arrived in the capital was 'Little Boney' himself. The First Consul was resident at the Tuileries, where he held court with a splendour surpassing that of the Bourbon kings. On 5 April in the court of the palace he reviewed five or six thousand soldiers, 'accoutred', as an English visitor reported, 'at an expense and with a magnificence that I suppose was never before lavished on an equal number of soldiers'. There one could see riding the generals whose exploits had amazed all Europe: Murat, Junot, Macdonald, Augereau, Masséna. But the cynosure of every eye was the conqueror of Italy and Egypt, with his pale face, melancholy grey eyes, and 'a look of calm and tranquil Resolution and Intrepidity which nothing could discompose'. There he passed above the rows of bearskins and bayonets, 'on his beautiful dun horse riding among the ranks attended by eight or ten officers and one Mameluc richly dressed'.

But English visitors provided with an introduction from their minister might approach closer than this. At a *levée* held at eleven in the morning they could walk into the palace and draw up in ranks in the Salle des Ambassadeurs for presentation. The First Consul would appear, walking quickly down the line, saying 'something to almost every one, and not much to any one'. But when he did speak, noted the same enraptured Englishman, his countenance 'relaxes into the most agreeable and gracious smile you can conceive'. Nor, despite the splendour, was all conducted with rigid formality. It was easy to wander through the halls to obtain a closer and longer look at the great man. A visitor, a young man in the Wiltshire militia, was standing gazing at the paintings in one of the galleries. He felt a tap on the shoulder, and turned to find General Bonaparte enquiring to what regiment he belonged.[10]

The first soldier in Europe would also undoubtedly have been intrigued by the visitor whose passport proclaimed him to be 'Mr John Rushworth', the travelling American merchant – and by a sinister object in Rushworth's possession. Alone in his room, Rushworth carefully cleaned and checked a deadly instrument.[11] To the uninitiated observer it was but a pistol: ordinary enough, with its shining octagonal barrel and rounded butt. The only unusual factor was a short lever curving alongside the barrel, which might perhaps have been a belt clip. There was also a little metal hinged door with a spring catch set in the stock on the opposite side from the lock.

Until the invention of the percussion cap, and hence of multi-barrelled revolving chamber pistols, the pistol was a clumsy weapon. It was accurate enough at close quarters, but after every shot the marksman had to perform the awkward procedure of recharging the barrel with powder, ramming down a wad, then the ball, then another wad, and finally repriming the pan and recocking the hammer. All this took time, and could not easily be done at all under conditions of stress or action. It was possible, of course, to carry more than one pistol, and for these in turn to be double-barrelled. One could then fire up to four shots without reloading, but this greatly increased the bulk and weight of metal carried. Such a procedure would be particularly impractical if one wished to carry a firearm concealed about one's person.

What Lord Camelford possessed was a small magazine pistol, capable of firing nine shots in succession without reloading. Cleverly concealed in the length of the butt were two parallel chambers: one held the powder and the other the balls. Once the two chambers had been filled and the little door closed, the procedure for firing was beautifully simple. Holding the weapon at a slight declination (to allow powder and ball to slide forward), the user rotated the lever screwed into the side through 220 degrees. This action caused two receptacles in a central revolving chamber to receive a ball and requisite charge of powder, and to drop them into the breech; a very slight tapering of the barrel retained the ball in position. Meanwhile, the same action had dropped priming powder into the pan, closed the pan-cover, and set the hammer at full cock.

To fire this pistol, therefore, all that was necessary between shots was to depress the gun and turn the little lever. A skilled mechanic reported after testing the pistol: 'I have discharged this course of balls several times, and I find that the whole nine balls can be fired in 30 seconds.'

The only snag was that the delicate mechanism was subject to clogging after repeated use – but this did not apply, of course, where it was to be used once for a specific purpose and was carefully prepared beforehand.[12]

For a fortnight Camelford – 'Mr Rushworth' – lived quietly in Paris. The city was alive with activity and excitement, for on 18 April was to be held a grand *Te Deum* at Notre-Dame to celebrate simultaneously the signing of the Peace of Amiens and the concordat with the Pope. The latter agreement was dreaded by French royalists as the ruin of all their hopes, since the aspirations of millions of French Catholics were no longer to be identified with the cause of the exiled King Louis XVIII. But the stability of the new order rested entirely on the life of the First Consul, a life that minister of police Fouché was determined would be preserved at all costs. For where would his own hard-won power and wealth be if the republic fell and the King returned?

For a fortnight his efforts to track 'Mr Rushworth' came to nothing. Couriers were despatched all over France, checking with prefects of police to establish his moves over the past five months. From the under-world of counter-espionage came mysterious reports on persons known or suspected to be working for 'Rushworth'. Why had a 'certain person' from Villiers ordered a coach to be brought to the rue de la Loi in preparation for another 'individual's' journey to Boulogne? Who was Citizen Duplessis, whose letters at the Hôtel d'Angleterre were to be intercepted and laid before Fouché? Watch must be kept on a Bernese named Mulach, and a check made on possible contacts between the conspirators and Lord Cornwallis, present in Paris after negotiating the Peace of Amiens.

Most disturbing of all were conversations behind closed doors, reports of which percolated through to the minister's ubiquitous agents. There had been talk of the late Tsar Paul of Russia, assassinated exactly a year before. True, the murder had originated in a court conspiracy: but had it not been greatly to the advantage of perfidious England, whose Indian possessions the Tsar had been on the point of invading with 20,000 Cossacks? Did not that treacherous 'Jean Boule', eternally jealous of the *Grande Nation*, 'secretly exult over the fall of a single man, bringing him greater advantage than the defeat of an army'?

For nine days all the police of Paris could report nothing. Apparently warned by a sixth sense of the danger, Mr Rushworth had deserted his lodgings at 11 rue des Bons Enfants. Then, on the afternoon of 3 April, came the first break-through. Someone who had been in London and knew well the familiar figure of Lord Camelford saw him in one of the alleys of the Palais Royal—a notorious haunt of royalist plotters. The disguised nobleman was gazing at a display of knives in the window of a cutlery shop. Camelford glimpsed the look of recognition, and disappeared once more.

On that day Fouché's men were too late. But now they had their quarry on the run. They caught him a week later near the Tuileries. Lord Camelford was arrested as a source of danger to France and her ruler. Fortunately, the lethal nine-shot pistol was not found on him.

A long interrogation followed, in which the Grand Judge's chief of secret police sought to establish Lord Camelford's motives in entering France under a false name. That his purpose had been hostile seemed certain. He was a reckless and dangerous man; and one who had no hesitation in killing when he felt justified. He was closely connected with the Pitts and Grenvilles, arch-opponents of the First Consul and of the present peace. In view of all this the conclusion seemed inescapable that he had come with the set purpose of assassinating the First Consul. What alternative explanation was there?

Lord Camelford expressed surprise at the interpretation placed upon his conduct. *He* wish to injure the government of France? This was very far from being the case. As he could explain, he was in fact a long-standing admirer of France and true Jacobin principles. In England he had greatly offended the advocates of war by joining Lord Stanhope and Horne

Tooke in opposition. He had in fact come to Paris to participate in the rejoicing at the conclusion of that unjust conflict.

Lord Camelford spoke convincingly — so convincingly in fact that the police chief's suspicions began to melt. Perhaps after all Camelford really was a friend of France. Fouché had reservations enough, however, to inform him that he must leave the country at once, never to return unless he had requested and received permission from the authorities. As a report later placed before Bonaparte pointed out, 'It is sometimes pointlessly provocative to embitter such characters, when their true instincts feel nothing hostile towards our Government.'

This was a charitable view. Others in France *were* convinced that Camelford's mission had directly menaced the life of the First Consul.

A French police report afterwards described Lord Camelford in the following terms:

> Lord Camelford, first cousin of Mr. Pitt, brother-in-law of Lord Grenville and near relative of Sydney Smith, gives much money to the émigré Chouans living in England, particularly to Limoëlan, whom he sees often. His close relationship with these scoundrels gave him the idea that he himself should assassinate the First Consul.[13]

Joseph Picot de Limoëlan was a devoted Breton royalist, who had fought the republicans in the west ever since 1793. His father had been guillotined in the Terror, and he became one of the most dreaded enemies of the Republic, operating under the *noms de guerre* of *Tap-à-Mort* and *Pour-le-Roi*. By the spring of 1800, however, it had become clear that the republic was too secure to be overthrown by military force, and a plot began to be hatched for the assassination of the First Consul as an alternative.

Limoëlan, more than any other, advocated this desperate course. In May 1800, he paid a brief secret visit to England, for the purpose of concerting the conspiracy. There he was decorated by the Comte d'Artois with the Cross of St Louis.[14] He never came again to England, so it looks as if his contacts with Camelford arose in direct connexion with the assassination plot. Only the year before, a French royalist leader had testified to Camelford's determination to enter France with a party of *émigré* gentlemen ('but he only chose very determined Royalists'), adding that 'it has always seemed to me that Lord Camelford wished to raise a crusade against the Directory and Bonaparte'.[15]

Two months later, in July, Lord Camelford had travelled to Hamburg.

Nothing is known of the purpose of his voyage, but it may be noted that this was the most convenient port for entering or observing France in wartime, Belgium and Holland being under French occupation. Then, in September, Camelford's friend Monsieur de la Brunerie sent him from Hamburg a detailed account of the procedure necessary to infiltrate a French *émigré* into Paris without attracting the hostile attention of Fouché's police.

On 15 November Limoëlan arrived in Paris as an *émigré* requesting to be struck off the proscribed list. On 24 December he arranged the discharge of the infernal machine in the rue St Nicaise, which was within an ace of destroying Napoleon. But the attempt failed, Limoëlan went to ground somewhere in Paris, and Lord Camelford himself entered France in disguise, armed with his formidable repeating pistol.

This succession of events suggests strongly that, in the first fortnight of April 1802, history was within a hair's breadth of being altered dramatically.

Lord Camelford was despatched under escort to Boulogne and thence to England. His return home was noted by *The Times* on 20 April with customary sarcasm.

A Morning Paper of yesterday informs us, that Lord Camelford is returned to England; and it adds, that his Lordship experienced *the most polite treatment from the Chief Consul*! It had been very differently reported in this Country, as it was said that Fouché's *Gentlemen* had been very anxious to find out his Lordship's address.

It was said, too, that Camelford had found opportunity to visit Parisian gambling houses, where he 'netted the nice little sum of £20,000'.[16]

Apart from this there seems to have been very little public notice taken of Camelford's adventure; Lord Grenville's efforts to ensure the matter was forgotten as swiftly as possible were presumably effective.

VIII

❧❧❧❧❧❧❧❧❧❧❧❧❧❧❧❧❧❧❧❧❧❧❧❧❧❧❧❧❧❧❧❧❧❧❧❧❧❧

The Peer and the Pugilist

It was not long before Lord Camelford was in the public eye again – but in an entirely different context. Frustrated in his political ambitions, he turned to sport. The summer of 1802 saw him an enthusiastic amateur of the turf, the ring and the cockpit. He acquired a reputation as a nonpareil. As his friend Anthony Carlisle, the famous surgeon at the Westminster Hospital, noted, Camelford 'desired ... to Have the best Horses'. On 3 June his three-year-old brown colt came ninth in the Derby, but the set-back did not disappoint him unduly.[1] A fortnight later there was a grand regatta on the Thames at Ranelagh Gardens, Chelsea. Most of the *ton* were present, and prominent among those who spent the long summer evening on the river were the Duke of Manchester, Lord Craven and Lord Camelford. At seven o'clock there was heavy betting on a race between six boats rowing from Blackfriars Bridge to Battersea Bridge. It was gloriously sunny weather, and scores of pleasure boats, wherries, skiffs and cutters appeared off Chelsea reach, 'happy-looking girls and assiduous gallants – all huddled together in most irreverent confusion'. Afterwards, the fashionable part of the company crowded into the Rotunda, dined and drank splendidly, and watched glittering cascades of fireworks crackling over the Thames. The party did not break up until four next morning.[2]

Lord Camelford's abiding enthusiasm was for the prize-ring. The great match he had arranged between Bourke and Belcher in the previous autumn had been frustrated by Belcher's temporary arrest. A month later, on 25 November, when Camelford was on the Continent, the two champions had met at Hurley Bottom, near Maidenhead. For twenty minutes the contest had raged ferociously, until Bourke's second had compelled the butcher to concede the victory. This he did with extreme reluctance, though in fact he had little choice as he had received so bad a cut on his forehead as scarcely to be able to see through the stream of blood pouring down his face. Though Belcher clearly deserved his victor's prize of 200 guineas, few people felt that the result was really indicative as to who was the better man. The punches on both sides had been clumsily delivered, Bourke had been largely incapacitated by his injury, and, above all, 'most men of science thought, that the battle was won by the *superior condition* of Belcher'.[3]

Lord Camelford's faith in Bourke was not lessened by the result of this contest. At Enfield Wash he had produced the Shropshire butcher in the pink of condition, whereas at Hurley Bottom, as he now learned, Bourke had been 'cajoled out of prison the night preceding the fight, without any *training*, or without any regard to his *condition*, which was exceedingly precarious from the confinement which he had suffered for debt'.[4]

At Newmarket one day it was agreed between several gentlemen, patrons of the Fancy, that another fight should take place on 17 June. The locality was the village of Grewelthorpe, near Ripon in Yorkshire, but again the host of enthusiasts assembled there was disappointed. Though Bourke and Belcher were both present, Bourke's second refused to allow him to fight. He gave no reason, but it seems he felt that Bourke was not yet in sufficiently good condition. Bourke had growled out threateningly that 'it would now be determined who was the better man', to which Belcher replied 'he was surprised he did not know that already'.[5] But once again the question of whether a fit Bourke could beat Belcher had been left unanswered.

However, steps to decide the matter for good were put in hand. The appointed day was 20 August, and the venue was kept a closely guarded secret, lest the magistrates attempted to pursue their vendetta against Lord Camelford by prohibiting the contest. The day before was that of Camberwell Fair, held at a little village just south of the Thames. Thither London annually disgorged its thousands, who flocked down to savour the delights offered by quack-doctors, tooth-drawers, Punch and Judy men, wise pigs, two-headed calves and other freaks of nature and humanity.

But it was two visitors who attracted more attention than all the hucksters, tumblers and fortune-tellers put together. Through one section of the crowd moved the gigantic figure of Joseph Bourke, accompanied by a group of his gentlemen backers and a host of lesser hangers-on. The day was hot and sultry, and the prize-fighter drank deeply from the mugs of ale proffered him by admirers. To the delight of the grinning spectators, the Shropshire butcher wiped his mouth with the back of an enormous fist and announced in ringing tones how he would 'serve it out' to Jem on the next day.

Next moment there were shouts on the fringe of the crowd; a passage was instantly cleared, and the unassuming figure of Belcher was seen approaching. Bourke's eyes lit up and, when the Bristol fighter invited him to another taste of what he had undergone at Hurley Bottom, he laughed scornfully. A way was at once made to a bowling green behind the Golden Lion Inn, and the fairground was virtually deserted as all swarmed towards the inn. There was little to see, however. Bourke was clearly quite *lushy* by now after all his midday refreshment, and flew at Belcher even while his opponent was removing his coat. Belcher knew his antagonist well enough by now to anticipate this. A few of the butcher's blows landed home, but Belcher sidestepped coolly and threw in a number of punches that left the drunken Bourke staggering and minus one of his front teeth. The *swells* of the Fancy interfered to prevent the unequal contest, and the two parted, uttering threats as to what would happen on the morrow.

The great fight finally took place on 20 August 1802, in a field behind St George's Chapel, near Tyburn Turnpike. So unprecedentedly large a crowd poured out of the city along Oxford Street and across Hyde Park that the magistrates were powerless to intervene. Everything had combined to make this long-postponed combat the most talked-of match of the age. The two men were the outstanding pugilists of their time. The contrasts in style and physique promised a fascinating struggle.

Joe Bourke was a giant of a man, but not, as is sometimes the case with large men, merely heavily built. His muscles and sinews stood out on his torso, shoulders and arms like knotted cables, and his whole appearance gave a suggestion of irresistible power. Added to this was the ferocity of his expression, his indomitable courage, and a resolution never to concede defeat, whatever his fate. He also bore a reputation, not unjustified, of being a bully and a ruffian.[6]

Jem Belcher was just twenty-one years old, slimly built, with gentle, handsome features. Many likened him in appearance to Napoleon.[7] His manner was mild, polite – even deferential. As to his boxing, he had developed a unique style entirely his own. His younger brother Tom, who was also to become one of the great names of the prize-ring, later described Jem's technique as follows:

> ... without appearance of superior bodily strength, [he] stripped remarkably well, and displayed much muscle. Considering him as a bruiser, he was *not* a man of science, according to the rules of the pugilistic art; he possessed a style peculiar to himself, capable of baffling all regular science, which appeared more intuitive, than gained by practice. He was remarkably quick, sprang backward and forward with the rapidity of lightning: you heard his blows, but never saw them. At the conclusion of a round, his antagonist was bruised and bloody, but he threw in his hits with such adroitness, that you could not discern them. This style was perfectly original, and extremely difficult to withstand.[8]

The event drew a large crowd to the fields across the Uxbridge Road from Hyde Park. Lord Camelford himself was not publicly in evidence, perhaps in an attempt to placate the wrath of the magistrates. Only half-a-dozen gentlemen amateurs were prominent, but many notables from the pugilistic fraternity were close to the ring. There was merry Tom Owen, ever partial to a bottle of *belch* in a *boozing ken*; big, bluff Bill Gibbons, victor of innumerable battles, though few of them in the ring; and old Joe Ward, already fifty years old and the patriarch of the Fancy, who continued to enter the lists and knock down his man for a further ten years.

Belcher and Bourke arrived

> about one o'clock, and there being no time to erect a stage, a most extensive ring was formed: the persons in the inner circle almost laying down, the second circle sitting, the third circle on their knees, and outside of them the others standing, till those on the very outside, who could not measure five feet ten, were glad of an occasional peep, by jumping up, aided by leaning on others shoulders.

Every eye was on the little green square in the centre of this multitude, kept clear only by the vigilance of the *vinegars*, who held hats before their eyes and struck impartially with their whips at anyone rash enough to press forward into the place of business. A great cheer was taken up and rolled back to the outermost skirts of the mob as the two champions entered the ring, attended by their seconds and bottle-holders. For the first time, there was no trace of drunkenness or ill-condition about Joe Bourke. There was a wicked look in his eye, which matched the power of his massive arms and fists. His nose bore a livid scar, memento of his defeat at Hurley Bottom, and it was clear that, so far as he was concerned, there was much more than the prize-money at stake in this contest. Glaring at his adversary, he demanded that the rounds be extended to three-quarters of a minute, instead of the customary half, but this the seconds resisted.

Now Belcher had stripped also, and the spectators marvelled at the contrast. His chest and arms, though clearly tough as whipcord, were slight and graceful; he seemed a mere boy who must be crushed by the bull-like strength of Bourke. But he shrugged his shoulders and smiled at the threats launched at him across the little green patch that was to be their battlefield. 'Time!' cried Mr Fletcher Reid, looking up from his time-piece. Then Bourke, who for all his bulk had immense agility, hurled himself forward in an attempt to bear his opponent to the ground. An untidy scrimmage followed, with a few indecisive blows given, but the round ended without obvious advantage to either party. The next followed a similar course. In the third Bourke slammed home a left-handed punch on to Belcher's right cheek-bone, and another on the chest. But once again they closed, and were only parted by Mr Reid's shout of 'Time!' By the fourth round murmurs of dissatisfaction were beginning to spread among the spectators, for Bourke was still attempting (quite permissibly by the then laws of the ring) to bear his adversary to the ground, with no decisive result.

The fifth round, however, at once convinced the crowd that what had occurred so far was but a preamble to the fight of fights. As before, Bourke dashed forward to close with his agile opponent. But this time he seized hold of the slight Belcher, gathered him up in his great arms and hurled him, head foremost, to the ground. For a moment Belcher lay stunned, and the crowd, believing his neck to have been broken by the dreadful fall, began to cry 'Foul!' But Belcher rose, pale, resolute and smiling. Pointing a scoffing finger at Bourke, he muttered, 'No, no — never mind.'

Now both fighters seemed to gain new vigour. In the sixth round Bourke hurtled forward as usual, but this time Belcher evaded the bear-hug and managed to keep him at bay with his fists. Here Jem's science gave him the advantage, and whop! whop! whop! went a flurry of punches to the butcher's head and neck. It was only as the round ended that Bourke managed to close in and wrestle. But he had suffered a set-back, and in the next three rounds appeared on the defensive. Jem scored a number of successful hits; in the contemporary account Bourke received

> three nobbers, a hit on the throat, one on the ear, and got pinked about the body — so that none could count the blows, and the fight was taken out of him. But he was a glutton, looked stupid, and knew not what to be at, which made Belcher laugh outright ... 'What dost think of it?' he asked; *whack, bang*! went his fists; 'There 'tis, vor thee' — Bang! bang! again and again.

The crowd was ecstatic. Cries of encouragement mingled with bets given and taken, punctuated by the crack of the vinegars' whips as they held back the pressing throng. The next round (number ten) was the decisive one, and exceeded all expectations. Bourke, sustained by his fierce courage, came out of his corner with his leg-of-mutton fists thudding forward with the force of a sledge-hammer driving in a gatepost. Despite the punishment he had received, his strength and resolution were unabated. But Jem Belcher was applying his amazing intuitive system of lightning fist-play: blows that moved so fast no man could see them begin or end. In danced Jem, and out; Bourke was bleeding from a cut under his left eye. In again, and blood was pouring from another under the right one. Then, before anyone could see what had happened, Jem's fist slammed in below Joe Bourke's chin with such dreadful force that the giant was knocked off his feet, and landed head first on the greensward some way off. So violent was the delivery of this punch that Belcher himself fell forward from its effect.

The two men seized hold of each other where they lay, Bourke managing to heave himself on top. Sucking up the blood from cuts in his mouth, he squirted it over Belcher's face. 'Damn thee, I'll pay thee out vor that!' gasped Belcher. Bourke muttered that it was an accident, the round ended, and both men staggered back to their corners. There were four rounds left of the fight, but it was clear that Bourke could take little more punishment. His face was a bloody pulp, but he would not give in and lurched forward to receive punches he could barely return. His seconds could hardly get him off the ground, and by the fourteenth round he could only lurch about, Belcher hitting him when and where he chose.

When the next round was announced, Bourke could no longer rise from Owen's knee, and Belcher was acknowledged the victor.

Three days later a dinner for supporters of the Fancy was held at the One Tun public house in St James's Market, and there Bourke rose before the assembled company, shook Belcher's hand and acknowledged him Champion of England.[9] Lord Camelford continued to support Bourke, but henceforward he became the especial patron of Belcher. Jem retained the Championship until 1807, when he was defeated by Tom Cribb. But it was universally conceded that it was 'only part of the man' that was beaten, for on 24 July 1803 he suffered an accident that would have led any other man honourably to quit the prize-ring. He was playing at rackets, when he was struck by a ball and lost the sight of an eye.

Soon after his retirement, he took a public house, the Jolly Brewer in Wardour Street. Camelford was a frequent visitor to it. By this time Camelford was interested in the fortunes of another martial champion. In the autumn of 1803, he bought a celebrated bull-terrier from another patron of the turf and prize-ring, Colonel Mellish. No other dog could stand against him, and it had not been long before Lord Camelford came to hear of this incomparable creature. Always desirous 'to be at the head in such matters, he made a successful bid for a purchase. The price was two guineas for each pound of the dog's weight: at around forty pounds, eighty-two guineas. 'This was satisfied in the following manner: A favourite gun, belonging to his Lordship, value forty guineas, and a case of pistols, value forty-four guineas. It would have been an insult to this noble animal to have paid the purchase in money, and, therefore, he was in a manner exchanged for these warlike articles.'

So he wagged his tail and entered Lord Camelford's service. He was renamed 'Belcher' in honour of the other Champion, and was famed as equally incomparable a warrior. He had fought and won 104 battles; three of his adversaries he actually killed, and he had grievously wounded many more. At the time Camelford was 'so pleased with his purchase, that he declares no money should part him and his dog'. Despite this, he shortly afterwards gave 'Belcher' to his namesake, declaring 'that two such invincibles would do well to reside together'. Jem was gratified, but with characteristic modesty renamed his new acquisition 'Trusty'. An engraving of the time portrays the dog as he must have appeared to his opponents: his hide covered in scars, and his upper lip drawn back to reveal a formidable array of *grinders*.[10]

Despite the informality of Lord Camelford's relationships with prize-fighters, his rank was always respected. A contemporary writer remarked:

The pugilists respected His Lordship, partly because he knew every-thing about their science and was no mean practitioner of it himself, and partly because he was always ready to open his purse to them. In consequence these fellows were very proud to boast of his friend-ship. But it must be appreciated that the relationship was absolutely correct; Camelford never forgot his rank even in the lowest society. He always received the respect due to his position, and if a coal-heaver or meatporter of his acquaintance attempted any insolence he was swiftly paid in his own coin. In good society, with his sister Lady Grenville, his mother and his friends, he was the best-bred and finest gentleman you could imagine. But this rough eccentric despised the customs, advantages and luxuries of the great world to which he was born as mere fripperies, unworthy of what ranked as a man in his estimation.[11]

IX

A Controversial Character

The contradictions of Lord Camelford's character have remained an enigma to this day. Charles Reade, the Victorian novelist, after summarising his contradictory qualities—consistent only in their vigour—confessed that: 'To those, who take their ideas of character from fiction alone, such a sketch as this must seem incredible; for fiction is forced to suppress many of the anomalies that Nature presents.'[1]

By those of his contemporaries who did not know him he was universally regarded as irrational and wild, even to the point of madness. But to his intimates he presented quite a different image. He had a close circle of friends who loved and respected him to a degree that suggests he possessed personal attractions unconnected with his rank and wealth. Barrie, Pakenham, Russell and Manby were all men of high reputation in their private and public characters, and their opinion must count for much.

When he chose, as Hester Stanhope testified, he could exert extraordinary charm. His experiences had been remarkable, and he could talk of them in a manner that excited rapt attention. Despite this, he remained largely isolated from society. Among people of his own rank he was shy and diffident. As someone who knew him closely explained, 'during the latter years of his life' he suffered from 'an absolutely unfounded jealousy that he was universally detested (with some, very few, exceptions) here, & that his treatment by the Country as a Country, & by its Powers and Jurisdictions, had been most unjust & most cruel ... '[2]

Fortunately, it seems that fresh light can be thrown on Lord Camelford's character from an unexpected source. In Anthony Trollope's novel *Phineas Finn*, published in 1869, much of the story is taken up with the hero's infatuation with Lady Laura Standish, an intelligent and beautiful woman with a strong interest in his welfare. A subsidiary character in the story is Lady Laura's brother, Lord Chiltern, and there appears to be little doubt that Lord Chiltern is a lightly disguised representation of Lord Camelford. Thus from a hitherto untapped source comes a perceptive picture of the man.

Lord Chiltern's origins bear some resemblance to those of Lord Camelford.[3] His sister, and consequently himself, 'was related to almost everybody who was anybody among the high Whigs'. Phineas's first glimpse of Lord Chiltern is ominous: 'There was something in the countenance of the man which struck him almost with dread, – something approaching to ferocity.' But Laura is devoted to him, explaining later that 'he is not half so bad as people say he is. In many ways he is very good, – very good. And he is very clever ... I think he loves me.'

But Chiltern drank, and was desperately violent. 'He had fallen through his violence into some terrible misfortune at Paris, had been brought before a public judge, and his name and his infamy had been made notorious in every newspaper in the two capitals.'

Like Camelford, Chiltern is ready to flare up at the faintest suggestion of an affront. Phineas Finn pays his addresses to Violet Effingham, to whom Chiltern had previously paid court without success, and who bitterly resented the intrusion. Finn felt an obligation to call and explain, but 'felt some palpitation at the heart ... knowing well the fiery nature of the man he expected to see. It might be that there would be some actual conflict between him and this half-mad Lord before he got back again into the street.' He was right to be apprehensive; Chiltern could barely suppress his rage when they met, and several times raised his clenched fist. However, he held himself in check with difficulty, explaining that he intended to fight a duel with his rival.

Phineas was greatly taken aback by this development; not because he was afraid, but because he 'felt at the moment that the fighting of a duel would be destructive to all his political hopes. Few Englishmen fight duels in these days. They who do so are always reckoned to be fools.' This was very true: the last duel fought by Englishmen on English soil had occurred over twenty years before the period (1866–7) of *Phineas Finn*.[4] The very weapons employed had become archaic in an age of revolvers and rifled barrels.

Trollope accordingly sets his duel on a beach in Belgium, where the participants could evade the legal prosecution that would undoubtedly have followed such an encounter in England. This procedure was rare but not unknown in Trollope's time, though would certainly not have involved people of the rank ascribed to his characters: a peer and a member of parliament.

Trollope was quite conscious of the anomaly, which he seems to have introduced not so much for dramatic purposes, but primarily because it sprang naturally from the character of his Lord Chiltern. Nonetheless he appears to have been embarrassed by a consciousness that he had introduced a scene inconsistent with the real men and manners of his day – a consistency on which he prided himself. Phineas is represented as thinking of the duel as 'an absurdity' and 'very silly'. It seems likely that the incongruity arose from Trollope's having borrowed the character of Chiltern from that of Lord Camelford. Chiltern behaved precisely as Camelford would have done in 1804, but it was an action quite inappropriate for 1864.

There is in addition, as has already been indicated, a reference that suggests irresistibly that Lord Camelford was consciously in Trollope's mind when writing this episode. After the duel, a radical newspaper gets wind of what has happened and publishes a sour attack on the principals: 'Here was a young lord, infamously notorious, quarrelling with one of his boon-companions whom he had appointed to a private seat in the House of Commons, fighting duels, breaking the law, scandalising the public – and all this was done without punishment of the guilty!' This description is too redolent of Lord Camelford to require comment, but it is the next sentence that is significant: 'There were old stories afloat, – so said the article, – of what in a former century had been done by Lord Mohuns and Mr Bests; but now, in 186–, &c, &c, &c.'

Both these names are linked to that of Lord Camelford. Lord Mohun, who was killed in a duel in 1712, was the last owner of Boconnoc before it was purchased by Governor Pitt. The coincidence of the same house having twice within a century passed from the hands of its owners as the result of a duel had often been remarked upon. Not too much emphasis can be placed on this, as Mohun's duel had become celebrated anew from its introduction into Thackeray's historical novel *Henry Esmond*, published in 1852. But the mention of Mr Best falls into quite a different category. As we shall see, Lord Camelford fought a famous duel with a Mr Best in 1804, and it is to this that Trollope is referring. But Best himself was not known as a duellist, and indeed would be quite unknown to history but for his encounter with Camelford. It is significant that Trollope refers to this duel, and in doing so singles out the name of the participant who was so obscure as only to be known as Camelford's antagonist.[5] The author must surely have deliberately avoided using the name of Camelford, which would have fitted the context so much more naturally. The avoidance is striking on two grounds: *Camelford* was the famous duellist, not Best (few of Trollope's readers can have known who Best was, whereas most would have heard of Camelford); and *Camelford* was a wild young nobleman, far more apt for the parallel with Lord Chiltern drawn by the *People's Banner*, the radical newspaper.

The parallels between the real and fictional peers seem to be far too marked for chance. Indeed, the 'Chiltern' picture of Lord Camelford almost certainly derives from sound authority.

Anthony Trollope was born eleven years after Camelford's death and wrote *Phineas Finn* sixty-two years after that event. Clearly he himself could possess no direct knowledge of Lord Camelford, but he could easily have spoken to many who did. And there was in any case one very remarkable survivor from the era of Lord Camelford, who died only two years before Trollope began to write *Phineas Finn*, and whom he may well have met.

Camelford's sister Anne was perhaps the person to whom he felt the closest attachment. Her husband, Lord Grenville, died in 1834 at the age of seventy-four, but she lived on for nearly thirty years until 1864, when she died at the advanced age of ninety-one.

It is not known whether Trollope ever met Lady Grenville, and if he did it is not certain that she would have spoken to the fashionable novelist about her brother, so misunderstood by the world, but whose finer qualities she had so valued. It is perhaps more likely that Trollope knew those who had themselves heard the story from Lady Grenville's lips.

If, as seems almost certain, Trollope had access to original accounts of Lord Camelford still current in the society of his day, then it is worth reading *Phineas Finn* for the light it throws on one other important but ill-documented aspect of the 'half-mad lord'. It is suggested throughout the novel that Chiltern's aggressiveness and suspicion of others' goodwill stemmed from his upbringing in the house of a cold and distant father. His trust in humanity had been warped at an early age, and he

145

consequently found difficulty in believing he could be loved. This was Camelford's experience.

Again, the novel may help to explain why Camelford's love affair with Lady Hester Stanhope came to nothing.

Lady Hester's uncle and aunt, Lord and Lady Chatham (in whose London house she frequently stayed), had been convinced that a marriage was imminent. But the relationship came to an end some time before September 1802. In the middle of that month, Lady Hester left her grandmother's house at Burton Pynsent for a tour on the Continent. She was accompanied by some old friends, Mr and Mrs Egerton, and planned to visit her brother, Lord Mahon, who was studying in Italy, where he was still living after having fled from their harsh parent's home at Chevening. Crossing Mont Cenis on a mule, she reached Turin in October and wintered in Italy. She did not return to England until July 1803, nearly a year later.

On her return she found herself homeless, for her grandmother had died in April and Burton Pynsent had passed to her uncle, Lord Chatham. It was Lord Chatham's younger brother, William Pitt, who came to her rescue and invited her to share his home and do the honours of his bachelor household. He was soon charmed by her glittering personality, and until his tragically early death in 1806 continued to enthuse over her beauty, liveliness, wit and intelligence.

Any thought of marriage to Camelford must have been far from Hester's mind when she moved into the establishment of her kindly uncle. In fact she must have known she would be severing all connexion with him. As she recounted later, 'Mr. Pitt liked him personally as much as I did; but considerations of propriety, arising out of his position, obliged him to keep him at a distance ... Mr. Pitt took little or no notice of him, out of absolute fear of the scrapes he was constantly getting into.'

There was no change, however, in the exceptionally high estimation and affection with which she regarded Lord Camelford. 'She admired Lord C's character, and, in some things, imitated him,' her doctor noted. After Mr Pitt's death in 1806, she retired to Wales in a melancholy state. Then, in 1810, she left Britain for good to begin the voyage that ultimately brought her to the celebrated refuge at Jôon, on Mount Lebanon in Syria, where she remained until her lonely death in 1839.

It was frequently conjectured that some unhappy love affair had led her finally to forsake everything that was familiar in order to retire among all the hazards attendant on life amongst the lawless peoples of the Levant. Many rumours as to the identity of her supposed lover were current; they included Sir John Moore and Beau Brummell, but both these conjectures have been authoritatively refuted.[6] Perhaps it was a recollection of Lord Camelford's adventure in the East that led her to take the remarkable step of becoming the first European lady of note to travel among the Arab tribes of the desert. Lord Camelford had crossed the desert from Suez to Alexandria in the spring of 1796, and it was Alexandria that was Lady Hester's first port of call in the Moslem East. There she may well have met an Italian gentleman, Marquetti Caravigis, who had brought camels to Lord Camelford at Suez and accompanied him on his return.

To Camelford the East was a land of adventure and romance. Before setting off for Suez he had declared himself 'zealous to try what possible hardships may be encountered between India and Europe';[7] two and a half years later he sat up all night in a coach travelling from Portsmouth to London, regaling a companion with an account of his Eastern travels.[8] He had probably talked similarly to Hester, for when he disappeared for France in 1801, she discounted the possibility of his having departed for India – a project which had presumably by inference been contemplated at some point. In the East Hester had her cousin constantly in mind. To Dr Meryon she spoke movingly of his finer qualities, unknown to the world. On another occasion she was able to reminisce at length with one who had loved him as dearly. In August 1811 she was visited at Constantinople by Robert Barrie; she recorded that 'Captain Barrie was poor Lord Camelford's greatest friend; therefore, I received him with great cordiality'.

In her hilltop refuge at Mount Lebanon, Hester Stanhope had frequent cause to fear the tyrannical caprices of local potentates and banditti, and the pressing attentions of her creditors. On such occasions she used to think of her fearless cousin, with his fierce blue eyes and deadly pistols. Were he by her side, her persecutors would make themselves very scarce. A year before her death, she learned that measures were on foot to distrain her for her debts, but 'certainly those who had ventured to charge themselves with such a message would have found that I was a cousin of Lord Camelford's'. The imagined threat continued, however, and she wrote to inform Sir Francis Burdett: 'I am now about building up every avenue to my premises, and there shall wait with patience, immured within the walls, till it please God to send me a little mouse: and whoever presumes to force my retirement, by scaling my walls or anything of the like, will be received by me as Lord Camelford would have received them.'[9]

No documentary evidence has survived to show what caused the cousins' separation. If Camelford, who had taken so much trouble to ingratiate himself with her father, had proposed marriage and she had been willing, there would have been no need for her to turn to her uncle for help. What is known is that for the rest of her life Hester never ceased to express the extent of her love and admiration for her cousin — yet by September 1802 she had irrevocably broken off all contact with him. It is possibly significant that Lord Camelford, who had earlier corresponded in friendly terms with his cousin the Prime Minister,[10] afterwards took to expressing extreme dislike for Mr Pitt.[11] The change may have resulted from resentment at Pitt's protection of Hester Stanhope.

Perhaps *Phineas Finn* will once again be found to supply the missing clues in this crucial aspect of Lord Camelford's life. Trollope's Lord Chiltern loves a girl named Violet Effingham, and there is much about her and her standing with Chiltern that reminds one of Hester Stanhope. Violet is not Chiltern's cousin, but their relationship is almost equivalent. Their fathers had been lifelong friends, and the young couple had known each other since childhood. It was perhaps the pre-existence of this unconstrained childish friendship that enabled Chiltern to relax his protective aggressiveness sufficiently to fall in love. He certainly did not love any other woman but his sister, and Violet he loved dearly. He proposes to her in his gruff manner that guarded against slights or rebuffs, and not surprisingly she refuses. Chiltern's sister Laura explained to Phineas Finn: 'Oh, I believe she loves him. I do indeed. But she fears him. She does not quite understand how much there is of tenderness with that assumed ferocity ... '

When Laura pressed Violet to marry him, urging that he loved her, Violet responded lightly, 'I know, – or fancy that I know, – that so many men love me! But, after all, what sort of love is it? It is just as when you and I, when we see something nice in a shop, call it a dear duck of a thing, and tell someone to go and buy it, let the price be ever so extravagant. I know my own position, Laura. I'm a dear duck of a thing.' But, urged Laura, you love him. No, replied Violet, 'It does not seem to me to be possible to myself to be what girls call in love. I can like a man. I do like, perhaps, half a dozen ... But as for caring about any one of them in the way of loving him, – wanting to marry him, and have him all to myself, and that sort of thing, – I don't know what it means.'

Just so was Hester Stanhope's light-hearted dismissal of a report that she was about to be married: 'Thank you for your news. I have been *going* to be married fifty times in my life; said to have been married half as often, and run away with once. But provided I have my own way, the world may have theirs and welcome.'[12]

Violet is presented as being a little frightened of her rough wooer: 'There was something in his eye that almost frightened her. It looked as though he would not hesitate to wring his wife's neck round, if ever he should be brought to threaten to do so ... No; – she did not think she could ever bring herself to marry him. Why take a venture that was double-dangerous, when there were so many ventures open to her, apparently with very little of danger attached to them?'

And later Violet says, 'The truth is ... that though we like each other, – love each other, if you choose to say so, – we are not fit to be man and wife ... We are too much alike. Each is too violent, too headstrong.'

The novelist, unlike the historian, can provide a happy ending. Lord Chiltern does succeed in overcoming Violet Effingham's reservations – ust – and Trollope clearly believes that the fiery lord would be a different man thereafter. From all that had passed it was not difficult to see that the lady was waiting to be won over; but won over she had to be, even if it were in Lord Chiltern's particular way.

Violet eventually 'takes the jump'. Hester Stanhope never did. Possibly Lord Cameltord ventured as far as the opening round of Chiltern's wooing, without being able to bring it to a successful conclusion. And possibly he failed for precisely the reasons which, for so long, threatened the courtship of his fictional counterpart. Mistrustful of others' affections, he guarded against wounding rebuffs by an abrupt and unsentimental approach which frightened Hester into thinking their marriage to be too risky a proposition. The cousins separated, never to meet again.

X

⚜⚜⚜⚜⚜⚜⚜⚜⚜⚜⚜⚜⚜⚜⚜⚜⚜⚜⚜⚜⚜⚜⚜⚜⚜⚜⚜⚜⚜

The Prisoner in the Temple

Within two months of Hester Stanhope's leaving for Italy, Lord Camelford had applied in his own name for a passport to travel once more to France. It appears odd that it was granted, in view of the circumstances under which he had left that country only a year previously. This passport was issued by the Foreign Office, and it seems odder still that the French embassy subsequently gave him a passport too. After the signing of the Peace of Amiens, France and England had exchanged ambassadors, and perhaps the French plenipotentiary, General Andreossi, had not been fully informed on the Camelford affair by his predecessor and locum tenens, Citizen Otto. In any case, Camelford made no use of the passport for several months; his mother was seriously ill, and he wished to be by her side.

The peace was uneasy. In the spring of 1803 Britain's strained relations with France were reaching breaking-point. The correspondence of French consuls in Britain had been intercepted, and proof obtained that they were engaged in espionage. Both countries were increasing their military establishments, and on 13 March occurred Napoleon's angry threat to the British ambassador, Lord Whitworth: 'If you will fight I shall also fight. You may possibly be able to destroy France, but never to intimidate her.'[1] War was near, and any Englishman with business to transact in France had clearly little time to lose.

Lord Grenville seems to have had an inkling that his brother-in-law was dangerously restive, and on 10 February wrote to Camelford: 'Your sister has mentioned to me that you had an idea of leaving town very shortly ... But before you take any final decision in this instance, there is a very painful communication which I have to make to you, & which it is of the utmost importance to yourself to know.' But whatever the communication was, it failed to avert the coming fiasco.

In the closing days of March Lord Grenville received a letter from Lord Camelford addressed from Calais, informing him that once again the young peer was a prisoner of the French authorities. The letter said:

> The same fatality, which has constantly attended me through life, has again rendered me an object of suspicion to the agent of the French Government here. Although my entire innocence of being concerned in any political Cabal whatever insures me a speedy release the moment I am arrived at Paris, yet I am in the mean time exposed to all the inconveniences of an arrestation. My object in informing you of this, is not that you should exert the springs of Government, in my favour, which is wholly unnecessary, and which I should besides decline, but simply that you may prevent its reaching my mothers ears, a circumstance which presents itself to me in such dreadful colours, that I can not allow myself to fix my thoughts upon it.[2]

Neither Lord Camelford's confidence that he would shortly be set free, nor the hope that Lady Camelford could be kept ignorant of his predicament, can have aroused much conviction for the unhappy Lord Grenville. *The Times* dispelled both hopes by publishing a gleeful article on 31 March:

> Lord Camelford was provided with the requisite passports to the very letter of diplomatic formality; but his Lordship, with his habitual eccentricity, preferred an open boat to a packet; and having little of the baggage generally thought to appertain to an English Nobleman, besides his pistols, awakened the supicions of Citizen Mengaud at Calais, who recollected his Lordship as a person once prevented, in very singular circumstances, by our own Government, from crossing the Channel.

Citizen Mengaud, 'Commissaire Général dans les Ports de la Manche et du Pas-de-Calais', was a dedicated servant of the republic and avid detector of spies and plotters. He regarded Englishmen with profound disdain, showing his contempt by decorating his antechamber with prints by Gillray which portrayed British ministers in an unflattering light.[3] The *commissaire* glanced at the passport, started at seeing the familiar name of Lord Camelford, and stared up at the tall, pale figure who held his head quizzically on one side. Recognising the look of suspicion that darkened Mengaud's broad republican brow, Camelford murmured airily that he was far from having any sinister motive for entering the country, and that he was incapable of intending harm to the First Consul, still less of ASSASSINATING him.

Possibly this was intended as a heavy-handed joke. It merely acted as a provocation. A search revealed that the milor carried with him a further passport, issued in the false name of Rushworth, an American merchant. The incessant fogs of London, or possibly a surfeit of *rosbif*, must have clouded the arrogant milor's understanding, causing him accidentally to muddle the two passports. Lord Camelford was at once placed under arrest and sent off under guard to the Grand Judge in Paris. He was, however, allowed to write the letter to Lord Grenville that caused such consternation at Dropmore a day or so later. Meanwhile Lord Camelford, deprived of his pistols, arrived at Paris in a chaise, under the watchful eye of a gendarme. Through the gate of St Denis they drove, and along crowded streets until they drew up at a great gateway guarded by soldiers. Camelford and his guard descended, crossed two courtyards, challenged by sentries at intervals, and came to a little lodge at the foot of a great stone wall. A porter emerged to examine the gendarme's pass, and then unlocked a door to allow the newcomers to pass on. Lord Camelford found himself in a garden planted with trees, and surrounded on all sides by the immensely high wall through which they had just passed. Before them towered an ancient stone keep, flanked by four round towers, their sharp spires dark against the sky. Another guard admitted the English nobleman through a gate at the foot of this donjon. Stone steps led up- wards into the gloom. A turnkey accompanied Lord Camelford in his ascent; he counted 130 steps, and ten times had to pause in the darkness as, with a rattle of bolts and shriek of unoiled hinges, great iron doors were opened and closed behind him. They were now presumably high up in this gloomy stronghold, but four further doors had to be unlocked before Lord Camelford was shown into a small cell. His companion left, locking the door behind him.[4]

Lord Camelford was, in fact, in the notorious prison of the Temple. An ancient mediaeval fortress, it had become the state prison of Paris after the destruction of the Bastille; characteristically, it now held four times as many prisoners as had been found in the old royal prison at its downfall on 14 July 1789. It was within these walls that the innocent Louis XVI, his queen, and his sister had been incarcerated, insulted, terrorised, and dragged off to execution. It might have been in this very cell that the ten-year-old Dauphin suffered republican cruelties that brought on his lingering death.[5] Innumerable lesser victims of the Revolution had been imprisoned, tortured and secretly murdered within these walls; many had entered who had never been seen again and whose fate could only be guessed at. The sinister significance of the Temple was familiar to Lord Camelford, for it was here that his cousin Sidney Smith had been immured for two years. In that very garden through which he had just passed, a mob of sansculottes had battered on the door and howled for the Englishman's blood.

An unaided escape from such a hold was clearly impossible. Yet who knew of his predicament? Perhaps the officious commissary at Calais had withheld the letter he had written to Lord Grenville. What was to happen to him? No word came from the authorities in Paris, and Camelford realised he was more alone than he had ever been in his life. A year ago he had received an unmistakable warning from the Grand Judge's chief of police not to return to France. But despite that, there could be no proof of ill intent on his part. How could they punish a British peer, allied to some of the first personages in the United Kingdom, merely for entering the country? But this brought a new, more sinister fear. They could prove nothing, so it seemed; yet how much did they know? What if the very fact of his virtual immunity from trial was leading them to contemplate a more private and efficacious means of removing the nuisance?

Lord Camelford hurriedly prepared a further letter to Lord Grenville:

My dear Lord, the doubts under which I labour, whether any of my letters have been permitted to come to hand makes me run the risk of a more rigorous confinement, simply to say, that I still continue to experience all the severity of secret detention, by the express order of the 1st Consul who has not condescended to explain the motives of this extraordinary proceeding which I must confess is not wholcy without its apprehension ... my Mother ... occupies my whole thoughts. I dare say but little, for my feelings upon that head are wound up to such a pitch that I dare not give vent to them.

He folded and stuck up this letter, writing on the back in French: 'If this paper falls into the hands of an honest man, he will help the cause of

153

humanity by arranging for it to reach Lord Grenville in London. He could indicate that this is being done by a signal to the relieving guard.'

The last sentence betrayed the fact that 'the gold of Pitt', so often denounced by ardent republicans, had in this case really been set to work. So the Grand Judge, Monsieur Régnier, remarked, when Lord Camelford's furtive message was laid before him. It had been thrown out of the window, and at once retrieved by one of the guards.

When it became clear that this attempt to communicate with his brother-in-law had failed, Lord Camelford sat down next morning to address an appeal through more regular channels. He requested the Grand Judge to forward the letter he enclosed to General Bonaparte. In it he begged in moving terms to be allowed to know with what he was charged, and either to be tried or discharged. He could not bear his present suspense much longer and, infinitely more important, his mother would certainly die if she learned of his predicament.

Lord Camelford would undoubtedly have been even more alarmed had he been able to see a long report the Grand Judge had received a week earlier from Citizen Mengaud. That lynx-eyed guardian of the coast had applied much thought to the question of Lord Camelford, and had come up with some startling conclusions. Lord Camelford, his researches showed, was held in England to be a violent opponent of Government. An ally of Lord Stanhope, he had earned in England and in Ireland the title of chief of the most fanatical Jacobins. Well, pursued Mengaud, this man, who is generally considered as the antithesis of his King and his ministers, does not seem to me to be altogether that. He, Mengaud, would lay his reasons before His Excellency.

Now, it was not as if Camelford had suddenly become a notorious character; he had always been such, and who knew this better than the English ministers? When in the navy he had shot dead his lieutenant. True, he had been obliged to leave the profession in consequence, but how had he escaped punishment for his crime? Because the hand of Mr Pitt had been secretly extended to protect him. And now Mengaud disclosed what really lay behind Camelford's conduct.

It was Camelford's excesses that provided the perfidious Mr Pitt with the pretext for suppressing all aspirations for liberty among the oppressed people of Britain. When Camelford came into conflict with the mob in Bond Street, he gave the Prime Minister an excuse to commit ghastly butcheries in Ireland, exile innocent people to the Botanical Bay in

Australia, and order the juridical assassination of Colonel Despard—executed only two months before for nobly plotting to raid the Bank of England and kill King George III. And why had Pitt protected Camelford from the consequences of his killing Peterson, if not to employ him as an agent in furthering his diabolical political schemes, surpassing as they did all the barbarities of a Turkish pasha? Camelford had been in France before, in disguise, and accompanied by a notorious enemy of the French nation, Colonel Williams. There was a clear pattern running through the whole evil story.

While Citizen Mengaud was pondering these deep matters, he was subjected to a slight which provided curious confirmation of his theory. A British official, named Jenkinson, passing through Calais a day or so after Lord Camelford's arrest, had been less than courteous to this great man, on whom lay the heavy responsibility of receiving the stiff-necked islanders on their arrival in the Republic.

'I presume,' concluded Mengaud's report to the Grand Judge, 'that the conduct of Mr. Jenkinson towards me arose from the fact that he had learned of the arrest of Lord Camelford and of his despatch to Paris under the guidance of a gendarme. He considers this treatment of a Peer of the United Kingdom as an insult to be washed out in the blood of the whole human race.' Jenkinson had begun this drastic course by being rude to Monsieur Mengaud.

The Grand Judge wrote to soothe the commissary's ruffled plumage, promising to investigate further Mr Jenkinson's strange conduct. Meanwhile he had to consider what to do with the young man held in the Temple. Setting aside Mengaud's elaborate theories, there was still much in the circumstances to alarm those responsible for maintaining public order and preserving the person of the First Consul—the two considerations being virtually identical at that period.

Interrogation of Lord Camelford and other enquiries had revealed a story full of inconsistencies and unanswered questions. Camelford had received his passport from Lord Hawkesbury on 13 November 1802, but had not applied for one from the French ambassador until 11 February 1803.[6] The motive for his visit, so he claimed, was to recover a sum of money owed him by a French bank; 900 louis, as he claimed. But could this really be the motive for so secretive a journey? Lord Camelford was famed both for his wealth and his indifference to money, and that he should go to such lengths to recover so relatively small a sum (a louis was equivalent to a pound) seemed highly improbable. In any case, the bank had already agreed to transmit the sum by the usual channels.

There was much to cause disquiet, considering Lord Camelford's ferocity, boldness and unpredictability. A police report noted that: 'It is claimed that this Lord said in London that *Bonaparte would die by his hand; and that on his first journey in France he would have assassinated him; that he was very angry that he had been prevented from fulfilling this purpose on his last journey; but that he would succeed another time.*' Against this, the evidence being as contradictory as the character of the young peer himself, was the promise of assistance in a highly delicate operation, which Camelford had given to the chief of police when last in Paris. At that very moment an agent named 'Laubeypie', with whom Camelford had planned to co-operate, had arrived in London. On whose side was Lord Camelford?

It was while the Grand Judge was revolving this dilemma in his mind that he received a visit from the British ambassador, Lord Whitworth, who had just learned from the prefect of police where Lord Camelford was. His distinguished relative Lord Grenville was making enquiries, and the ambassador wished to know what was Lord Camelford's situation. Monsieur Régnier explained the suspicious circumstances connected with the prisoner's journey to France, and confessed himself to be at a loss to know how to proceed. He naturally made no mention of the possibility that Camelford was working for *them*.

Seeing the Grand Judge's indecision, Lord Whitworth urged him to solve the problem by getting rid of the troublesome visitor as soon as possible. If he did not, then he as ambassador would have to make the strongest representations for the instant restitution of an Englishman of such high rank, held without charge. The Grand Judge began to feel that this was probably the easiest solution.

When Napoleon was told of the ambassador's request, he at once concurred with the Grand Judge in thinking the immediate repatriation of Lord Camelford to be the best way out of an embarrassing situation. He knew better than anyone that war would soon cause the frontiers to be closed against further visits; and it was scarcely a propitious moment to place an English nobleman on trial for – what? Orders were speedily issued and passes signed. A smart cabriolet escorted by mounted gendarmes drew up in the rue de la Corderie below the grim walls of the Temple. A tall, pale young man appeared in the gateway, shook hands with officials, and sprang in.

To his delight and surprise, Lord Camelford found an old friend sitting smiling inside — it was Monsieur de la Brunerie, with whom he had struck up an acquaintance in 1799 when he had travelled to Switzerland to serve under the Archduke Charles. The friendship had been maintained, and Monsieur de la Brunerie had recently helped Lord Camelford in a curious business which may have had something to do with the real purpose of Lord Camelford's present visit to France.

With the restoration of peace and order under Napoleon, and the concordat with the Pope, many French *émigrés* had reconciled themselves to the new government and returned home. Among these was de la Brunerie, who settled down in Paris with his wife at number 396 rue de l'Université. Lord Camelford helped them with money. It is not known whether he was in touch with them during his few weeks' stay in Paris in 1801 and 1802, but it was about that time that he arranged for de la Brunerie to purchase for him two estates, one in Picardy and the other near Lausanne. The arrangement was presumably very secret, as the estates continued in Lord Camelford's possession even after war broke out again.[7]

De la Brunerie knew of Camelford's incarceration in the Temple, and had received permission to accompany his friend to Boulogne. He watched Camelford depart on the French packet-boat for Dover early on the afternoon of 11 April, and returned home.

Fortunately for Lord Camelford, his latest exploit excited less public attention than might have been expected. A young Scotch doctor attached to the embassy in Paris regaled English visitors with stories of the adventure, but Lord Grenville was able to make arrangements with London newspaper editors to prevent undesirable publicity. From Dropmore he wrote to his wife at Camelford House, assuring her that the whole business had been a storm in a teacup. The fact was that the public were too much preoccupied with the possibility of war to concern themselves overmuch with Lord Camelford's peccadilloes. The same consideration doubtless made many sympathise with his treatment at the hands of a ruler who was increasingly regarded as an arbitrary despot.[8]

Lord Camelford returned from the part-comedy, part-melodrama of his fortnight's stay in France to find a tragedy impending at home. His mother was lying very ill at Camelford House. It had been Thomas himself who, in the previous June, had first noticed that her health was taking a serious turn for the worse. She had 'long laboured under an unpleasant tumor in her breast which keeps increasing and has given room to Heaviside [the family doctor] to pay more attention to it'. He wrote to his sister Anne, anxiously urging that a second opinion be called in, 'but you know I cannot bear much influence at headquarters [Camelford House] therefore I write to see if you can be more successful. Do not let it be known that I have wrote to you for God's sake.' Now, nearly a year later, Thomas and Anne, Lord Grenville and Mrs Holroyd (a faithful old family servant[9]) were gathered in deep distress by Lady Camelford's bedside.

Dr Heaviside could no longer offer words of hope; the illness had been long drawn out, and it was clear the end was approaching. The only consolation was that she was 'free from pain and is on the whole so tranquil'. On 5 May Lady Camelford died peacefully. Anne was ill with grief for a considerable time, and Thomas suffered the anguish of a son who had always shown the greatest tenderness towards his mother.

Clearly, however, the true nature of the relationship between mother and son was not known to others. Indeed, Camelford was subsequently held in large part responsible for his mother's death. The *Dictionary of National Biography* claimed that Lady Camelford died 'pining from grief at the career of her son'; while Sir Tresham Lever asserted that she was not 'suffering from any bodily infirmity. She was dying of a broken heart'. He also imaginatively pictured her lamenting an incident in her son's career that almost certainly occurred after her death!

On 12 May a funeral cortège set off on the 250-mile journey westwards, bearing Lady Camelford's body home to Boconnoc. Anne was too ill to travel, but numerous relatives and friends requested to be allowed to follow in their carriages. Lord Camelford, grief-stricken but calm, declined that request, as he wished for no distraction on this last journey. In the little church by the great house at Boconnoc Lady Camelford was laid to rest, alongside her husband in the family vault. After the service Lord Camelford stayed only a night or so in his house before returning to London. Boconnoc and Camelford House conjured up thoughts too poignant for recollection; only on the little green Île de St Pierre, its trees swaying in breezes ruffling the deep-blue surface of the lake of Bienne, had Tom known happiness untinged by bitterness. One day he would return there.[10]

Almost immediately after his return to town, Lord Camelford notified his solicitor that he intended to let Camelford House. The great mansion, built by his father in 1784, stood on an incomparable site at the corner of Oxford Street and Park Lane, looking out over the green expanse of Hyde Park. With its Adam mantelpieces, red damask drawing-room, massive service of silver and well-stocked wine-cellars, it was a setting worthy of a great peer.[11] But Lord Camelford preferred his humbler, less painfully evocative lodgings at 148 New Bond Street.

Installed once again in his old residence, Camelford now became as wild as ever Trollope's Lord Chiltern had threatened to be. In this new phase of boisterous behaviour he had as his companion his old friend Robert Barrie, who had come to share a berth with him in January. Barrie had been stationed in the West Indies, but after the Peace of Amiens returned home to his mother's home in Lancashire. Before Christmas he came to London, and in the New Year of 1803 was staying at the Spring Garden Coffee House near Charing Cross. There he was suddenly confined to bed with rheumatism: 'The torture I endure is more than I can describe,' he wrote to his mother; 'as soon as it is possible to move me I shall go to Lord Camelfords – who with his usual Friendship for me has provided a quiet sick appartment, attendants &c.'

On 17 January Camelford himself wrote to Barrie's mother, explaining that Robert was now living at 148 New Bond Street and, despite the fact that his swollen hands prevented his being able to write, he was under the care of a skilful physician and mending fast. Camelford lavished every care on his friend, exerting his influence on Sir Sidney Smith in an attempt to secure him a new command. Then came Camelford's visit to France. The day after his arrest at Calais, Barrie casually informed his mother that 'Camelford is gone to France to endeavour to get some money due him there before hostilities break out, but I much doubt wether he will recover mony from the French Government'. After his return and the death of his mother, Lord Camelford was able to share his grief at the bereavement with his old shipmate. 'Poor Lady Camelford,' wrote Barrie again to his mother on 6 May, 'died last night & tho: this event has been long expected it is a severe shock to my good Friend.'

Barrie's mother, Mrs Clayton, had probably by now revised her earlier opinion of Lord Camelford, whom she had considered a very bad influence. On 30 September 1800, before his departure for the West Indies, her son had written to allay her fears:

Be assured your advice relative to my professional conduct shall not been thrown away—perhaps I have been a very wild fellow but I think I may say I never was a brutal one—As to Camelford be not alarmed at my intimacy with him, I have known him nearly ten years—& his excentricities aside I know not a more brave, generous, or friendly fellow & I hope I've *now seen* too much of the world to practise over again my follies—C. is now in town, I heard of him the other day.[12]

However, three years later, when he was back in London, Barrie seems to have quite forgotten that all his youthful follies were supposed to be behind him. Like his bosom friend Lord Camelford, he was 'a strong-limbed, powerful man', much given to practical jokes and larking about.[13] One night in the summer of 1803, he and Lord Camelford were returning home to Bond Street after an evening's revelry. It was one o'clock in the morning, and the ill-lit streets were deserted. Camelford and Barrie 'flown with insolence and wine', came swaggering into Cavendish Square. Before them they beheld a nightwatchman snoring in his box, while on the pavement beside lay sleeping three of his comrades. Their symbols of authority—lanterns, rattles and staves—lay beside them on the pavement, as did a near-empty gin bottle.

'Shall we teach these lazy *dambers* a lesson, Bob?' whispered Lord Camelford, with a wink to his comrade. Barrie joined his friend in the task of waking the slumberers. They overturned the box, and delivered a number of sharp blows with their canes on the watchmen's heavily caped shoulders. Angry oaths arose, and the outraged *Charleys* struggled to their feet. Blows were exchanged, and the two swells managed to floor a couple of their assailants, who toppled back on to the pavement. The gin bottle was also a casualty, but meanwhile the two surviving watchmen had hastily sprung their rattles.

Reinforcements were not far off, and a dozen or more watchmen came pounding into the square. Barrie and Camelford set themselves back to back, and a battle royal began. Though heavily outnumbered, they put up a formidable defence. Fighting back with their canes and fists, they kept up the unequal struggle for nearly an hour. Finally there was a sudden rush forward of the peace-keepers, and the two bucks were swept off their feet and borne to the ground. They were dragged off to the nearest roundhouse (presumably that at Marylebone)[14], to be brought before the night-constable.

Lord Camelford was covered in bruises but was clearly enjoying the whole procedure hugely. Poor Barrie, however, had received a *snorter* on the *nob* (head), rendering him temporarily *groggified*. In the roundhouse he appeared to recover, and began shouting indignantly that he did not like this berth and would have to cut out a port hole in the cabin side. The burly sailor rose to his feet and, with an inarticulate bellow, cannoned forward among his captors, knocking them headlong before him. The battle was on the point of raging once more, but Barrie was carrying too much liquid ballast and was swiftly floored.

Next morning the revellers, their heads and limbs aching, were brought before a magistrate in Marlborough Street. The watchmen testified to the damage done to their persons and property, the magistrate hinted that compensation might not come amiss, and the parties withdrew to the street. Lord Camelford bestowed a guinea apiece on the watchmen and he and Barrie returned home rejoicing. An odd consequence of this exploit was that Camelford became friendly with the watchmen, and was a frequent late-night guest in the roundhouses of the West End. It was his practice to eject (by force or persuasion) the constable from his seat, and take his place. When offenders were brought in, he would interrogate them solemnly and admonish them on the errors of their ways. He then invariably discharged them without punishment.[15]

Not all Lord Camelford's exploits excited public disapprobation. The day after his return from his mother's funeral he was following the fashionable practice of strolling on the gravel walk in Kensington Gardens. But that day

> there was a great riot in Kensington Gardens. Two well dressed women, whose dress attracted notice, were mobbed and grossly insulted by men like labourers in Sunday clothes. Lord Camelford, at the head of a party of gentlemen, went to their assistance at last; a scuffle ensued and he knocked down everyone in his way, giving them his card.[16]

The next day Britain declared war on France, but even against the background of that overriding topic, Lord Camelford's eccentricities continued to attract attention. He was frequently at horse-races, cock-fights and prize-fights. He fought no duels, but could not keep away from them. Robert Barrie was second to Captain Macnamara, who killed Colonel Montgomery in a quarrel arising from a squabble over their pet dogs. They fought on Primrose Hill on 6 April (a month before Lady Camelford's death), and Camelford afterwards called on the wounded Macnamara to congratulate him on his courage.[17]

It was this or a similar encounter that occasioned a hasty pencilled note to Lady Grenville:

My Dear Sister
Pray apologise to My Mother for my not calling this Evening. I have a friend who has had the misfortune to be concerned in a duel that has ended fatally, and he requires my assistance to get out of the way.[18]

Lord Camelford's servants were expected to mirror Camelford's robust character. When engaging a new footman, valet or coachman, he always selected fine, manly-looking fellows. After a few days he would provoke the new employee by finding unnecessary fault; the servant would turn surly, and then Lord Camelford would strike him. This no Englishman of whatever rank would stomach, and a regular set-to was the result. If the servant showed science and 'bottom', Camelford would halt the struggle, congratulate the man and present him with a £20 note. All his servants were handsomely looked after; in turn they were expected to stand by him in numerous ugly or peculiar situations.

Lord Camelford had no time for feeble-spirited fellows, of whom he believed tailors to be the prime example. One day he informed his own tailor that he wished to have a 'hell-fire jacket' made for him. This was a sort of leather waistcoat, much patronised by hedgers and ditchers in the miry lanes of Devonshire. The knight of the thimble hesitantly confessed that he did not know what such a jacket was.

'I'm not surprised,' replied Lord Camelford, 'you London ninnies fly from anything with a bit of fire in it. Tell me, my friend, have you ever fired a pistol?'

'Oh! no, my lord, I've never had anything to do with such dangerous things.'

'Well, you had better try now. Here's a loaded pistol – take it – now, stand in front of the mirror here, while I take this other one (it's loaded too). There, I'll stand here opposite you, and we'll shoot.'

Lord Camelford walked over to close the doors and returned. The poor tailor could scarcely speak for terror, and stood trembling from head to foot before the mirror.

My dear Sister

          Pray apologise
to my mother for my
not calling this Even[in]g
I have a friend who
has had the misfor-
tune to be concerned
in a duel that has
ended fatally, and
he requires my assis-
tance to get out of
the way.
          Your very Affecte
                    Brother
Friend[?]

Camelford

Note from Lord Camelford to his sister

'You had better fire first,' urged Camelford genially, but the wretched man's hand was quivering so much he could scarcely hold the pistol.

'I shall have to do it, then,' cried the peer, raising his pistol and pulling the trigger. There was a deafening report, the room was filled with smoke, and the mirror was shattered. The tailor slumped to the ground, groaning that he was shot. His ears were still ringing from the noise of the explosion, but he could hear somewhere in the distance the voice of Lord Camelford, summoning his servants to remove the corpse. He soon recovered, however, when set down before a splendid meal in the servants' hall. Lord Camelford, feeling some compunction for having ill-treated the poor fellow, gave him a £50 banknote. With this the enterprising tailor managed to set up his own business, his most munificent patrons being Lord Camelford and his friends.[19]

This and similar stories received wide circulation, and in July the newspapers made play with yet another adventure of Lord Camelford's. The Royal Circus in St George's Fields was greatly resorted to by pleasure-seeking Londoners. The renewal of the war had caused much popular demand for continual renditions of 'Hearts of Oak', 'Rule, Britannia', and other patriotic ditties, interposed in the regular programme at junctures appropriate and otherwise.

On Wednesday, 20 July, during the evening performance, there was a general call for 'God Save the King', accompanied by yells of 'Stand up! Hats off!' All hats were at once doffed; all, that is, save one. A drunken naval officer named Shaw noticed a gentleman in the next box still wearing his *castor*, or beaver hat. Being equipped with a heavy oak cudgel, he leaned across and knocked off the offending headgear, shouting out, 'Take off your hat, sir!' The stranger turned round, and proved to be Lord Camelford, who returned a punch that knocked Shaw to the floor.

Both parties thrust their way out into the lobby and flew at each other. Lieutenant Shaw's cudgel gave him an advantage that did not last long. Camelford dodged his blows, threw in several smart *facers*, and then closed with Shaw, wresting away the weapon. Shaw now received a drubbing from his own stick, and he might have suffered severe injuries but for the arrival of the constables.

Both men were taken to a coffee house adjoining the Circus, but as they would come to no agreement they were required to appear before the magistrates next morning, who urged the parties to make up their difference. Lord Camelford, who insisted that he had kept his hat on quite inadvertently, offered to meet Shaw halfway in an apology, but the latter refused. Camelford departed, vowing to take legal proceedings for assault.

Two young brothers named Smith had been witnesses of the affray. 'The devil is not so black as he is painted,' said one to the other. 'Let us call upon Lord Camelford, and tell him we were witnesses of his being first assaulted.'

They were received by Camelford in his drawing-room, where they saw the cherished collection of bludgeons and horsewhips suspended over the fireplace. As they wrote later: 'Lord Camelford received his visitants with great civility, and thanked them warmly for the call; adding, that their evidence would be material, it being his intention to indict the lieutenant for an assault. "All I can say in return is this," exclaimed the peer with great cordiality, "if ever I see you engaged in a row, upon my soul, I'll stand by you." The brothers expressed themselves thankful for so potent an ally, and departed.'

Mutual threats of legal proceedings by Camelford and Shaw continued for several weeks, but by 21 September Robert Barrie informed his mother: 'Camelford is at Brighton. I believe I shall be able to settle the dispute he had at the Circus, tomorrow I meet the party involved & the the gentlemen of the law &c.' A few days later he was able to report further that 'I was successful in settling Lord Camelford's affair and you will hear no more of it'.[20]

Sporadic incidents of this nature continued until Christmas 1803.[21] Meanwhile, two hundred miles away, in Paris, certain gentlemen were displaying pertinacious interest in quite another aspect of Lord Camelford's career. On 26 April 1803, a fortnight after his expulsion from France, the ministry of police at the quai Malaquai had received a report from an agent employed to spy on British visitors crowding Paris. 'J.M.', as he signed himself, had heard several times that the days of the First Consul were numbered. For some time he was puzzled by this sinister remark, but finally he managed to extract a detailed account from a certain Major Sharp.

After providing an accurate résumé of Camelford's background and previous activities in France, Sharp remarked warningly that 'he is the more dangerous for being very rich, having an income of thirty thousand pounds a year; he can hire scoundrels, or spare no expense to achieve his ends'. So sinister was Sharp's account that 'J.M.' believed it essential to take the most stringent precautions to guard the First Consul when he visited the Channel coast. This report merely confirmed the French authorities in their strong conviction that Lord Camelford still represented a very potent danger. His assurances that he was working in the interests of France could no longer receive any credit at all, and the French were now convinced that he had really threatened to destroy Bonaparte with his own hand.

One of Camelford's associates, to whom he was held to have confided this abominable scheme, was a certain Colonel William Whaley, brother-in-law of Lord Clare, former Lord Chancellor of Ireland. Whaley was an Irishman from County Wicklow,[22] and was as wild and eccentric as Lord Camelford himself. His brother Thomas had once walked to Jerusalem in his riding boots for a bet, and William was capable of even more extravagant deeds. Like Camelford, ran a report drawn up for the Grand Judge, 'his boldness made him capable of the most dangerous and atrocious ventures'. A ferocious duellist (like many Irishmen of the period), he had left his regiment after killing his colonel and wounding the major. He was financially ruined, a social outcast, and plainly ready material for any desperate project.

It was reported soon after Lord Camelford's departure from France that Whaley was planning to enter the country secretly, and on 29 April the Grand Judge ordered officials at Dieppe and Calais to ensure that he was not admitted. But on 21 May Monsieur Régnier reported to Napoleon that this dangerous man had managed to cross the frontier undetected (probably via Holland or Belgium), and was in Paris. Napoleon, who had already taken a close interest in the affair of Lord Camelford, ordered this disreputable accomplice to be arrested.[23] On 8 June, at three o'clock in the morning, troops despatched by General Junot arrived at Whaley's lodgings and bore him off to the Abbaye military prison.

Under interrogation, Whaley asserted that his purpose in visiting Paris was purely to recover money owing to him over the sale of a famous racehorse, named Vivaldi, to a French banker whom he had met at Epsom.[24] This banker, named Michel, had declined to pay, and Whaley strongly suspected that Michel had denounced him to the police to avoid payment.

And what of Lord Camelford? Whaley had been on terms of close friendship with him, and might possess information that could throw light on the plot supposed to be being hatched against the First Consul.

But Whaley claimed that he had rejected all Camelford's attempts to embroil him in such matters. Further, he offered to provide the police with 'certain facts on Lord Camelford, facts which prove that, far from participating in his schemes, he was on the contrary ready to reveal them'. Lengthy reports were submitted again on this subject to Napoleon, but, as the Grand Judge admitted, much still remained obscure in this mysterious business. Whaley was held in prison, though under unusually comfortable conditions, for the next eleven years – until Napoleon's empire fell.[25]

Whaley's arrest and revelations, whatever they were, had not established precisely what were Lord Camelford's intentions. But they inevitably made the young English peer an even greater object of suspicion and, indeed, fear than before.

General Savary, who as commander of the *Gendarmerie d'Élite* held direct responsibility for the protection of the person of the First Consul, summed up what leading Frenchmen saw as the main danger to their country in the great struggle which was then in its opening phase. The English ministers

had doubtless observed that the wonderful restoration of things in France, and that in so short a time, was purely the work of a mighty genius, which conceived, arranged, and executed, with the rapidity of thought; that the First Consul was the legislator, the magistrate, and the absolute master, of a country and of an army, of which he was at the same time the general and the first soldier; that it was consequently at him that the blow which was to preserve England from ruin ought to be aimed; and that the success of this single blow would suffice to plunge France back into the abyss of calamities from which he had drawn her, and to sink her to that depth to which the powers of the continent that had made war upon her could not reduce her.[26]

Ironically, the evidence suggests that, at the very time that Lord Camelford thus became a greatly increased object of fear and suspicion to the French secret police, he may have been abandoning the reckless project that had thrice brought him dangerous notoriety. In the spring of 1803 he authorised the publication of an account of his repeating pistol. This may imply that he no longer contemplated actions involving the use of so lethal a weapon, even though it also revealed, for the first time, the full extent of the danger which had threatened Napoleon.[27]

Whether or not Lord Camelford had entirely abandoned his private campaign against the French, there is no doubt that at this time his attention became largely absorbed in more respectable activities. *A Journal of Natural Philosophy*, in which details of the pistol were published, was edited by an enterprising scientist named William Nicholson. Nicholson, a fifty-year-old Londoner who, like Camelford, had travelled in the East Indies, was well known for having perfected a number of ingenious inventions, including a machine for printing designs on linen. He lived at 10 Soho Square; and there, it seems, Lord Camelford frequently visited him to conduct experiments and discuss matters connected with chemistry and engineering. Nicholson also maintained a school for twenty pupils on the premises. Lord Camelford greatly interested himself in this, lending Nicholson £1500 'for the expanding of his Establishment'; the loan was later converted into a gift.[28]

Camelford also studied chemistry with another distinguished scientist, Friedrich Accum, a pioneer of the gas-lighting that began to illumine London's streets a decade later. He paid large sums in the first months of 1804 to this brilliant German, presumably subsidies in return for consultations on the experimental study of chemistry in which Camelford was deeply absorbed. Much of this work was conducted in Lord Camelford's own laboratory, presumably at 148 New Bond Street.[29]

Camelford's interests at this time were intensive and wide-ranging. It is probable that he was consciously making up for the lack of formal education he had received as a boy. Perhaps, too, an instinctive feeling that the old social order was being threatened from below led him to follow Rousseau's advice to acquire manual skills, and also a knowledge of chemistry.[30] Even those with the bluest blood needed to prove themselves as men in this age of revolution. This had also been the view of the crazy old Lord Stanhope.

We are told, for example, that Lord Camelford 'understood architectural drawing almost as well as some of our most eminent professors. His Lordship had made the arts his peculiar study for several years, and he was no bad proficient even in the Old School'.[31] This at least was an achievement that would have gratified his father, who had been a gifted amateur architect. Anthony Carlisle, the surgeon and close acquaintance of Lord Camelford's, assured a friend that 'he was industrious to acquire knowledge of many things. He was a good Chemist, – a most excellent geographer, – a good seaman, – could do the business of a Turner, & work in *fineering* as a Cabinet Maker'.[32]

Yet another, hitherto unsuspected, aspect of this versatile character was revealed by a close friend, a clergyman:

> Lord Camelford was always passionately fond of science, and though his mind, while a young sailor, had been little cultivated, yet of late years he had acquired a prodigious fund of information upon almost every subject connected with literature. The world will perhaps with difficulty believe, what however I assert from my own knowledge, that Christianity was the constant subject of his reflections, his reading, and his conversation. In early life he had gloried much in puzzling the chaplains of those ships in which he served; and to enable him to gain such triumphs, he had read all the sceptical books he could procure; and thus his mind became unwillingly tainted with infidelity. As however his judgment grew more matured, he discovered of himself the fallacy of his own reasonings; and convinced of the importance of religion, he often applied to me and to others for the best books he could consult upon the evidence of Christianity. Many were the conversations I had with him on this subject, and [recently] ... he had dined with me, and staid as was his custom till twelve o'clock, conversing on his favourite topic. He left me at length with this important remark, 'No sensible and well-informed man can presume to assert that Christianity is false; I do not yet venture,' said he, 'to assert positively that it is true, but I confess the probabilities are in its favour.'

Camelford's practical Christianity led him to spend much time, trouble and money helping people in misfortune. The Rev. William Cockburne gave a category of sufferers who aroused Thomas's particular sympathy:

> The warmth of disposition which prompted him so unhappily to great improprieties, prompted him also to the most lively efforts of active benevolence. From the many prisons in this metropolis, from the various receptacles of human misery, he received unnumbered petitions; and no petition ever came in vain. He was often the dupe of the designing and crafty suppliant, but he was more often the reliever of real sorrow, and the soother of unmerited woe. Con-

stantly would he make use of that influence which rank and fortune gave him with the government, to interfere in behalf of those male-factors whose crimes had subjected them to punishment, but in whose cases appeared circumstances of alleviation.[33]

To his immediate friends, relations and dependants the warm-hearted Camelford was invariably kind and attentive. On 30 December 1803 Robert Barrie, depressed by illness and his failure to obtain a ship, wrote to his mother that: 'I was at Down House near Blandford, looking at a cottage Lord Camelford wants me to live in. I must turn it over in my mind. The country abounds in game &c. & Camelford will furnish the House from Bocconoc.' Instead, however, he returned to 148 New Bond Street, and Lord Camelford exerted his influence on Lord Grenville to find a command for him.[34]

Camelford's mother's old companion, Mrs Holroyd, fell ill in February 1804, and he wrote to her and his sister at Dropmore, confessing to Anne that 'I really feel for the good old woman an affection little short of what I once bore a parent, not to dwell longer upon a subject so painful to us both ... '

To Anne he sent gifts and fond messages. Five partridges he had shot 'humbly beg leave to offer their services and to request to be devoured at Dropmore'. In January came a similar note and present.

My Dear Sister
As I never know when you are in town, I have no other way of recalling myself to your recollection than by sending you from time to time, some little token of my remembrance. On the present occasion my Ambassador is a very fine Haunch of Prize, Grass fed, Mutton; which Mr. Giblet assures stands with out a rival. His Excellency desires that he may be treated in every respect like a Haunch of Venison, in which case he promises to repay your care by every exertion on his Part, which can tend to throw a dignity and lustre on his mission not doubting but that he will meet with a kind and favourable reception at Dropmore in consideration of him, from whom he comes. I remain my Dr. Sister your most affectionate Brother.[35]

XI

❀❀❀❀❀❀❀❀❀❀❀❀❀❀❀❀❀❀❀❀❀❀❀❀❀❀❀❀❀❀❀❀❀

A Dangerous Challenge

Lord Camelford was apparently becoming tamer, but his temper could still flare up where he suspected an affront. Drawing on the knowledge he had gained during the voyage of the *Discovery*, he decided that there was money to be made in the Pacific Ocean. At his expense, and in collaboration with William Nicholson, he fitted out two ships to be despatched to the South Sea fishery. His fat little steward John Borlinder joined the venture, put up £500 of his own capital, and sailed as master of one of the ships, the *Weldon*.

After the ships had sailed something arose to make Lord Camelford feel Borlinder was cheating him. To Camelford the steward abruptly became 'perhaps one of the worst Men that ever disgraced humanity', who was capable of using 'every artifice in his power to defraud my heirs'. In 1805 the *Weldon* returned to England, but in the Channel Borlinder had the ill-luck to be ordered to haul to by H.M.S. *Brilliant*. Captain Robert Barrie was in command and, remembering Camelford's complaints, placed an armed party on board to ensure Borlinder put in at London and accounted for all his actions. However, Lord Grenville's subsequent investigations appeared to establish that Camelford had been mistaken.[1]

Camelford's intimates at this time included the faithful 'Bob' Barrie; the Hon. Henry Devereux, two years younger than himself, son of Lord Hereford, and a cornet in the fashionable 10th Light Dragoons; Captain Macnamara, the duellist; and Captain Thomas Best, a wealthy West Indian. Best was, like Camelford, an avid attender at boxing-matches.[2] He was 'a slim person in figure, & not of a strong constitution', but bore a reputation for being 'false and faithless' with women.[3]

One of these was a Mrs Loveden, described as 'a very pretty little woman, abt. 5 or six & twenty years old'. She seems to have been well able to take care of herself, however. Some years previously, when she can have been only about twenty-one, she had an affair with Best. Then, in 1801, she met Lord Camelford, and became his mistress. No ill-will arose from the transfer, and it was in fact Fanny Loveden's introduction that brought Best and Camelford together as friends. She did not come to live at Bond Street, but was maintained in a house of her own, where she lived 'in a very dashing style'.

The relationship, it seems, was largely one of physical convenience on both sides. By 1803 Camelford's interest seems to have become fairly perfunctory, and he was little concerned when

a young West Indian of the name of Simmonds coming over became acquainted with Her, & she had fascination enough to induce Him to marry her. She was to have gone with Him to the West Indies, but when on Ship board, was so unmanageable, that the Captain put Her into a boat, & sent Her on Shore, and she returned to Lord Camelford who she had before been with.

The unfortunate Simmonds was also a friend of Best's. By the spring of 1804, Camelford himself ceased his liaison with Fanny Simmonds (as she now was), though he continued to provide for her maintenance.[4]

Camelford, Best, Barrie and other intimates of their coterie dined regularly in the Prince of Wales Coffee House in Conduit Street.[5] In the New Year of 1804 Camelford and Best had been eating in one of the boxes, when the conversation turned on marksmanship. Camelford accepted a bet that he would hit a given mark within three shots. The stakes were Captain Best's blood mare against a hundred guineas. Pistols were fetched from Bond Street, a waiter set up a lighted candle on a table ten yards off, and Lord Camelford took careful aim. His first shot missed, the second actually snuffed the wick, and the third hit the candle. As he had not shot out the flame, though, he lost his wager and duly paid the hundred guineas.[6]

On the evening of Saturday, 3 March, Best was attending a performance at the Opera House in the Haymarket. To his surprise he was accosted there by his former mistress, Fanny Simmonds, who coolly asked him to take her home after the performance. Best declined, out of consideration to Camelford who still had her in keeping. The lady's bright eyes flashed, and she remarked in meaning tones that Best would have cause to repent of his refusal, for she would set Lord Camelford on his back. She left the Opera House, crossed Piccadilly, and knocked up Lord Camelford. She told him a tale to which he listened with mounting indignation: Best, she said, had made insulting proposals to her in public at the opera. She had remonstrated, and said she would inform Lord Camelford if he did not restrain himself. 'Lord Camelford may be damned!' Best had cried loudly; all around had heard the contemptuous dismissal. So convincing was this circumstantial account, that Camelford was now beside himself with rage. He called in Robert Barrie, who agreed to visit Best and settle the matter.

Next morning, Sunday, Barrie walked over to Captain Best's house at 3 Wimpole Street, and explained the unpleasant nature of his mission. But Best had no sooner heard the story than he explained in astonishment that it was utterly untrue, and he had certainly never uttered the alleged expression. Captain Barrie realised there had been a misunderstanding, and assured Best he would set out the real facts before Camelford.

Barrie hastened back to Bond Street to assure Thomas that he had been deceived, and the story was false. Camelford was still very angry; so much so that Barrie, fearing mischief, begged him to promise not to fight Best. Camelford, who was soon won round when tactfully treated, finally concurred that 'upon *His Honor He would not*'. Barrie left the house, content that he had settled what might have been a very unpleasant business.'

But Lord Camelford's resentment soon welled up again. Whether he recalled Fanny Simmonds's very convincing account, or whether she visited him again, is not known. But on Tuesday, 6 March, early in the evening, Camelford strode across to the Prince of Wales Coffee House in a very stormy mood. He demanded of a waiter whether Mr Best had been there.

'My lord, I expect him here to dine,' replied the man. Camelford waited, becoming increasingly agitated. Eventually, at half-past six, Best came in, accompanied by two friends. Camelford went straight up to him and blurted out: 'Mr Best, I understand you have been traducing my character, and insulting my girl Fanny, in a most ungentlemanlike manner. Such conduct, sir, is infamous, and you must be a damned scoundrel!'

Taken aback by this outburst, Best replied indignantly, 'My Lord, I do not understand what you mean by the first remark, but the last no one can misunderstand.'

Camelford angrily demanded an apology; but Best continued to deny that he had done or said anything to his friend's prejudice, assuring him on his word of honour that the report was false. But with Lord Camelford continuing to heap insulting epithets on him, such as 'scoundrel', 'liar', 'ruffian', he finally saw no alternative but to suggest their friends named a time and place of meeting.

Thus both men were committed to an absurdly unnecessary duel – and all because of the accusations, almost certainly false, made by a woman of doubtful virtue. It is therefore necessary to examine Fanny Simmonds's motives and role in this bizarre affair. Was she just an irresponsible, mischief-making woman? Or did she have some more specific reason for precipitating a quarrel between Camelford and Best which, in view of Best's reputation as a marksman, would be likely to end in injury or death for his opponent? There is one explanation which, though at first sight far-fetched, cannot be totally excluded. It is possible that Fanny Simmonds was acting under instructions – from the French security services.

It must be remembered that throughout the early years of the century there were ceaseless rumours, some well founded, of plots against the life of the First Consul. Those responsible for ensuring Napoleon's safety were driven frantic with anxiety. Napoleon's most dreaded enemy was a powerfully built Breton of peasant origin, Georges Cadoudal. Georges (as he was generally known) had continued the struggle abandoned by most of his fellow *Chouans* in 1800, and had thereafter a single purpose in mind, the removal of Bonaparte, in order to pave the way for the restoration of Louis XVIII. In 1801 he had been obliged to flee to England, but in London he redoubled his efforts to bring about a successful *coup*. With the outbreak of war he received British official assistance. On 21 August 1803 a Royal Navy cutter landed him with some companions on the French coast, and a week later he was in Paris.

So elaborate were the precautions taken by Georges and his followers that his presence in the city was not established with certainty by the police until six months later. A colossal manhunt was set up; the gates and walls were vigilantly guarded, patrols were everywhere, and a death sentence was imposed on anyone providing shelter for the conspirators. Meanwhile the same British ship was found to have landed further parties in December, and January of 1804. Among these was the celebrated former Republican General Pichegru; on 28 January Pichegru met France's most distinguished soldier after Bonaparte, Moreau. The ramifications of the plot were widening, but already the French police were closing in. Moreau and Pichegru were arrested in February, and about the same time a captured servant of Georges revealed under torture his master's whereabouts. On 4 March two noblemen, Georges's close associates, were taken. Finally, on 9 March, Georges himself was found and surrounded. The desperate *Chouan* fought his way through the cordon, killing a policeman; but he was pursued, captured, and carried to the Temple.

The plot was crushed, but it had been a very close-run business. The formidable courage and resource of Georges were known to all, and the public fear excited by his reputation was heightened by his apparent immunity from arrest. For months his spectre stalked the great capital, and the life of the First Consul hung on a hair .'This plot against the life of the First Consul produced a profound impression upon the public opinion,' wrote General Savary, whose gendarmes had the task of capturing the hidden *Chouans*. 'Every functionary, whether present or at a distance; every officer, of every rank whatsoever, and particularly all who aspired to favour, thought of nothing but how to avail himself of this circumstance to prove his devotedness to the person of the First Consul.'

The climax of this alarming crisis, the most serious internal threat to his rule ever experienced by Napoleon, coincided precisely with the death of Lord Camelford in London. Indeed, notices of the fatal duel appeared in English newspapers alongside reports of the arrest of Pichegru and the trial of Moreau. The question arises whether the two events were merely coincidental, or whether an unsuspected connexion may link them.

For six months before the capture of Georges, the French state organs of security had been in a permanent state of alert. 'For some time dark rumours had been afloat,' wrote Savary, 'and without affording the certainty of a completely organised conspiracy, they still gave warning that something was going forward which it was daily more and more important to sift to the bottom.

'A thousand sinister reports were circulated, as if to prepare the public mind for some event; the possibility of arresting the political career of the First Consul was talked of: letters from London even stated that he would be assassinated, and that the information was derived from an authentic source. The certainty of this intelligence, though it was not incontestable, was nevertheless sufficient to excite the alarm and consequently to deserve the attention of the government.'

Among suspected authors of such an attempt, the name of Lord Camelford figured high. His previous efforts to accomplish this dire end were now notorious. The French police maintained spies in London,[8] and these kept a close watch on Lord Camelford. In the summer of 1803, an agent known only as 'No. 6279' despatched an alarming report to the Grand Judge's secret police division in Paris:

Some Englishmen have said that Lord Camelford is likely to return soon to the Continent, via Holland. This remarkable persistence is really extraordinary; one must never lose sight of the fact that this man is inflexible in his resolutions, skilful at concealing them, and that there can be for him no insurmountable obstacles, as his nature demands that the world take notice of him. Lord Camelford will be the author, one day, of some of those actions which lead rapidly to glory – or the scaffold.

Could this planned expedition be linked with the plots of Georges Cadoudal? It seemed highly probable. Camelford had long enjoyed the confidence of St Amand, Limoëlan and other *Chouans*, and in December 1801 a police report on his activities had concluded with the direction that the documents: 'be attached to the dossier of Georges as relevant to that person'.

The last attempt on the First Consul's life had been by means of an infernal machine, and Camelford, an amateur chemist of distinction, was again reported to have a dangerous competence in this direction. Another report recalled spies' observations on Lord Camelford's activities when preparing the *Charon* for secret operations in 1798: 'The Lord ... sought to recruit several French émigré artillery officers, particularly La Marteliere and another; none wished to go with him. While he was equipping his ship, he had constructed several boxes or cases which he filled with explosive matter and incendiary devices, and had carried on board his frigate.'

Then there was the highly suspicious conduct of his accomplice, Colonel Whaley, now a prisoner in the Abbaye. One of Georges Cadoudal's seven companions who had entered France with him on 21

August 1803 was a man named Querel. On 11 October the police in Paris had caught him, and he too was placed in the Abbaye. In the following February he was sentenced to death; as a result he made a full confession of his activities, and it was in this way that the government learned for the first time that Georges was in Paris. After this Querel was returned to the Abbaye. There Colonel Whaley somehow learned of the betrayal, and was so incensed that he attempted to kill the traitor.[9]

Thus there were strong indications that Camelford's plans were linked with those of Georges Cadoudal. But his very unpredictability made him the more menacing. Paris was being combed for Georges, while Camelford remained outside the net, free to strike when and where he chose. That he was preparing to make some quite extraordinary move seemed confirmed from a widespread report in London 'that he had been for some time employed in preparation for the disposal of his property in this country, and had sent persons to value the timber on his estates in Cornwall and Dorset'.[10]

On every side Camelford appeared to have links with the tangled threads of conspiracy now being painstakingly unravelled by the French. Lord Camelford planned to enter France through Holland? How very convenient that the commodore of the British squadron blockading the Dutch coast was his first cousin, Sir Sidney Smith![11] The officer commanding the Royal Navy cutter that landed Georges and two successive parties of *Chouans* on the cliff de Belville was Commander John Wright, a close friend of Sir Sidney's, who had been a prisoner with him in the Temple.[12] Then again, a French double agent had recently exposed the complicity of the English minister at Stuttgart, Spencer Smith. Spencer Smith was the brother of Sir Sidney, and Lord Camelford's first cousin.

Camelford possessed the skill, daring, inclination and resources to perform that dread act the French state was straining every resource to combat. Could any official concerned for the safety of the First Consul's life have failed to take this consideration into account, or to adopt any measure, however extreme, likely to counter it? Certainly the French government acted at this time with exceptional rigour against the exceptional danger. France's enemies had stooped to unlawful means of striking their treacherous blow, and the servants of the Republic were fully justified in replying in kind. The laws of nations were temporarily suspended as the underground struggle reached its ruthless climax.

Agents were despatched across France's frontiers to arrange the abduction of those regarded as the directors of the conspiracy. The *émigré* Comte d'Antraigues, Royalist intelligence agent at Dresden, evaded surprise by fortifying his house, but others were less fortunate. On 24 October 1803 a body of 250 French troops landed secretly near Hamburg, and kidnapped Sir George Rumbold, British minister to the Hanseatic Towns. Sir George was lodged in the Temple, and all his papers examined by the police. Finally, and most notoriously, the Duc d'Enghien was seized on neutral territory in Germany, brought to Paris, and sentenced to death by a court-martial. This dramatic and highly dangerous venture was decided upon at a meeting of the privy council held on 10 March 1804 (the day Lord Camelford died), at which the three Consuls, the Grand Judge, Fouché and Talleyrand were present.[13]

The judicial murder of the Duc d'Enghien showed the lengths to which the servants of Napoleon would go to protect their master. There may have been other such 'executions'. On 6 April Pichegru was found strangled in his cell in the Temple. This was perhaps suicide, but much more suspicious was the case of Commander Wright, R.N., who had landed Georges in France. His ship, the *Vincejo*, was captured by the French on 8 May, and he was carried a prisoner to the Temple. A year later, on 27 October, he too was discovered dead. A razor was in his hand, and his throat cut back to the bone.[14]

The kidnapping or murder of Lord Camelford in London would have been a well-nigh impossible task. There were the usual obstacles against operating any such project in a closely guarded island, where every Frenchman was an object of intense suspicion. There was moreover the daunting reputation of Lord Camelford himself. It would have been no easy matter to have laid hands on the muscular peer, who was generally accompanied by his black pugilist footman, Mungo.

But what if Lord Camelford could be drawn by his own irascible nature into some trap from which there was no extricating himself? In Captain Best he had selected as opponent the best shot in England, the one man perhaps with a more deadly aim than his own. Spies watched Lord Camelford's every movement; could they have fixed upon the volatile Fanny Simmonds as the instrument that would bring about his downfall? There is in the nature of the case little direct evidence on which to proceed. In a biography of Lord Camelford the novelist must frequently wish to elbow aside the historian. But let the novelist exercise his imagination as he will—make Fanny Simmonds the willing agent or the dupe of a persuasive Citizen X – it is hard to think of any circumstance where documentary evidence would be kept. Nor would the French police, if responsible, keep a record of so dubious, if neccessary, a transaction.

There is only the circumstantial evidence to set in the balance alongside established facts. The French government had the motive, the ability and the opportunity to eliminate Lord Camelford in the manner suggested. The duel took place in the very week that the Cadoudal affair reached its climax. Lord Camelford was, it is true, an exceptionally choleric man; once he became involved in the quarrel with Best it was his own intransigent nature that prevented any reconciliation.

But it is unfair to label him, like the *Dictionary of National Biography*, as a 'duellist'. His name is connected with only one duel apart from that with Best, when he is said to have killed Lieutenant Tremlett in 1798 at Martinique. But tempers then were heated after the Peterson affair, and in any case no supportive evidence for such a dual has been traced. One who knew him claimed: 'So far was Lord Camelford from being inclined to quarrel, or to encourage the enmity of others, that he has absolutely prevented more meetings of that nature, than any man in existence'.[15]

Mrs Simmonds's action appears singularly provocative and motiveless in the fairly full accounts preserved. She appeared, after all, more or less out of the blue to play her part, having been the mistress of neither Best nor Camelford for some considerable time. Yet there again we cannot know all the circumstances. Other questions raise themselves. Were the French authorities right in thinking that Lord Camelford's existence menaced the security of Napoleon, or had he unknown to them abandoned his murderous project? What was Colonel Whaley's true role in all this? If the French police were indeed prosecuting a secret war against Lord Camelford, who was involved: the official police of Grand Judge Régnier? Or the agents of Fouché, whose ministry was not yet reconstituted, but who was working industriously behind the scenes to destroy Georges and so restore his lost prestige?

One thing is certain: the French police were very interested in Lord Camelford's intransigent nature and love of duelling. A secret-police report of 1803 told of his visit to a badly wounded duellist. Camelford had felt bound to congratulate the man on his courageous conduct, though the cause of the quarrel was a trifle, and the man unknown to him.[16] The Grand Judge may well have pondered the implications of this report as the crisis drew near.

XII

⚜⚜⚜⚜⚜⚜⚜⚜⚜⚜⚜⚜⚜⚜⚜⚜⚜⚜⚜⚜⚜⚜⚜⚜⚜⚜⚜⚜⚜⚜

Pistols for Two

After the encounter at the Prince of Wales Coffee House, Lord Camelford returned to his lodgings and sent a servant to call Henry Devereux. Barrie was out, and other messengers sent to find him returned without success. When Devereux arrived, Camelford explained that he had been challenged by Best, and asked Devereux to make the necessary arrangements. If more were known of the manner and substance of Mrs Simmonds's tale it would no doubt be possible to understand Lord Camelford's perturbation. There was another factor, which had perhaps by now superseded the original provocation. 'The fact was,' as the Rev. William Cockburne pointed out, 'his Lordship had an idea that his antagonist was the best shot in England, and he was therefore extremely fearful lest his reputation should suffer, if he made any concession, however slight, to such a person.'

Devereux reluctantly consented, and went to the Prince of Wales Coffee House to confer with Best's second, a Mr Nihell, who was dining with him there. It was again explained to Devereux that the insult complained of was imaginary, but messages to this effect were despatched to Lord Camelford with no effect. At nine o'clock Best returned to his own lodgings in Wimpole Street. A quarter of an hour or so earlier, one of the waiters in the coffee house, a man named John Collins, slipped out and made his way to the magistrate's office in Marlborough Street. Anxious to prevent the bloody encounter whose arrangement he had witnessed, Collins explained the danger to the official on duty. The man explained that the magistrate, Mr Conant, was out, but that he would place the particulars on his desk to await his return.

Collins was greatly alarmed at this prospect of delay, and begged the

official to contact Mr Conant at once. The man shrugged his shoulders
and Collins was obliged to leave, still extremely concerned. Mr Conant
did not return to his home in Sloane Street until eleven o'clock, and it
was not until an hour later that the persistent John Collins was able to
provide him with details of the challenge he had witnessed. Police
officers were despatched to watch Lord Camelford's door; lurking in the
street, they saw his carriage draw up outside at half-past one. Presuming
that this was to conduct His Lordship to the field of honour some time
before dawn, they felt confident of being able to prevent the conflict
and settled down to maintain their vigil.

Camelford was determined that the duel should take place. After
Devereux had arranged a time and place with Nihell, he sent for his
solicitor, Richard Wilson, and drew up a codicil to his will. This included
a note emphasising

> that in the present contest I am fully and entirely the Aggressor as
> well in the Spirit as in the letter of the word should I therefore lose
> my life in a contest of my own seeking I most solemnly forbid any of
> my friends or relations ... from instituting any vexatious proceedings
> against my antagonist and should notwithstanding the above declara-
> tion on my part the Law of the land be put in force against him I
> desire that this part of my Will may be made known to the King in
> order that his Royal Breast may be moved to extend his Mercy to-
> wards him.

About one in the morning, Camelford left his lodgings by the back door.
In the mews he instructed his coachman to take the carriage round to the
front door and await further orders.

'Thomas,' he added, as the man clambered on to his seat, 'I have
quarrelled with Best, and he has challenged me to a duel.'

The coachman replied bluntly, 'You have done a very wrong thing,
My Lord; he'll shoot you, by God!'

While the coach was being brought to the front of the house, Lord
Camelford walked through the dark and silent streets to Soho Square.
At number 10 he knocked up his friend, the chemist William Nicholson.
For an hour or so they walked slowly round the square, deep in conversation.[1] The clock of nearby St Anne's Church chimed stilly over the
sleeping houses, and Camelford finally bade his companion farewell. It
was still night-time when he walked into the coffee house in Oxford

Street where Best and he had arranged to meet. Best was there with his second, Nihell, and Camelford's friend Devereux. The young men conferred in subdued voices. They were pale and unshaven: Best, like Camelford, had not been to bed that night.

Best made one final attempt to heal the breach.

'Camelford,' he pleaded, 'we have been friends, and I know the unsuspecting generosity of your nature. Upon my honour, you have been imposed upon by a strumpet. Do not insist upon expressions under which one of us must fall.'

But Camelford had committed himself too deeply: 'Best, this is child's play; the thing must go on.' But a moment later, when conferring privately with Devereux, he confessed that he realised now he had been wrong. Thomas Best was too much a man of honour to persist in a falsehood. But how could Camelford honourably withdraw now? Best's reputation as a dead shot was such that all the world would hold Camelford a coward were he to back down after the harsh words he had uttered in so public a place.

The matter was settled now, and the four men stepped out into the street. Two horses, saddled and bridled and attended by grooms, were waiting, together with a post-chaise. Best and Camelford mounted the horses, while the seconds entered the chaise. Henry Devereux bore under his arm an oblong leather-cased box. It was five o'clock in the morning when the little cavalcade set off westwards along Oxford Street.

About the same time a frantic Captain Barrie, who had known nothing of the final arrangements for the duel, was enquiring in vain of his friend's whereabouts at the house in Bond Street. He had finally been tracked down and warned of what was happening. The servants could say nothing, save that His Lordship had gone out some hours before. Barrie departed, watched by the impassive constables, who believed their man to be still within. He hurried to Anthony Carlisle's home to see if he knew anything. Despite the early hour (it was six o'clock), the surgeon was up. To him Barrie explained in agitated tones he was certain that if only he could reach Camelford in time, he could still prevent the duel. Carlisle, though sympathetic, knew nothing, and Barrie hurried out to continue his search.

Meanwhile the duellists' party had arrived in the little village of Kensington. Glimpsing ahead the Jacobean splendours of Holland House, its forest of chimney-tops blending with the surrounding trees, they dismounted at the Horse and Groom Inn. Consigning their chaise and horses to ostlers, they continued along the road on foot and walked up a small lane. Day was dawning, and the bare branches of trees above showed black against a pallid sky, and were reflected in large clear puddles below. On their left lay bare fields; entering a gateway, they crossed an enclosure in silence and, passing though a gap in a fence, came to a halt in a meadow beyond. A large pond glinted dully at the far end, and the ground was sodden beneath their feet.

Best looked up at his friend, and made one last entreaty for Camelford to withdraw his offending remarks; but Camelford was inexorable.

'Mr Best,' he replied stiffly, 'I do not come here to be trifled with: take your ground and prepare yourself.' There was nothing more for it, the two principals stepped apart, and the seconds discussed distances. Devereux proposed eight paces, to which Nihell strongly objected. He had not come to see the men murder each other, and would withdraw unless the customary twelve paces was accepted.[2] Devereux consented, and also agreed to provide the signal. He presented the open case, containing Lord Camelford's pistols, to each antagonist in turn. They took their weapons, beautiful and deadly saw-handled pistols by Tatham and Egg, their polished octagonal barrels the hard cold colour of the sky above.[3] There followed the unpleasant interval remarked by Lord Byron:

> It has a strange, quick jar upon the ear,
> That cocking of a pistol, when you know
> A moment more will bring the sight to bear
> Upon your person, twelve yards off or so.

Slowly the pistols were raised and levelled. Camelford could see that Best was deliberately aiming to one side, and called across firmly, 'That won't do.' Best's aim shifted, and the muzzle stared directly at his adversary.

'Be quick!' shouted Devereux, which Camelford took to be the signal, and at once squeezed his trigger. Best saw the flash and heard the ball whizz past his ear. Expecting the word 'Fire!', he had momentarily delayed, but at once fired back. For a moment the scene froze, smoke hung in the air, and the four men gazed at each other. Then Lord Camelford staggered and slumped to the ground.

Tom Best threw down his weapon and ran to kneel by his friend. Raising the stricken man's head, he cried out: 'Camelford, I hope you are not seriously hurt?' Camelford spoke with difficulty. 'I suspect I am, but I forgive you.'

'I again declare,' called out Best in anguished tones, 'I am innocent of the charge you made against me.'

'I believe you are right,' admitted the victim faintly, 'but you had better provide for your safety.'

There was need for the warning. Men could be seen staring through the gap in the nearby hedge. Best rose, looked about agitatedly, and then, accompanied by Nihell, brushed past the bystanders and ran to the high-road and the waiting chaise. Devereux had remained to support Camelford's shoulders, but when one of the labourers who had approached came up, he told the man to take his place. Devereux ran to Kensington village, knocked up a surgeon named Thomson, and then made off himself. Shouts followed his flight, but he sprang into the chaise outside the Horse and Groom, where Best and Nihell were anxiously waiting, and they drove off at breakneck speed past the Hammersmith Turnpike. They did not slacken their pace until they had dashed through the streets of London, and on to the house of a cousin of Best's at Dunmow in Essex. They were none too soon, for the Bow Street Runners had already started in pursuit.

Surgeon Thomson hurried to the place of the duel. Lord Camelford was surrounded by a group of gardeners from Lord Holland's park. He was very weak, but repeatedly implored his hearers to make no attempt to stop the fugitives. He was the aggressor, he groaned out, he forgave the gentleman who shot him, and trusted God would do the same. Their names he declined to reveal: 'I know nothing, for I am a dead man.'

A wheelbarrow was fetched from the park, and Lord Camelford was transported in it to a neighbouring house. He was carried upstairs and laid in bed. When his cravat was removed and his shirt opened, a wound was seen in the right side of his chest, below the shoulder.

Mr Otley, the owner of the house, despatched men into town to summon the best surgeons. It was not long before Dr Nicholson, of Sackville Street, arrived and made a full examination. Camelford told him of a burning pain in his chest, but far worse were terrible shooting spasms that racked his body from chest to back, particularly when he spoke. There was also an agonising ache lower down, and Nicholson felt certain that the ball had passed through the patient's lung and was lodged in his spine.

Minutes later Robert Barrie arrived, bounded up the stairs and stood in a sweat of apprehension by his friend's bedside. By now there were three or four surgeons present, and from them he learned that they expected the worst. Convinced that had he been in time he could have dissuaded Camelford from his course, he was in an agony of self-reproach. Camelford smiled wanly, however, and pointed out that it was he that was to blame for having broken his promise not to fight Best. Barrie stayed, grief-stricken, by the bedside.

Other friends began to arrive. The Rev. William Cockburne learned the news within half an hour of the event, hastily despatched a message to Lord Grenville at Dropmore, and was himself at Little Holland House within a short time. At first the surgeons believed Lord Camelford was failing fast, but in the afternoon he made some recovery and spoke with those about him. But by eleven that evening he was suffering excruciating pain once again. Muscular spasms were gripping his spine and side with ever-increasing malignancy. Heavy doses of laudanum began to have some effect, though, and he managed to get some sleep. Next morning he was seemingly much better. He talked about friends and relatives, and asked for some of his belongings to be sent over.

By midday there was a serious relapse. All feeling had vanished from his legs, and his kidneys had ceased to function. It was at this unhappy moment that Lord and Lady Grenville arrived in their barouche from Dropmore. Anne was in a poor state of heath, and when she entered the house she became so agitated at the picture conjured up of Thomas's sufferings that she nearly fainted. The surgeons warned Lord Grenville in the strongest terms that under these conditions a meeting might be fatal to brother or sister — or both. Anne stayed downstairs for some hours, and then returned to Dropmore. Next day she drove again to Little Holland House, but once again it was felt unwise to admit her.

That evening Lord Grenville conferred with the surgeons, and learned that there could be no hope of his brother-in-law's survival. He remained with Barrie at Thomas's bedside, talking of happier days. The failure of sensation in Camelford's body proved an even greater relief from pain than laudanum, and when Captain Macnamara called, the dying man joked faintly, 'Is not this a wonderful cure?' For over three days Lord Camelford lay in this state; at one point he was even strong enough to write a letter to his cousin Sidney Smith, absent on board ship. Frequently

185

he begged William Cockburne to pray by him, and when he could he uttered a faint 'Amen'.

But by midday on Saturday 10 March he began to fail fast. The torturing spasms of pain returned with increasing frequency. He exerted great control over himself to prevent giving way to his torments, and asked in calmer moments, 'Why do they not perform the proposed operation? I am ready to undergo it whenever you please.' But suddenly the convulsions gripped his spine again, and he could not avoid crying out, 'This is suffering indeed!' He turned to the faithful Barrie and asked him to say what his chances were. 'Tom, you must die,' murmured Barrie, gripping his hand.

Thomas lay silent, and then expressed a hope that what he was now suffering, coupled with what good he had managed to achieve in his life among all the ill, might operate in his favour in the next world. He begged Barrie to give up the fruitless life they had both led, and to leave London. He knew his life was ebbing, and turned to Lord Grenville with a request to take care of all his servants, whom he had not named in his will, but wished to be well provided for. Finally, at half-past eight in the evening, came the closing moment. He looked up at Robert Barrie, and murmured the words '*Tanash Mamathi*'.

Barrie recognised the words used by the Indians of Nootka to signify the soul, which they pictured in the form of a little bird. In his dying hours Camelford's mind had dwelt much on his boyhood and youth; now he had flown back in his thoughts to those stirring days when two young midshipmen had spent a long summer surveying creeks and promontories along the North American coast.

Lord Camelford died peacefully. Barrie rose reluctantly and left the room. Lord Grenville came with him; outside, the statesman told Barrie of his conviction that the dead man 'possessed such abilities that could He have survived 10 years longer till the heat of Youth shd. have passed away & the mind have settled, *He would have been the first Man of the age*'. Only in death could the noble brothers-in-law, so entirely different in temperament, bring themselves to express the full warmth of their mutual regard. In Lord Camelford's will, Grenville read for the first time of Thomas's affection for 'Lord Grenville whose repeated acts of kindness to me can never be erased from my memory and have made a stronger impression on me than I have been at times inclined to think he imagined'.

22, 23   Joe Bourke (left) and Jem Belcher (right) from vol. 1 of *Boxiana*
by Pierce Egan

24   Belcher, afterwards Trusty, from vol. 1 of *The Fancy*

25 Celebration of the Peace of Amiens outside Citizen Otto's house in Portman Square

26 In the watch-house, by I. R. and G. Cruikshank from *Life in London* by Pierce Egan

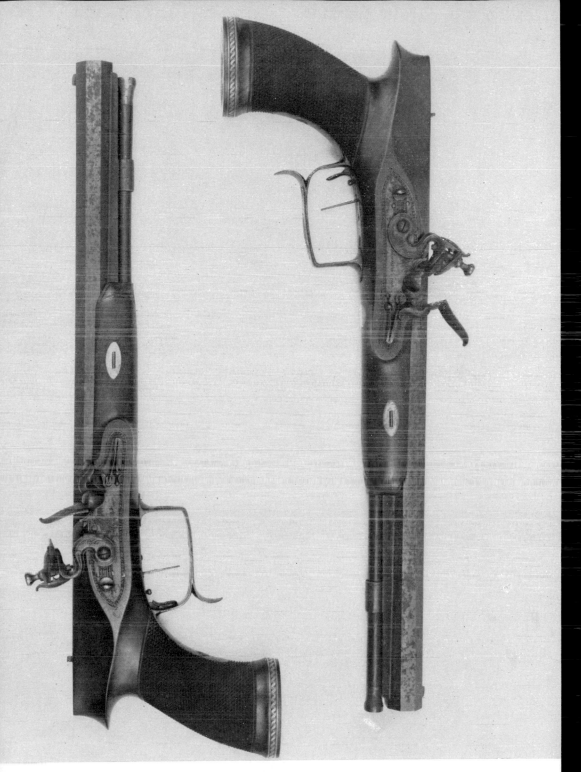

27   Lord Camelford's duelling pistols

28 The death of Lord Camelford. An engraving from vol. IV of *The Eccentric Mirror*

29 The Île de St Pierre on the Lac de Bienne, where Lord Camelford wished to be buried

Friend and relative departed for London, leaving the body in the care of servants. Barrie went to see Anthony Carlisle, and gave him a full account of the distressing scenes of the past three days. Carlisle possessed a keen insight into the workings of the human mind. Camelford had frequently unburdened himself to his friend, and Carlisle had come to understand the pattern reconciling Camelford's seemingly contrary character.

He was much acquainted with the late Lord Camelford. He said He was a man of superior abilities but of singular character. That His prevailing feeling was *ambition*. – That He had declared to him (Carlyle) that He had no *animal courage* and laboured by any means to get the better of a weakness of nerves in this respect, by attending Cock-fightings, – pugilism, – &c. &c. That in Him courage was a struggle of sentiment against Constitution ... He was very desirous of being reckoned much upon as *a Man* independent of his title & wished his friends to lay that aside and to adress Him *familiarly* – But He desired to be at the head notwithstanding, – to Have the best Horses, – in points of dress, and in other things to be first.

When in a passion it was a kind of phrenzy it disordered Him in so great a degree. – But otherways His mind was gentle and easy. His generosity was great & *His Charity very extensive.* One person known to Carlyle had paid on charitable accts. more than £11,000 for Him and that to persons who did not know whence it came.

Next morning Dr Nicholson performed an autopsy on Lord Camelford's body,

when it appeared that the ball had passed into the right breast, between the fourth and fifth ribs, breaking the latter, and making its way through the right lobe of the lungs into the sixth dorsal vertebra, in the substance of which it was found, having completely divided the spinal marrow. In the right side of the chest there was above six quarts of blood and serum, and the lung was so compressed, as to be rendered entirely useless. From the time of the wound taking place, all the parts below the divided spinal marrow were motionless and insensible; and as his Lordship could not expectorate, the left lung became filled with mucus, which produced suffocation and death.

On Monday 12 March an inquest was held by the coroner of Middlesex in the White Horse Inn at Kensington. Dr Nicholson described his findings, and Lord Holland's gardeners described what they had witnessed in the field beyond the park. The jury, following the coroner's direction, unanimously returned a verdict of wilful murder, or felonious homicide, by some person or persons unknown. This they were obliged to do, but in view of the general social acceptance of the code of duelling, and the victim's expressed exculpation of his adversary, it seems to have been accepted that no effective measures would be taken to bring Best or the two seconds to trial.[4]

Lord Camelford's body was brought to Camelford House. Funeral hatchments on the great façade in Oxford Street reminded the passing multitude of the death of a young man, killed, as the uncharitable noted, vindicating 'a fashionable prostitute'.[5] Opinions varied widely on the merits of the dead lord. By the men he was on the whole little regretted. A Dr Hayes spoke to Farington, the artist, 'of the danger of such men as Lord Camelford ... being in society. No man's life is safe where such men are'. And Westmacott, the sculptor, 'mentioned that Lord Camelford is little regretted. At Lord Darnley's He heard some gentleman say "that it was dangerous to sit in company with such a man." ' A popular preacher spoke before a huge congregation on this example of the evils arising from duelling, but dwelt too on Lord Camelford's Christian end.[6]

The ladies were more sympathetic. Eugenia Wynne feared 'he certainly was half mad', but Lady Bessborough felt that, 'with all his wrongheadedness he shew'd so much anxiety to save Capt. Best, his antagonist, and has behav'd with so much generosity, it is impossible not to be sorry for him ... How dreadful a lesson against violent passion his whole life and death have been!' One woman mourned his passing with especial feeling. The day after the duel, Lady Hester Stanhope wrote to a friend that 'Lord Camelford has been shot in a duel, and there is no chance of his recovering. You know my opinion of him, I believe, therefore can judge if I am not likely to lament his untimely end. He had vices, but also great virtues, but they were not known to the world at large.'[7]

Lord Holland, on whose land the fatal contest had taken place, erected on the spot a commemorative block, surmounted by an antique Roman altar. For years it stood alone in the dank meadow adjoining some ornamental fishponds known as the Moats. Then houses began to be built along what is now Addison Road, and workmen damaged the little column around 1827. By the time King Edward VII ascended the

The altar erected by Lord Holland on the spot where Lord Camelford
fell, from Thomas Faulkner, *History and Antiquities of Kensington*, 1820

throne, an opulent villa named Oak Lodge had enclosed part of the field
for its garden, but the altar remained. Oak Lodge in its turn departed,
and today the spot where Best and Camelford met is covered by the
west end of a block of flats known as Oakwood Court. A surviving
fragment of Lord Holland's altar was transferred to a spot near the
Japanese Garden by Holland House. Today all trace of it has vanished.[8]

XIII

Envoi

On Friday, 16 March 1804,

... the shop of Mr. Dawes, undertaker, in Dean Street, Soho, was
surrounded, for several hours, by a concourse of people, anxious to
see Lord Camelford's exterior coffin. The covering of it is a beautiful
crimson velvet, with double rows of silver nails on the lid, beside a
multitude of escocheons and silver ornaments; a baron's coronet is
placed at the head; at the feet a smaller one; and between both a
square silvered plate, with the arms of Camelford engraved upon it,
and the following inscription:

> The Right Honourable
> Thomas Lord Camelford
> Died March the 10th 1804
> Aged 29.

The sides of the coffin are superbly adorned with silver cherubims,
coronets, handles, and a variety of ornaments. At 5 o'clock it was
carried to Camelford-house, where the body, shrouded in white satin,
and laid in a leaden coffin, was placed in it ...

Thus in death Lord Camelford was accorded all the splendid pageantry
due to his rank, though in life he had often disdained it. Early on the
morning of the next day the cortège moved slowly along still-darkened
streets. This exceptionally early hour had probably been chosen to avoid
undue public attention; despite this, great crowds lined the way. The
procession was as impressive as the coffin.

Ten outriders with white scarfs and bands
A plume of white feathers and two pages

The hearse and six horses adorned with white plumes
A coach and six containing mourners
Captain Barrie
Mr. Wilson formerly his Lordship's solicitor
Two of the principal domestics
The deceased's carriage
With two servants behind in mourning, and the coachman seated
on a black velvet hammercloth.

The cortège halted outside St Anne's Church in Dean Street; a stone's
throw from Soho Square, round which Camelford and Nicholson had
paced ten nights before. The service over, the coffin was carried below to
the north vault. Guttering lights threw the mourners' shadows into
ludicrous relief on the walls, final prayers were recited by the curate, and
the company ascended to the daylight. A stout door was softly drawn to
and locked, and Lord Camelford remained alone in the darkness.[1]

Robert Barrie returned to the lonely rooms at 148 New Bond Street.
Seated at Lord Camelford's desk, in the room where so many merry
gatherings had taken place, he wrote to his mother:

I am just return'd from performing the last sad office to my poor
departed friend. He was buried at nine o'clock this morning in a
vault of St. Anne's Church ... Lord Grenville is kind enough to me.
Poor Lady G I have not seen since she came to Little Holland House
to see her brother, but I hear poor Camelford's end has reconciled her
to his fate. He died nobly – a memorable example to us all.[2]

In his will Thomas left the major part of his inheritance to the Grenvilles.[3]
Generous sums were left to Monsieur de la Brunerie and the chemist
William Nicholson.

'I likewise bequeath,' continued the codicil penned on the dreadful
night of 6 March,

to my good friend and old Ship Mate Captn Barrie a full discharge
of all his debts to be paid by my heirs as soon as may be together
with the redemption of his half pay which I have reason to fear he
has sold and I further more bequeath to him a yearly annuity of 200 £
whenever he is not employed on Service on condition that he does
not reside in town or within one hundred miles of it. To my friend

Devereux I bequeath my little Brown Hunter together with my Guns Dogs and other sporting Apparatus which I think will amuse him and tend to drive away the recollection of the tedious hours I have made him spend; he will understand what that means ...[4]

Lord Camelford was dead, but not buried. The night before the duel his mind had dwelt much on that lone haven of peace he had found and lost in boyhood. In the codicil to his will, he wrote pathetically:

With respect to myself, I have ever entertained an anxious desire that my remains may be deposited in some region of the Earth distant from the place of my Nativity and where the surrounding Scenery will smile upon me. Others adorn their abode while living, and it is my fancy to adorn mine when dead. For this purpose I beseech most earnestly that whenever the times will permit, my body may be removed in the cheapest manner to the Island of St. Pierre in the Lake of Bienne in Switzerland; there to be deposited in the centre between the 3 trees that stand on the right of the pavillion. A bush or some such thing may be planted over me, but without any stone or masonry in any shape or form whatever; and for the permission to have this my last wish carried into execution I bequeath one thousand pounds to be paid to the Hospital at Berne to whom the Island belongs. I appoint Devereux my Executor for all these things relating to my burial, on which I attach more importance than a sensible Man perhaps ought to do.[5]

But there was a war in progress, and it was not thought possible to fulfil Lord Camelford's wishes until more peaceful times. The gorgeous coffin lay in its dark vault year after year.

Six years after Camelford's death, there was an intriguing postscript to his short but eventful life. Lord Grenville suddenly received a mysterious letter suggesting that Camelford had fathered a child. A man signing himself only as 'C.T.' explained that he had adopted a little girl, but now wished on her behalf to make 'application to those most able, most bound, and most likely to be willing to protect her'. Lord Grenville consulted a legal adviser, Charles Cowper, who was sceptical: why had the writer adopted the child *before* approaching those he clearly believed to have a prior claim on her?

'Yet,' Cowper went on, 'where "incontestable proofs" are averred to exist, I dare not go the length of attempting to thwart them ... ' Accordingly he would take up the matter, making careful enquiries.

On Thursday, 23 August 1810, 'C.T.' called on Cowper at his rooms in Albany. He proved, surprisingly, to be a respectable gentleman named Charles Trebeck, land agent to some of the first families in Ireland and England. He spoke very candidly about the business mentioned in his letter, and explained 'that the Mother knows nothing of the application made by him ... she has been principally abroad for several years'. Now that he had Lord Grenville's approval, he (Trebeck) would seek to obtain from her factual evidence such as would satisfy Lord Grenville's mind on the subject. His own was already fully satisfied, but his opinion rested entirely on the very high estimate he had formed of the mother's veracity and good character. Neither Mr Trebeck nor the mother was seeking money; as Cowper explained, 'his sole object is, if he can establish the fact, is to have reasonable hopes in his own mind while bringing up the girl above mere labour, that she will not be wholly deserted in case of his death'.

Charles Cowper was clearly impressed by Trebeck's account, but there the story tantalisingly ends.[6]

Meanwhile, Lord Camelford's body still lay in the vault of St Anne's Church in Soho. But when at last the war with Napoleon ended, the question of his dying request was at once raised by his friend Devereux, who had by then succeeded his father as Lord Hereford.

As he explained to Lord Grenville, he felt the removal of the body to the desired spot 'a Duty I owe to the memory of the most esteem'd Friend I ever possessed imposed upon me not only by his will but imprinted upon my Memory in the most awful & impressive manner, at a time that I thought he had but a few moments to exist'.

The owners of the Île de St Pierre, the Hospital of Berne, were quite willing to comply, as a senator of Berne explained. The directors had received in 1804 a notice of the terms of His Lordship's will:

The very place on the island was marked [in the will] so that it imediately was discovered ... the Directors ... had that piece of ground cleaned, smoothed, and this spot where the tomb should be, and where stand the Trees mentioned in this will, surrounded with plantations of Pappel [poplar] trees and weeping willows, which already are of such growth as to beautify much this aspect ... they will be bound to take special care of a spot where the remains of so distinguished a friend of the Swiss nation are deposited ... I remember very well Lord Camelford having been in Switzerland in the year 1799 and having shewn great kindness to all our Officers fighting there against the French in the Austrian and Russian Armies.

It seemed as if Lord Camelford's wish would be accomplished, but then Lord Grenville pointed out that there were strong reasons for not embarking on a course which would inevitably attract public attention, much of it adverse. At the time of Camelford's death there had been a widespread view that he could not have been completely sane. Now, in the turmoil of the war, his escapades had been largely forgotten. But this final eccentricity – an Englishman asking to be buried abroad – would set malicious tongues wagging again.

Despite many friends' urgings along these lines, Hereford reluctantly felt duty bound to honour Camelford's wishes. In the event he was relieved to find his crisis of conscience resolved for him. Ecclesiastical permission was required before the body could be moved. The chancellor of the diocese of London, Sir William Scott, refused to grant it.[7]

And so the body of the second Lord Camelford stayed in the vault at St Anne's in Soho. In the middle of the nineteenth century, the vaults ceased to be used and were sealed up.[8] Strange rumours began to circulate concerning the hidden coffin. The novelist Charles Reade was assured that Camelford's body in the vault reposed in 'an enormously long fish-basket, fit to pack a shark in'.[9]

In October 1940, a century later, St Anne's Church was severely damaged by bombing, and after the war all the building except the tower had to be demolished. Today there is a car-park within the ruined walls. The vaults remain intact beneath, and there can be little doubt that Lord Camelford still lies somewhere towards the eastern end of the north vault. Possibly underpaid Victorian sextons removed the splendid silver trappings, but traces of these should ensure identification.[10]

The second Lord Camelford found little happiness in life, and in death made but one heartfelt request. Perhaps it may yet be possible to fulfil his dying prayer, and to reinter him, as he wished, on the Île de St. Pierre.

‡❀

Appendix

The article published in 1803 in
A Journal of Natural Philosophy, Chemistry, and the Arts
describing Lord Camelford's repeating pistol.

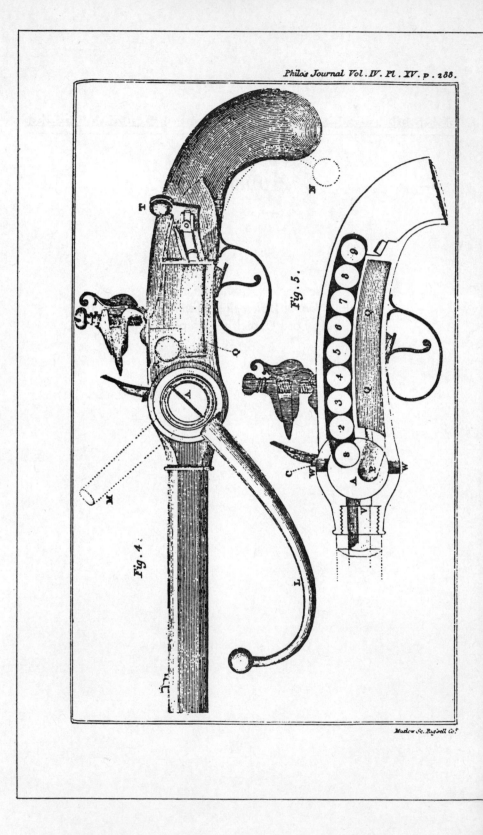

A

JOURNAL

OF

NATURAL PHILOSOPHY,

CHEMISTRY,

AND

THE ARTS.

VOL. IV.

𝔍llustrated with 𝔈ngrabings;

BY WILLIAM NICHOLSON.

LONDON:

PRINTED BY W. STRATFORD, CROWN-COURT, TEMPLE-BAR FOR

THE AUTHOR, No. 10, SOHO-SQUARE

AND SOLD BY

G. AND J. ROBINSONS, PATERNOSTER-ROW.

1803.

This method is shorter than that of the anagrammatic scale, and is preferable when there is much to write; but it is less secure, and requires a more complicated apparatus.

XI.

Description of a Magazine Pistol, which when loaded is capable of being discharged Nine successive Times through the same Barrel. W. N.

Account of a magazine pistol.

I AM indebted to the liberality of the Right Honourable Lord Camelford for the accurate drawings of the curious and valuable piece which forms the subject of the present Memoir, as well as for permission to use and examine it in any manner I might think proper. It is of German make; the workmanship very good, and it has been used by his Lordship without any particular care in various parts of the world. Its construction does, in effect, shew that its use is attended with neither danger nor uncertainty; but I shall postpone my remarks till I have given the description.

Description by reference to the drawings.

Figs. 1 and 4 in the Plates XIV. and XV. exhibit views of the two sides of the pistol. Fig. 5. is a section to shew the magazines, and Figs. 2. and 3. shew what may be called the chamber piece. The large face of this last (Fig. 2.) is slightly taper or conical from X towards Y, where the diameter is smallest, and the small part B is cylindrical, excepting that a portion is scooped out on one side marked by the dark space D in Fig. 3. Its proper place in the pistol is in the breech, crossing the line of direction at right angles. When the lock is off, it goes into its cell from the side Fig. 1. which it fits with considerable accuracy, but does not come to rub hard, because the Plate X forms a projecting face which stops it. In this situation its small cylindrical part B projects outwards, and is received in an hole of the same diameter in that part of the lock beneath the hammer where the pan is usually placed. In fact, the cavity D, Fig. 3. does constitute the pan when its position is such as to be immediately beneath the covering face of the hammer. The screw B which goes into the cylindrical piece, and Z, which goes into the stock, are the fastenings by which the lock is secured. At the opposite end

A,

A, Fig. 2. the chamber piece terminates in a fquare, upon ich the broad head of the lever L, Fig. 4. is fitted, and kept down by the fcrew A, which goes into the chamber piece. It is to be underftood that the cock and hammer are conftructed, and act in the fame manner as in the beft fire
arms, and do not therefore require to be defcribed. The
lever is capable of being moved from the pofition M to thofe
of L and N; but is prevented from defcribing the remaining
part of the circle by an interior ftop, which may be eafily imagined without any attempt at minute explanation.

Description of a piftol which fires nine balls in fuc- ceffion by once charging.

Fig. 5. being a fection through the middle of the ftock,
breech, and part of the barrel, fhews the relative fituation of
the magazines, with the chamber piece, and other parts. The
balls S, 2, 3, 4, &c. are lodged in their proper receptacle,
being put in through the hole R, Fig. 4. and the powder is
lodged in its magazine Q Q. both which are clofed by the
door T, which is then faftened by a fmall bolt and back fpring.
A, Fig. 5. fhews the fituation of the chamber piece at the
time when the lever is brought to the pofition M. This is
done with the muzzle of the piece pointing towards the
ground, and the effect is, that powder runs into the chamber
P (fee alfo Figs. 2 and 3) and a ball into the chamber S. The
lever is then moved from M to L and N, by which procefs
the ball chamber drops its ball into the barrel as it paffes oppofite to N, where the ball remains, becaufe the actual bore
of the fcrew barrel is not wide enough to allow it to pafs far-
ther than juft to clear the moveable chamber. As foon as the
lever has arrived at the pofition N, the powder chamber P is
exactly oppofite the ball, and ready to be difcharged againft
it. After the difcharge the muzzle is to be again depreffed,
and the lever moved from N to M: the chambers become
again charged with powder and ball; and by returning the
lever back to N, this ball and powder become duly placed
for a fecond difcharge. It is obvious that thefe difcharges may
be repeated until all the balls have been fired out. The fmall
bridge in the powder chamber P (Fig. 2.) is to prevent any
impediment from the entrance of part of one of the balls into
the receptacle, and the perforations W, W, in the breech,
ferve to clear the furface of the chamber piece from any foul-
nefs it might acquire.

Thus

Description of a piftol which fires nine balls in fucceffion by once charging.

Thus far we have fpoken only of loading and difcharging; but this piece would admit of little rapidity of effect, if it did not at the fame time cock and prime itfelf. It may be obferved, that the projecting part, or ftud C, is fixed to the chamber piece Fig. 2. and 3. a very little behind the fhot chamber; fo that it ftands at the top of the lock at the time of charging. A thin flat bar of iron proceeds from the cock, and flides with it along the face of the lock plate, withinfide the hammer: againft this plate the ftud C acts, and brings it to full cock a little before the lever arrives at the pofition M; at the fame time that the more prominent part of C preffes on the back of the hammer, and fhuts the pan. The lock is therefore put into the condition to give fire by the fame fimple operation, and precifely at the fame moment as the charge is taken from the magazines.

It now remains only to be fhewn how the priming is given. The excavation D in the fide of the fmall cylinder B, Fig. 3. conftitutes the pan, and the fmall dot reprefents the touch hole paffing through the metal into P the powder chamber. When the lever is in the pofition M, Fig. 4, the cavity D is exactly placed beneath the covering face of the hammer G: but at the time of charging it has the pofition Fig. 3. confidered with regard to that of Fig. 1. In this laft figure the dark fhaded fpace H denotes a refervoir for priming, the door of which may be opened and fhut under the action of an ingenious back fpring, operating nearly like that of a clafp knife. A long perforation or flit communicates from this refervoir to the fpace in which the cylinder B revolves: fo that when the excavation D paffes that flit (during the return of the lever) it becomes filled with powder, which it carries round to the laft pofition, which is exactly that in which it muft receive the fire whenever the piftol is to be difcharged.

The hiftory of this conftruction feems to be imperfect; but there is reafon to fuppofe that it is of fome antiquity. The magazine air gun of *Colbe* conftructed for carrying ten balls, and lodging them fucceffively in the barrel by a crofs cylindrical piece was made early in the laft century, and is defcribed in Defagulier's Lectures, and moft elementary books. In the prefent arm the contrivances are highly judicious, as well with regard to mechanifm as to arrangement. If it were poffible for the powder magazine to be fet on fire at the dif-

tance

tance of a femi-circumference of the chamber piece from the Defcription of a pistol which fires nine balls in fucceffion by once charging. explofion, the only effect would be that the door would be blown open, and this is fituated in a place where it could do no harm. The fame remark is alfo applicable to the magazine for priming.

How great the advantages muft be in battle, for a man to be able to reload his piece by a fimple movement of one fecond of time, without taking his eye off his enemy; or how confiderably ufeful this invention might prove in the defence againft robbers need not be ftated. It can indeed be ftated, that the opponent may alfo provide himfelf with the like advantage; and then we have only to urge the argument, that the duration of wars have been diminifhed, and its humanity diminifhed by rendering the means of annoyance more perfect.

I have difcharged this courfe of balls feveral times, and I find that the whole nine balls can be fired in 30 feconds.

XII.

On the Diffemination of Plants. By CIT. L. REYNIER *.

THE hiftory of vegetables affords fome facts to which I think it my duty to call the attention of naturalifts; they relate to the diffemination of plants, and to the means by which this is effected. I have already collected feveral obfervations on this fubject in the dictionary of Agriculture of *L'Encyclopédie Méthodique*, article *Diffemination*. Diffemination of plants,

There are two natural means of reproduction: one of thefe is by the roots, which, fpreading outwards, form new ftems round the mother plant; this reproduction is flow, and can only take place gradually and without intervals; the other is by the feeds, which being carried by the winds, or by the hooks with which they are provided, or by animals which fwallow them, and afterwards depofit them, unchanged, in their excrements, are removed to greater diftances, though ftill within a limited circle. It is not therefore wonderful, to fee a plant fpring up in a fpot, where the fame fpecies is known to exift at no great diftance; its introduction is in the clafs of poffibilities. by the fpreading of the roots, or tranfportation of feeds.

* Decade Philofophique, No. 13. An. XI.

But

Notes

ABBREVIATIONS

Addn. MSS.   Additional manuscripts in the British Library
ADM.   Admiralty records in the Public Record Office
HO   Home Office records in the Public Record Office
PRO   Public Record Office
PROB.   Probate records in the Public Record Office

Chapter I: 'Wellcome little Stranger'

1 Sir Tresham Lever, *The House of Pitt: A Family Chronicle* (London, 1947), pp. 11–13, 46–7.
2 Ibid., pp. 80–2, 86–90, 134–6.
3 Ibid., p. 141; Michael McCarthy, 'Eighteenth Century Amateur Architects and their Gardens', Sir N. Pevsner (ed.), *The Picturesque Garden* (Dumbarton Oaks, Washington, 1947), pp. 53–4.
4 Lever, op. cit., pp. 90, 136, 222.
5 Ibid., pp. 216–17, 220–3, 229, 231. He was one of those who offered to help William Pitt out of his financial difficulties in 1789 (pp. 282–3).
6 *An Act for Rectifying Mistakes in the Marriage Settlement of Lord and Lady Camelford; and for making a further Provision for the younger Children of the said Marriage* (1786), pp. 1–3. A further large sum was inherited when Pinckney Wilkinson died in 1784 (cf. his will, Fortescue MSS., Cornwall County Record Office, D.D.F. acc., 3).
7 I am indebted to Lady Margaret Fortescue for her kindness in lending me the first Lord Camelford's own copy of his *Narrative and Proofs* (London, 1785). Cf. also Lever, op. cit., pp. 174–8, 206–10
8 Ibid., p. 196.

203

9 The Bible (Authorised Version, published in 1717: the year Governor Pitt bought the house) is still kept at Boconnoc.
10 I am grateful to the Rev. Geoffrey G. Pinnock, Rector of Braddock, for kindly supplying me with an extract from Boconnoc parish register. A contemporary pencil sketch of the font by S. Lysons is to be found in Addn. MS. 9462, folio 20b.
11 Lever, op. cit., p. 196.
12 Ibid., p. 267.
13 John Nichols, *Illustrations of the Literary History of the Eighteenth Century* (London, 1817–48), v, p. 860. For the Rev. Benjamin Forster, Rector of Boconnoc until his death in 1805, cf. also Nichols, *Literary Anecdotes of the Eighteenth Century* (London, 1812–15), IX, pp. 648–50.
14 e.g. Addn. MS. 59491, 42, 44.
15 W. S. Lewis *et al.* (eds), *Horace Walpole's Correspondence with Sir Horace Mann* (Yale, 1967), VIII, p. 411.
16 C. S. Gilbert, *An Historical Survey of the County of Cornwall* (Plymouth, 1820), II, pp. 908–13; Fortescue Hitchins and Samuel Drew, *The History of Cornwall* (Helston, 1824), II, pp. 80–6; Eric R. Delderfield, *West Country Historic Houses and their Families* (Newton Abbot, 1968), pp. 14–17. I am indebted to the present owner, Mr J. D. G. Fortescue, for his hospitality and kindness during my visit to Boconnoc.
17 Sir Robert Barrie MSS., William R. Perkins Library, Duke University, North Carolina (henceforth cited as 'Barrie MSS'.); Davies Gilbert, *The Parochial History of Cornwall* (London, 1838), I, p. 70; cf. Addn. MS. 58904, 4; PRO 30/70/3, 159. The first Lord Camelford had been taught Latin by the parson of Boconnoc in 1754 (Lever, op. cit., p. 87).
18 Compare the experience of Sir Jonah Barrington, *Personal Sketches of his own Times* (London, 1827), I, pp. 53–7.
19 Lever, op. cit., p. 222. There are allusions to her illness in Addn. MS. 59490.
20 Compare the sufferings of the young Talleyrand and his contemporaries: J. F. Bernard, *Talleyrand: A Biography* (London, 1973), pp. 19–25.
21 Addn. MS. 59490, 5.
22 One may compare again Sir Jonah Barrington's vividly recalled experiences (op. cit., pp. 2–5).
23 Addn. MS. 59491, 7–10; F.-A.-M. Jeanneret and J.-H. Bonhote, *Biographie Neuchâteloise* (Locle, 1863), II, pp. 80–4. The last reference was kindly supplied to me by Monsieur Jean-Pierre Jelmini, Curator of the Neuchâtel Museum. I am grateful to MM. Jelmini, Alfred Schnegg and R. Vionnet for help in identifying de Meuron's school building.
24 G. H. Wilson (ed.), *The Eccentric Mirror* (London, 1807), IV, p. 30.
25 Compare Lady Elizabeth Foster's pilgrimage in 1783: Dorothy Margaret

Stuart, *Dearest Bess* (London, 1955), p. 14; William Waldvogel, *L'Ile de Saint-Pierre et le lac de Bienne* (Neuchâtel, 1949), p. 10. (I am grateful to my friend Jasmine Maag-Božin, who sent me a copy of this monograph, together with other related material.) The Camelfords visited Edward Gibbon at Lausanne in 1788: J. E. Norton (ed.), *The Letters of Edward Gibbon* (London, 1956), III, p. 144.

26 *Oeuvres de J. J. Rousseau* (Paris, 1819), III, pp. 221–3, 228.

27 Ibid., pp. 246–7. Compare Murray's *Hand-Book for Travellers in Switzerland, and the Alps of Savoy and Piedmont* (London, 1846), pp. 137–9.

28 *Oeuvres de J. J. Rousseau*, III, pp. 294–5. The pavilion still stands; for a photograph, cf. Waldvogel, op. cit., p. 36.

29 Information from Mr Martin Pope, Dept. of Archives, Charterhouse; R. L. Arrowsmith, *Charterhouse Register 1769–1872* (Chichester, 1974), p. 297; W. P. Byrne, *Gossip of the Century* (London, 1892), I, p. 95.

30 Compare Martin Tupper, *My Life as an Author* (London, 1886), pp. 14 24.

31 Gilbert, op. cit., I, p. 70.

32 Compare the print published by Carington Bowles (National Maritime Museum, negative no. 8705).

33 ADM. 107/21, 169.

34 ADM. 51/997.

35 Michael Lewis, *A Social History of the Navy 1793–1815* (London, 1960), pp. 165–8; David Hannay, *Naval Courts Martial* (Cambridge, 1914), pp. 98–104. In 1790 the nine-year-old William (later Admiral) Dillon was offered a similar certificate as 'Captains Servant': Michael Lewis (ed.), *A Narrative of My Personal Adventures by Sir William Henry Dillon*, K.C.H. (London, 1953), I, pp. 9–10.

36 It is on this inference that I assume that Thomas's enrolment on to the complement of the *Tobago* followed his visit to Plymouth, and hence that the visit took place in 1781.

37 1st Lord Camelford, op. cit., p. 59; Sir John Barrow, *The Life and Correspondence of Admiral Sir William Sidney Smith*, G.C.B. (London, 1848), I, pp. 5–16.

38 ADM. 107/21, 169.

39 A. Aspinall (ed.), *The Later Correspondence of George III* (Cambridge, 1962), I, p. 475; PRO 30/8, 77, 79.

40 Archibald Duncan, *The Mariner's Chronicle* (London, 1804–5), I, p. 54; cf. pp. 49–54; IV, 36–48; reference kindly supplied by Patrick O'Brian. The foregoing account of the voyage and escape of the *Guardian* is based on 'The Log of the Guardian' in Christopher Lloyd (ed.), *The Naval Miscellany* (Navy Records Society, London, 1952), pp. 295–358; MSS. RUSI/ER/1, 2, 3 at the National Maritime Museum, Greenwich; Isaac Schomberg, *Naval*

Chronology (London, 1802), II, pp. 204–15; Lever, op. cit., pp. 270–1. The National Maritime Museum has two prints of the departure of the *Guardian's* boats: an aquatint after Dodd, and a mezzotint published by Carington Bowles. For Riou's appearance and character, cf. Lewis (ed.), op. cit., I, p. 69.
41 ADM. 1. 2400; cf. ADM. 1. 2807.

Chapter II: The Caning in Conduit Street

1 Sir Tresham Lever, *The House of Pitt: A Family Chronicle*, p. 271.
2 *The Manuscripts of J. B. Fortescue, Esq., Preserved at Dropmore* (Historical Manuscripts Commission, London, 1892), I, p. 611.
3 Bern Anderson, *Surveyor of the Sea: The Life and Voyages of Captain George Vancouver* (Toronto, 1960), p. 46.
4 *Memoirs of Madame Vigée Lebrun* (London, 1904), p. 57. Lord Camelford may not have paid for the portrait until 1 August 1792, when he instructed Drummond's Bank to pay her £100. There existed an earlier portrait which a young friend thought 'looks too old' (Addn. MS. 59491, 96). It was probably painted in or before 1784, as Blanchard's balloon ascent is alluded to in the same letter (cf. R. H. Cholmondeley, *The Heber Letters, 1783–1832*, London, 1950, p. 27), and it was also in 1784 that Lord Camelford instructed Hoare's Bank to pay 'Mrs Le Brun' the sum of £20 5s. 0d.
5 For a full account see John Ehrman, *The Younger Pitt: The Years of Acclaim* (London, 1969), pp. 554–71. Thomas may well have read John Meares's *Voyage from China to North America*, a copy of which is still at Boconnoc.
6 George Godwin, *Vancouver: A Life 1757–1798* (London, 1930), p. 153.
7 ADM. 107/21, 169.
8 Anderson, op. cit., pp. 47–8.
9 A list is provided by Robert Barrie in a letter of 15 January 1791 (Barrie MSS.).
10 Michael Lewis (ed.), *A Narrative of My Personal Adventures by Sir William Henry Dillon*, K.C.H., I, p. 31; Barrie MSS., letter of 13 February 1791; ibid., biographical sketch by Julia Boodle (Barrie's daughter).
11 *The Naval Chronicle* (London, 1812), XXVIII, pp. 3–4; (reference supplied by Patrick O'Brian and Tom L. Brock).
12 For midshipmen in the Royal Navy at that time, compare further Michael Lewis, *A Social History of the Navy 1793–1815* (London, 1960), pp. 267–9; Patrick O'Brian, *Men-of-War* (London, 1974), pp. 29–32.
13 Addn. MS. 59491, 11.
14 Godwin, op. cit., pp. 38–9; Anderson, op. cit., pp. 48–9.
15 ADM. 107/21, 169.
16 Lewis, op. cit., p. 267.

17 Addn. MS. 59492, 4. The letter quoted by Sir Tresham Lever (op. cit., pp. 271–2) must be misdated. It appears to refer to the earlier voyage on the *Guardian*, but could not in either case be dated 1 July.

18 Anderson, op. cit., pp. 50–9.

19 Owen Rutter (ed.), *The Court-Martial of the 'Bounty Mutineers'* (Edinburgh, 1931), pp. 32–3, etc.

20 Sir Joseph Banks, the famous naturalist, collected evidence of Thomas Pitt's ill-treatment at Lady Camelford's request. Cf. Banks Correspondence (Natural History Museum, 1796–7), x, pt. i, pp. 80, 84, 87; the *True Briton*, 5 October 1796 (obviously Lord Camelford's own account).

21 Compare Anderson, op. cit., pp. 65, 66–7, 68–9, 88, 148, 150, 255; Godwin, op. cit., pp. 141, 166–7.

22 Barrie MSS., 15 January 1791.

23 Ibid., 12 October 1796.

24 Anderson, op. cit., p. 220.

25 Ibid., pp. 139–40, 172.

26 Godwin, op. cit., pp. 187–8, 192–3, 240.

27 Banks MSS., p. 83. For the arrangement, compare Lewis (ed.), op. cit., I, p. 21.

28 Anderson, op. cit., p. 190.

29 Ibid., pp. 112–13, 196; cf. pp. 208–9. It was, of course, easier to send letters home than to receive them.

30 Banks MSS., pp. 80–8; for the watch, compare Lewis (ed.), op. cit., I, p. 14. This appears to be the only surviving account of Pitt's punishments on board the *Discovery*. Relevant logs and journals which must have recorded them are missing from the collections in the Public Record Office. Admiral Anderson suggests they were collected together to facilitate an enquiry called for by Vancouver in 1797, and that excerpts relating to Thomas Pitt were not returned to the central office (Anderson, op. cit., pp. 220–1). Some such explanation is doubtless correct, but as logs relating to Pitt are missing for the whole period of his naval service, it seems more probable that they were collected together early in 1799. It was then that Lord Spencer decided that Pitt's record was such that he could no longer be entrusted with a command. To provide but two examples: the ADM, 51 logs in the Public Record Office are missing for the *Favorite* from 13 September 1797 to 4 May 1798, and for the *Terror* from 5 May 1798 to 22 April 1799. These cover precisely the weeks that Pitt served on each vessel.

31 Oliver Warner, *The Life and Letters of Vice-Admiral Lord Collingwood* (London, 1968), pp. 24–5.

32 Godwin, op. cit., p. 223.

33 ADM. 107/21, 169.

34 Addn. MS. 59492, 20.

35 The date is supplied by ADM. 107/21, 169.

36 Anderson, op. cit., pp. 174, 217.

37 Lever, op. cit., p. 272.

38 Addn. MS. 58979, 1. In 1797 the sculptor Flaxman was commissioned to erect a monument to Lord Camelford in Boconnoc church, but the project apparently fell through (Addn. MS. 59492, 44–6). His will is amongst the Fortescue MSS., D.D.F. acc., 5, in the Cornwall County Record Office, Truro.

39 For the threadbare uniform, compare Anderson, op. cit., p. 205. A contemporary view of Port Jackson is reproduced in J. Christopher Herold, *The Age of Napoleon* (London, 1963), p. 296; cf. *The Naval Chronicle* (London, 1809), XXII, pp. 385–90, 477–81.

40 Lever, op. cit., pp. 267–70. Lord Camelford had long been a political ally of the Grenvilles (ibid., pp. 151, 172, 174). The marriage settlement is to be found in the Cornwall County Record Office, Fortescue MSS., D.D.F. acc., 4.

41 Addn. MS. 59487, 218.

42 Addn. MS. 59492, 20.

43 Stamford Raffles Flint, *Mudge Memoirs* (Truro, 1883), p. 159; Addn. MS. 59492, 31–4, 147–8.

44 Ibid., 27–30.

45 Compare Sir Evan Cotton, *East Indiamen* (London, 1949), p. 184. For a plan and description of Malacca, compare Abbé Antoine-François Prévost, *Histoire Générale des Voyages* (Paris, 1746–68), VIII, pp. 326–7.

46 Michael Roe (ed.), *The Journal and Letters of Captain Charles Bishop on the North-West Coast of America, in the Pacific and in New South Wales 1794-1799* (Cambridge, 1967), p. 216. Bishop himself was offered Camelford's appointment a year later (ibid., p. 212).

47 Addn. MS. 59491, 13–16; Addn. MS. 59492, 35–41, 49–50; Banks MSS., p. 81. For the movements of the Madras squadron against the Dutch in 1795, compare William James, *The Naval History of Great Britain* (London, 1837), I, pp. 302–4.

48 Rev. William Neil (ed.), *The Cleghorn Papers: A Footnote to History* (London, 1927), pp. 261–2, 266, 285–6. (I am indebted to Colonel Geoffrey Powell for drawing my attention to this source; cf. his article 'Delinquent Pitt', *British History Illustrated*, London, 1976, I, pp. 6–8). For the loss of the *Union*, cf. also ADM. 107/21, 167; a 'country ship' was one 'which plied between port and port in the Eastern seas', (Cotton, op. cit., p. 25).

49 Addn. MSS. 59491, 17–19; 59493, 11–12, 195. For the hazards facing a voyager in those seas, cf. the 'Journal of a Levant Pirate', *The Edinburgh*

Annual Register for 1810 (Edinburgh, 1812), III (2), pp. LI–LXIII. (Reference kindly supplied by Patrick O'Brian).

50 Addn. MS. 59491, 19; National Library of Wales, Pitchford Hall Collection: Cotes MSS. (henceforward cited as Cotes MSS.).

51 Addn. MS. 59492, 83–90.

52 Ibid., 92–135; Cotes MSS.; the *True Briton*, 9 September 1796, 30 September 1796, 3 October 1796, 11 October 1796, 24 October 1796, 26 October 1796; *The Times*, 30 September 1796; the *London Chronicle*, 4–6 October 1796; Thomas Wright and R. H. Evans, *Historical and Descriptive Account of the Caricatures of James Gillray* (London, 1851), pp. 81–4; Mary D. George, *Catalogue of Political and Personal Satires ... in the British Museum* (London, 1942), VII, pp. 264–5; Godwin, op. cit., pp. 152–3; Banks MSS., p. 80. King Kamehameha's feathered cloak was belatedly presented to King George in 1797) Anderson, op. cit., pp. 143, 178, 218).

53 Banks MSS., pp. 81–2.

54 Barrie MSS., 12 October 1796.

55 Flint, op. cit., p. 160.

56 Addn. MS. 59492, 135.

57 Addn. MSS. 59491, 19; 59492, 35, 47, 51; cf. G. C. Boase and W. P. Prideaux, *Bibliotheca Cornubiensis* (Truro, 1878), II, p. 501.

58 ADM. 107/21, 169; ADM. 51/1187. There is a fine painting by Rowlandson of a ship fitting out at Deptford dockyard (Godwin, op. cit., opposite p. 30).

59 Banks MSS., 82; Barrie MSS., 3 November 1796; Addn. MS. 59492, 136

Chapter III: Blood on the Quayside

1 The *True Briton*, 27 October 1796. The National Maritime Museum possesses an engraving of the *London*, published by Carington Bowles in 1781.

2 Addn. MS. 59491, 21, 23; 59492, 135.

3 Ibid., 51, 137, 167; Barrie MSS., 23 February 1797; ADM. 107/21, pp. 164–9.

4 *Journals of the House of Lords* (London, 1798), XLI, p. 84; cf. pp. 177, 204.

5 Barrie MSS., 7 December 1796.

6 Verbatim conversation and description taken from Cotes MSS.; Addn. MS. 59492, 150–2. Charles Vancouver was temporarily obliged to return to Holland, as he could not find the required sureties. When Lord Camelford returned to England in the following summer, he too was required to provide similar security for good behaviour.

7 Ibid., 140. On 13 April Camelford's lawyer took out nearly £50 in Spanish dollars for him from Drummond's Bank at Charing Cross. The Spanish

dollar was the principal coin circulating in Barbados, valued at some three to the pound sterling (John Waller, *A Voyage to the West Indies*, London, 1820, p. 7).

8 Julian S. Corbett (ed.), *Private Papers of George, second Earl Spencer* (London, 1914), II, p. 115.

9 Sir John Barrow, *The Life of Richard Earl Howe*, K.G. (London, 1838), pp. 325–39.

10 Addn. MS. 59491, 35; Michael Lewis, *A Social History of the Navy 1793–1815*, pp. 296–7. Camelford appears to have crossed the Atlantic in the sloop *Scourge* (cf. ADM. 12/72; ADM. 3/118, 37).

11 Addn. MS. 59493, 160. The National Maritime Museum possesses an engraving by T. Stevens of the *Vengeance* off Martinique.

12 Anon., *The Life, Adventures and Eccentricities of the Late Lord Camelford* (London, 1804), p. 3.

13 *The Naval Chronicle*, XXII, pp. 323–4. Lord Spencer notified Lord Grenville of this long-awaited move on 10 December (Addn. MS. 59492, 153), and the rank was confirmed two days later: *The Commissioned Sea Officers of the Royal Navy* (? London, n.d.), I, p. 140; *Steel's Original and Correct List of the Royal Navy ... corrected to May 1797* (London, 1797), p. 28. Captain Russell's initial order was dated 13 September (*The Naval Chronicle*, XXII, p. 491). Either Admiral Harvey owed much to the Camelford-Grenville interest, or he thought very highly of Lord Camelford, for there was an acute shortage of vacant command postings on the Leeward Islands station in 1797 (Michael Lewis, ed.), *A Narrative of My Personal Adventures by Sir William Henry Dillon*, K.C.H., I, pp. 307–8).

14 Addn. MS. 54942, 154–9, 195; 54943, 17.

15 *The Annual Register ... For the Year 1798* (London, 1800), p. 11. It seems unlikely the author had any real conception of Lord George Gordon's appearance a quarter of a century previously.

16 *The Naval Chronicle*, XXII,. p. 489.

17 Compare Lewis, op. cit., pp. 111–12. In 1798 an affray, similar in some respects to Lord Camelford's at Bridgetown, occurred at Mevagissey. There, however, Lieutenant Hicks was dismissed his ship, though justified in several of his measures (David Hannay, *Naval Courts Martial*, pp. 88–94).

18 Compare William Dillon's threats when faced by a similar situation off the Mexican coast in 1800 (Michael Lewis, ed., op. cit., I, pp. 391–2).

19 For events at Barbados on 6 and 7 November 1797, see Addn. MSS. 59492, 160–208, 217–22; 59493, 1–10, 15–17, 22–7; *The Manuscripts of J. B. Fortescue, Esq., Preserved at Dropmore* (London, 1899), III, pp. 165–6; R. C. Wellesley (ed.), *The Wellesley Papers* (London, 1914), I, p. 49; Sir John Barrow, *The Life and Correspondence of Admiral Sir William Sidney Smith* G.C.B., II, pp.

121–2; Lady Granville (ed.), *Lord Granville Leveson Gower ... Private Correspondence* (London, 1916), I, p. 193. A contemporary account of Barbados, with an engraving of Bridgetown, is contained in Waller, op. cit., pp. 1–28; cf. also J. Holland Rose, A. P. Newton and E. A. Benions (eds), *The Cambridge History of the British Empire* (Cambridge 1929), I, pp. 820–2.

20 Addn. MS. 54942, 194, 196.

21 Eighteen months previously, Mainwaring himself in the 32-gun frigate *Aimable* had been engaged in a fierce fight with the elusive *Pensée*. He will the more have appreciated Camelford's courage in attempting against all odds to seize so much more powerful a vessel than his own (cf. William James, *The Naval History of Great Britain*, I, pp. 339–40).

22 Guy E. Cooper, 'The Last Lord Camelford', *The Mariner's Mirror* (London, 1922), VIII, p. 163; (reference supplied by Tom L. Brock).

23 Mainwaring 'was an active, gallant officer, and a thorough good seaman. Although hot and passionate, he knew how to soften these failings'. (Lewis, ed., op. cit., I, p. 251.)

24 Sir John Barrow, *The Life of Richard Earl Howe*, K.G., pp. 330–1.

25 Lord Camelford had been, as was noted earlier, confirmed in the rank of commander the previous December. But as this was still unknown on the Leeward Islands station it is irrelevant to the case.

26 In a letter to his brother, my generous informant Mr Tom L. Brock.

27 *The Naval Chronicle*, XXII, pp. VIII, 303.

28 Hannay, op. cit., p. 146. By a curious coincidence a marine had killed a sailor on the very same spot twenty years earlier. Though there appeared to be no real justification for this action, 'the Court Martial acquitted him because he had been attacked while on duty'! (ibid., pp. 154–5). There had been a serious mutiny on board the frigate *Santa Monica* in English Harbour in 1781 (ibid., pp. 131–5).

29 The original of the court-martial proceedings is at the Public Record Office: ADM. 1/5343. Mitford's letter is in ADM. 1/321,3; the Antigua coroner's verdict is in ibid., 4, and Parsons's application (13 May 1798) to return home on account of chronic rheumatism and other ailments on p. 62. The court-martial appeared in printed form twice:*Minutes of the proceedings of a court-martial, assembled and held on board His Majesty's ship the Invincible, in Fort Royal bay, Martinique, on the 20th of January, and continued ... until the 25th, to try—,for the death of—.* (London, 1799); 'Trial of Captain Lord Camelford, R.N.', *The Naval Chronicle*, XXII, pp. 303–24, 423–32; 481–92. Cf. also the *Gentleman's Magazine* (London, 1798), LXVIII, p. 345; *The Mariner's Mirror*, VIII, pp. 162–7; Addn. MS. 59492, 209–16; Sir Kenneth Blackburne, *The Romance of English Harbour* (5th edition, Antigua, n.d.), (note by Tom L. Brock); John Luffman, *A Brief Account of the Island of*

Antigua (London, 1788); Lewis (ed.), op. cit., I, pp. 252–7 (for the *Perdrix*, cf· p. 262). An early woodcut of the shooting of Peterson, reproduced in *British History Illustrated*, I, p. 9, is in the possession of the Radio Times Hulton Picture Library. The Library informs me that it is an unidentified cutting from a contemporary magazine.

30 Hannay, op. cit., p. 147.
31 *The Annual Register* (1798), p. 11.
32 Addn. MS. 59493, 160.
33 *The Naval Chronicle*, XXII, p. 303; Charles Meryon, *Memoirs of the Lady Hester Stanhope* (London, 1845), I, p. 323.
34 Addn. MS. 59493, 18, 25–6.
35 G. C. Boase, *Collectanea Cornubiensia* (Truro, 1890), p. 739. Tremlett appears to have been no very pacific character himself, as on 13 October 1797 he had been stripped of his rank 'for riotous and contemptuous conduct, and disobedience of Orders' (ADM. 12.27c). A year or so later Captain Mitford instituted legal proceedings (for libel?) against Lord Camelford, but the affair was settled out of court (Addn. MS. 59493, 116).
36 Addn. MS. 59493, 17–21, 47–50, 77–83, 87; J. S. Udal, 'A West Indian Military Buriel Ground', *Notes and Queries* (10th Series, London, 1906), V, pp. 104–5.
37 Addn. MS. 59493, 21. For an account of Colquhoun, the prize-master, *see* Lewis (ed.), op. cit., I, p. 260.
38 The captain of the *Terror*, Joseph Westbeech, was transferred to the *Favorite* (ADM. 51/1204). For the *Terror* herself, see Lewis (ed.), op. cit., I, p. 236. Westbeech and Camelford had applied for this exchange (ADM. 1/321, 67). Camelford had quarrelled with his bosun on the *Favorite*, John Davies, and expelled him from the ship. The Admiralty disapproved of this action, performed without a court-martial (ibid., 109; ADM. 1/1625, 17).

On 28 July 1798 Camelford, newly arrived in London, wrote to the Secretary of the Admiralty requesting a new command, 'His Majestys Bomb Vessel Teror late under my command being no longer in commission ... ' (ADM. 1/1624).

Chapter IV : A Secret Expedition

1 Twelve days after his capture, Lady Camelford sent Smith £105 (Messrs Drummond's Accounts Ledger, 1796; cf. Addn. MS. 59492, 56–8).
2 See Smith's letter of 11 October 1796 to Lady Camelford (Addn. MS. 59490).
3 Sir John Barrow, *The Life and Correspondence of Admiral Sir William Sidney Smith* G.C.B., I, pp. 182–225.

4 Cotes MSS.; Addn. MS. 59493, 29.
5 Michael Lewis (ed.), *A Narrative of My Personal Adventures, by Sir William Henry Dillon*, K.C.H., I, pp. 323–4.
6 Addn. MS. 59493, 31–4.
7 Ibid., 35–9.
8 Sir George Leveson Gower (ed.), *Hary-O: The Letters of Lady Harriet Cavendish* (London, 1940), pp. 297–8.
9 Rear-Admiral H. W. Richmond (ed.), *Private Papers of George, second Earl Spencer* (London, 1924), IV, pp. 61–3. Smith must have arranged matters with Camelford during the first three weeks of October, after his appointment to the *Tigre* and before his departure for the Mediterranean (compare Barrow, op. cit., I, pp. 234–5).
10 Camelford appears to have settled in at Camelford House on his return; at any rate he was there on 13 July 1798 (Cotes MSS.).
11 George Godwin, *Vancouver: A Life 1757–1798*, pp. 134–7, 262–7.
12 For Warren's victory over Bompard, cf. H. F. B. Wheatley and A. M. Broadley, *Napoleon and the Invasion of England: The Story of the Great Terror* (London, 1908), I, pp. 152–4; and for the exchange of cartels, William James, *The Naval History of Great Britain*, II, p. 147.
13 The prime source for Lord Camelford's abortive enterprise is the bundle of Home Office depositions held at the Public Record Office (HO 42/46). Further material was derived from the following sources: the *London Chronicle*, 12–15, 15–17, 17–19 January 1799; *The Times*, 14, 16, 17 January 1799; the *True Briton*, 14, 15, 16, 17 January 1799; Addn. MS. 59493, 53–72, 75, 91, 102–5; A. Aspinall (ed.), *The Later Correspondence of George III*, III, pp. 180, 183–4; the Countess of Minto (ed.), *Life and Letters of Sir Gilbert Elliott First Earl Minto* (London, 1874), pp. 45–7; Lady Granville (ed.), *Lord Granville Leveson Gower … Private Correspondence*, I, pp. 236–7; John Marshall, *Royal Naval Biography* (London, 1824), II (pt. 1), pp. 202–4. The timetable of the Dover mail is drawn from *Cary's New Itinerary* (London, 1806), pp. 1–5; the description of Dartford from David Hughson, *London … the British Metropolis and its Neighbourhood* (London, 1805–9), V, pp. 151–60; of Dover from anon., *A Guide to all the Watering and Sea-Bathing Places* (London, 1806), pp. 210–15, and anon., *Journal of a Party of Pleasure to Paris in the Month of August, 1802* (London, 1814), pp. 1–5; and an inimitable account of the pleasures and perils of coaching from James Beresford, *The Miseries of Human Life* (London, 1806), pp. 126–40. For Turnbull the Mint robber, see *The New Annual Register … For the Year 1799* (London, 1800), p. 13 ('Principal Occurrences'). Lord Wycombe was another of those who considered Camelford a madman: William Hazlitt (ed.), *Memoirs of the late Thomas Holcroft* (London, 1852), p. 247.

14 Addn. MS. 59493, 69–71; the *London Chronicle*, 15–17 January 1799; *Royal Naval Biography*, II (pt. I), p. 204. Camelford's letter to the Admiralty (24 January 1799) revealingly alludes to 'the late imprudent measure I took of embarking for France, through a too ardent Zeal for the service of my Country' (ADM. 1/1626, 2): he had forgotten, presumably, his earlier plea that he had been travelling as a simple tourist!

15 Messrs Drummond's ledger; for the National Lottery, cf. John Ashton, *The Dawn of the XIXth Century in England* (London, 1906), pp. 290–2.

16 R. C. Wellesley (ed.), *The Wellesley Papers* (London, 1914), I, pp. 89–90; Addn. MS. 59493, 87. Yonge's appointment dated from 3 April 1799, *The New Annual Register*, 1799, p. 179 ('Principal Occurrences'). A year later Camelford offered to use his influence with Yonge to obtain a posting for his friend Robert Barrie on the Cape station (Barrie MSS.).

17 Ibid.

18 For the box-lobby scene, cf. Pierce Egan, *Life in London; or the Day and Night Scenes of Jerry Hawthorn, Esq. and ... Corinthian Tom* (London, 1821), pp. 172–8; and Rowlandson's 'Box Lobby Loungers': John Hayes, *Rowlandson: Watercolours and Drawings* (London, 1972), p. 93.

19 The *London Chronicle*, 16–18 May 1799: *The Times*, 15 May 1799; the *Sporting Magazine* (London, 1799); XIV, pp. 36–7, 88–92.

20 Camelford's will was drawn up on 24 May 1799 (PROB. 2. 1412, 262–3).

21 For a contemporary description of Cuxhaven, cf. *The Naval Chronicle*, XXII, pp. 297–8.

22 The demand for girls is recorded in Edith J. Morley (ed.), *Crabb Robinson in Germany 1800–1805* (Oxford, 1929), p. 63.

23 For Camelford's exploits on the continent, see Addn. MS. 59491, 109–33; for his journey back, see *The Times*, 23 October 1799; ADM. 1/522, 473.

Chapter V: The Lion Tamed: Lord Camelford in Love

1 Henry B. Wheatley, *London Past and Present* (London, 1891), I, p. 90.

2 Barrie MSS.

3 Addn. MS. 59487, 218.

4 Addn. MS. 59493, 85.

5 The Duchess of Cleveland, *The Life and Letters of Lady Hester Stanhope* (London, 1897), pp. 1–4.

6 Earl Stanhope, *Life of the Right Honourable William Pitt* (London, 1861–2), III, pp. 210–18; Ghita Stanhope and G. P. Gooch, *The Life of Charles Third Earl Stanhope* (London, 1914), pp. 187–8; Addn. MS. 59493, 204–5.

7 Lloyd C. Sanders (ed.), *Lord Melbourne's Papers* (London, 1889), pp. 21, 23, 25.

8 Lord John Russell (ed.), *Memoirs, Journal, and Correspondence of Thomas Moore* (London, 1854), VI, p. 345.

9 The *Sporting Magazine* (1800), XV, pp. 296–7; Addn. MS. 58898, 26, 33, 35; Addn. MS. 59493, 73–4, 109–10, 116.

10 Charles Meryon, *Memoirs of the Lady Hester Stanhope*, I, p. 282; II, pp. 16–21. Unfortunately no portrait was painted of her in the bloom of her youth (ibid., p. 17; III, p. 344).

11 Ibid., II, p. 23; the Duchess of Cleveland, **op. cit.**, p. 230.

12 Ibid., pp. 1–5; Meryon, op. cit., II, p. 24.

13 Ibid., I, pp. 321–5. There is no other evidence of Lord Chatham's designs on Boconnoc, but he was certainly impecunious (cf. Sir Tresham Lever, *The House of Pitt: A Family Chronicle*, pp. 359–60).

14 Meryon, op. cit., I, p. 23.

15 Ibid., p. 38.

16 PRO. 30.8/142, 440 – a reference kindly supplied to me by Mr John Ehrman. Lord Camelford declared his intention of staying at the Black Bull for some weeks. The inns of Highgate were celebrated for some quaint and convivial local customs (David Hughson, *London ... the British Metropolis and its Neighbourhood*, VI, p. 386).

17 PRO. 30/70/6, 381.

18 Meryon, op. cit., I, pp. X, 183–4.

19 *The Reports of the Society for Bettering the Condition and Increasing the Comforts of the Poor* (London, 1802), III, p. 34. Another estimate supplies a figure of 2,712 deaths from various types of fever in the year 1800 (p. 213).

20 Ibid., pp. 283, 284.

21 Ibid., p. 291.

22 Charles Marsh, *The Clubs of London* (London, 1832), I, pp. 41–3.

23 Addn. MS. 59494, 52.

24 Meryon, op. cit., I, pp. 322–3.

25 Addn. MS. 59493, 111–15.

26 The Duchess of Cleveland, op. cit., p. 21.

27 Ibid., p. 84; Meryon, op. cit., II, pp. 287–91.

28 The Duchess of Cleveland, op. cit., p. 127.

Chapter VI: *Politics and Prize-fighters*

1 The *Morning Post*, 28 March 1804.

2 'Bernard Blackmantle', *Fitzalleyne of Berkeley: A Romance of the Present Times* (London, 1825), I, p. 62.

3 J. G. Millingen, *The History of Duelling* (London, 1841), II, p. 171.

4 Pryse Lockhart Gordon, *Personal Memoirs or Reminiscences of Men and Manners* ... (London, 1830), I, pp. 307–8.

5 The *Sporting Magazine* (1802), XIX, pp. 23–4, 217–19; John Ashton, *The Dawn of the XIXth Century in England*, pp. 251–5.

6 G. H. Wilson, *The Eccentric Mirror*, IV, pp. 20–1.

7 James Greig (ed.), *The Farington Diary* (London, 1923), II, p. 202.

8 Camelford's hat and coat are depicted in Gillray's caricature of 'The Union Club'. The monocle and belcher cravat appear in the engraving issued on 31 January 1805 by R. S. Kirby, 11 London House Yard. For Jean de Bry coats, cf. Ashton, op. cit., pp. 250–1; and for the cant expressions, *The Monthly Magazine; or, British Register* (London, 1798), VI (II), p. 173.

9 Greig (ed.), op. cit., II, p. 201.

10 Sir Tresham Lever, *The House of Pitt: a Family Chronicle*, pp. 305–6; Charles Meryon, *Memoirs of the Lady Hester Stanhope*, II, p. 21; the Duchess of Cleveland, *The Life and Letters of Lady Hester Stanhope*, p. 10.

11 Draper Hill, *Mr. Gillray the Caricaturist* (London, 1965), plate 88; Mary D. George, *Catalogue of Political and Personal Satires ... in the British Museum* (1947), VIII, pp. 4–6, 11–12.

12 Edward Porritt, *The Unreformed House of Commons* (Cambridge, 1903), I, pp. 35, 97.

13 Lever, op. cit., pp. 4, 217, 223.

14 Ibid., p. 254; *The New and Complete Newgate Calendar* (London, n.d.; ?1795), VI, pp. 333–48.

15 Compare Gillray's cartoons of 18 April and 1 October 1798 (Hill, op. cit., pp. 70, 101; plates 76, 77).

16 Addn. MS. 59493, 124.

17 Meryon, op. cit., I, p. 374; II, p. 23; Ghita Stanhope and G. P. Gooch, *The Life of Charles Third Earl Stanhope*, p. 135.

18 This account of Camelford's abortive attempt to place Tooke in Parliament is based on Alexander Stephens, *Memoirs of John Horne Tooke* (London, 1813), II, pp. 236–9; the Countess of Minto (ed.), *Life and Letters of Sir Gilbert Elliott First Earl of Minto*, p. 201; Sir Herbert Maxwell (ed.), *The Creevey Papers* (London, 1903), I, p. 60; Thomas Sadler (ed.), *Diary, Reminiscences, and Correspondence of Henry Crabb Robinson* (London, 1869), I, p. 82; Francis Bickley (ed.), *The Diaries of Sylvester Douglas (Lord Glenbervie)* (London, 1928), I, p. 170; W. P. Byrne, *Gossip of the Century*, I, p. 95; Alicia Bayne (ed.), *Autobiographic Recollections of George Pryme* (Cambridge, 1870), p. 237; Mary D. George, op. cit., pp. 16–17; Joshua Wilson, *A Biographical Index to the Present House of Commons* (London, 1807), pp. IX, 483; Porritt, op. cit., I, pp. 126–7.

19 Wilson, op. cit., pp. 54, 400, 485; Addn. MS. 59493, 111, 115, 120, 147,

178–80; Addn. MS. 59494, 32–8, 49, 57. Lord Camelford's influence had obtained the grant of a new charter for Bodmin on 27 August 1798: Sir John Maclean, *The Parochial and Family History of the Deanery of Trigg Minor* (Bodmin, 1873), I, p. 218; cf. also Addn. MS. 41885, 68; Cornwall County Record Office, Fortescue MSS., D.D.F. acc., 516, 38; *The Manuscripts of J. B. Fortescue, Esq., Preserved at Dropmore* (1899), III, pp. 76–7. For Camelford's continuing friendship with Horne Tooke, see Stephens, op. cit., II, pp. 299–300.

20 He was presumably the 'Lord C.' who lost £1,000 at a fight on 1 July 1800 (the *Sporting Magazine*, 1800, XVI, p. 185). One hopes, on the other hand, that he was not the 'Nobleman, well known on the town as a fighter and bruiser ... black-balled at the Jockey-Club at Newmarket', (ibid., p. 91). A more congenial fraternity would have been the eccentric Crudiverous Club (ibid., 1802, XIX, pp. 115–16). There is an interesting account of Camelford's sporting activities in 1800 in James Brady, *Strange Encounters: Tales of Famous Fights and Famous Fighters* (London, n.d. ?1946), pp. 30–2, though unfortunately neither the author nor I can trace the original source of his story.

21 The *Sporting Magazine* (1801), XVIII, p. 172; Pierce Egan, *Boxiana; or Sketches of Ancient and Modern Pugilism* (London, 1823), I, pp. 132–3; Fred Henning, *Fights for the Championship: The Men and their Times* (London, 1903), I, pp. 195, 198, 206, 209. Camelford had first displayed interest in promoting Belcher in August 1799 (pp. 184–6).

22 The *Sporting Magazine* (1802), XIX, p. 44.

23 Ibid., pp. 35–6. For Margate at that time, cf. anon., *A Guide to all the Watering and Sea-Bathing Places*, pp. 286–311. The famous Mrs Jordan was a regular performer at the Theatre Royal at this time (Brian Fothergill, *Mrs Jordan: Portrait of an Actress*, London, 1965, pp. 192–3), and possibly the gallant Jackson was one of her company. The Hon. Mr T–N is clearly that Mr Tufton whose presence at Margate on 6 October was recorded by the *Morning Post*, 13 October 1801. For Tufton's cricketing prowess, cf. J. Pycroft, *The Cricket Field: or, The History and the Science of the game of Cricket* (London, 1854), pp. 65, 88. Margate was frequently the scene of holiday jokes and absurdities, cf. the *Sporting Magazine* (1802), XX, pp. 315–16.

24 Ibid., XIX, pp. 47–8, 49–50; *The Times* 12 October 1801; H. F. B. Wheatley and A. M. Broadley, *Napoleon and the Invasion of England*, I, pp. 256–64. There are some fine prints of the illuminations by Edward Orme of Bond Street in the British Museum Crace Collection, folio XXIX, 100, 101, 102.

25 *Report on the Manuscripts of J. B. Fortescue, Esq., Preserved at Dropmore* (1910), VII, p. 53.

26 Lord Grenville had sold his town house in Cleveland Row in the spring of 1801 (ibid., p. 8; the *Morning Post*, 13 March 1801; 31 March 1801).

27 James Smith and Horace Smith, *Rejected Addresses: or, The New Theatrum Poetarum* (London, 1851), p. 57.

28 Francis Grose, *A Classical Dictionary of the Vulgar Tongue* (London, 1785), s.v. 'file'.

29 For precise statistics, *see* P. Colquhoun, *A Treatise on the Police of the Metropolis* (London, 1797), pp. 208–11.

30 The foregoing account of Lord Camelford's famous battle with the mob is based on the following sources: *London und Paris* (Halle, 1804), XIII, pp. 13–15; G. H. Wilson (ed.), op. cit., IV, pp. 18–19; the *Porcupine*, 8 October 1801, 12 October 1801; *The Times*, 8 October 1801, 9 October 1801, 12 October 1801, 17 October 1801, 24 October 1801; the *Morning Post*, 9 October 1801; Henning, op cit., I, p. 213. The Edwardian penny journal *Famous Fights* (1902), V, p. 45, carried an imaginative picture of the Bond Street battle (copy kindly loaned to me by Mr James Brady).

31 Compare the example illustrated in John Hayes, *Rowlandson: Watercolours and Drawings*, p. 101.

32 Enfield Wash is illustrated in an engraving opposite p. 407 of David Hughson's *London … the British Metropolis and its Neighourhood*, vol. VI. The inn is the Bell.

33 The *Sporting Magazine* (1802), XIX, pp. 43–5; the *Morning Post*, 13 October 1801; Fred Henning, op. cit., I, p. 215.

Chapter VII: Dangers and Disguises

1 PRO. 30/70/6, 383. It is possible, but less likely, that the reference is to Lord Chatham.

2 Camelford accounts, Messrs Hoare, 37 Fleet Street. Camelford had significantly added a codicil to his will on 16 October. He tore off part of a sheet, which had perhaps contained some indication of his plans (PROB. 2. 1412, 263).

3 Compare A. M. Broadley (ed.), *The Journal of a British Chaplain in Paris during the Peace Negotiations of 1801–2* (London, 1913), p. 224; Lady Jackson (ed.), *The Diaries and Letters of Sir George Jackson* (London, 1872), I, p. 60.

4 The Duchess of Cleveland, *The Life and Letters of Lady Hester Stanhope*, p. 26.

5 Compare the interesting first-hand account published in *The Anti-Jacobin Review and Magazine* (London, 1803), XIV, pp. 498–502.

6 David Darrah, *Conspiracy in Paris* (New York, 1953), pp. 85–144.

7 Compare R. H. Cholmondeley, *The Heber Letters 1783–1832*, p. 138; anon., *Journal of a Party of Pleasure to Paris*, pp. 16–17; L. Hebert and G. Dupont,

An Actual Survey and Itinerary of the Road from Calais to Paris (London, 1814), p. 21.

8 Vere Foster (ed.), *The Two Duchesses* (London, 1898), p. 176.

9 For the route, compare *État Général par Ordre Alphabétique des Routes de Poste de l'Empire Français* (Paris, 1813), pp. 129-31.

10 Vere Foster (ed.), op. cit., pp. 170-8; *Journal of a Party of Pleasure to Paris*, pp. 69-70.

11 I have drawn what I feel is not an unwarranted conclusion. The account (*see* note 12) of Lord Camelford's pistol was published in the early spring of 1803. It is there stated that 'it has been used by his Lordship without any particular care in various parts of the world'. The first question is, are we to take this as implying that he took it beyond the confines of Europe? He is perhaps unlikely to have taken it on Vancouver's voyage, when in any case his pistols are said to have been thrown overboard on the captain's orders. It is certainly possible that he obtained it before going to the Leeward Islands in 1797. But probably the most likely suggestion is that he bought it on either of his visits to the Continent in 1799 and 1800, as it was 'of German make'. Be all this as it may, since we know he took it abroad on some occasion or occasions before April 1803, it seems scarcely conceivable that it should not have accompanied him on his most recent and dangerous journey in the winter of 1801-2. It must surely have been designed for just such an expedition. It may be recalled that Camelford took with him on his attempt to assassinate Barras a dagger *especially designed for the purpose.*

12 See Appendix on p. 195 for a full account of Lord Camelford's pistol.

13 The preceding account of Lord Camelford's activities on the Continent in 1801 a is based on Archives Nationales, Paris, F⁷ 6307, dossier BP 6386 and 6402; F⁷ 6334, dossier BP 7051; F⁷ 6339, dossier BP 7155; Addn. MS. 59493, 150-77.

14 Darrah, op. cit., pp. 75, 190. He had paid other secret trips to England in open sailing-boats in 1796-7 (p. 67).

15 Addn. MS. 59493, 68.

16 Fred Henning, *Fights for the Championship: the Men and their Times*, I, p. 235.

Chapter VIII: The Peer and the Pugilist

1 James Greig (ed.), *The Farington Diary*, II, p. 202; Edward and James Weatherby (eds), *The Racing Calendar ... 1802* (London, 1803), pp. 33, 314; the *Sporting Magazine* (1802), XX, appendix p. 13.

2 Ibid., pp. 168-9; cf. Sir Jonah Barrington, *Personal Sketches of his own Times*, I, pp. 436-7. The cost of such an evening was about a guinea (John Ashton, *The Dawn of the XIXth Century in England*, p. 360). For a full account of

Ranelagh, cf. William Gaunt, *Chelsea* (London, 1954), pp. 76–80, plate 19.
3 The *Sporting Magazine* (1802), XIX, pp. 61–2; ibid. (1803), XXII, p. 89.
4 Ibid., XIX, pp. 271–2.
5 Ibid., XX, pp. 126–8, 221–2.
6 Pierce Egan, *Boxiana; or Sketches of Ancient and Modern Pugilism*, I, pp. 318–20.
7 He was born on 15 April 1781, at his father's house in St James's Church-yard, Bristol (ibid., p. 140). The likeness to Napoleon can be seen in the engraving published at the beginning of that volume. A fine half-length painting, possibly the original of this engraving, was with Messrs Sotheby in 1973 (I am indebted to the firm for supplying me with a photograph). Another full-length by Ben Marshall was sold at Christie's to an American buyer: cf. the *Connoisseur* (London, 1959), CXLIV, p. 203. I owe these references to the kindness of Mr Robin Gibson of the National Portrait Gallery.
8 Thomas Belcher, *The Art of Boxing, or Science of Manual Defence* (London, 1819). p. 31; cf. Egan, op. cit., I, pp. 120–1; anon., *The Fancy* (London, 1821), I, p. 131.
9 The *Sporting Magazine*, XX, pp. 237–40; *The Fancy*, pp. 156–7; Egan, op. cit., I, pp. 135–8. A magnificent contemporary (1791) painting of Hyde Park, reproduced in Ivor Brown, *London: an Illustrated History* (London, 1965), plate 93, clearly shows the open space of the contest (at the top left). Camelford House can also be glimpsed at the top of Park Lane.
10 Egan, op. cit., I, p. 144; *The Fancy*, I, p. 125 and engraving opposite (cf. p. 140); the *Sporting Magazine* (1804), XXIII, p. 43; Trusty may also be the dog shown in the Ben Marshall portrait noted above (note 7). For Colonel Mellish, see Pierce Egan, *Sporting Anecdotes* (London, 1825), pp. 375–9.
11 *London und Paris*, XIII, pp. 15–16.

Chapter IX: *A Controversial Character*

1 'What has become of Lord Camelford's Body?' *Belgravia* (London, 1876), XXIX, p. 318.
2 Addn. MS. 59493, 52.
3 T. H. S. Escott in *Anthony Trollope: His Work, Associates and Literary Originals* (London, 1913), p. 259, suggested an identification with the 8th Duke of Devonshire. The Duke's character, however, was in no way similar to that of Chiltern.
4 John A. Atkinson, *Duelling Pistols* (London, 1964), p. 109.
5 Compare Sir Bernard Burke, *The Romance of the Aristocracy* (London, 1855), II, pp. 350–69 – a book much to Trollope's taste. A similar account by

Grantley F. Berkeley, *Anecdotes of the Upper Ten Thousand* (London, 1867), I, pp. 351, 378–86, appeared just as Trollope was completing *Phineas Finn*.

6 J. H. Jesse, *The Life of George Brummell, Esq.* (London, 1844), I, pp. 141–4; the Duchess of Cleveland, *The Life and Letters of Lady Hester Stanhope*, p. 58; Major-General Sir J. F. Maurice (ed.), *The Diary of Sir John Moore* (London, 1904), II, pp. 110–11.

7 Rev. William Neil (ed.), *The Cleghorn Papers: A Footnote to History*, p. 262.

8 HO 42/46 (testimony of Monsieur Bosset).

9 Charles Meryon, *Memoirs of the Lady Hester Lucy Stanhope*, II, p. 227; III, pp. 308–9; Frank Hamel, *Lady Hester Lucy Stanhope* (London, 1913), p. 115.

10 In 1798 he wrote concerning Pitt's duel with Tierney: J. Holland Rose, *William Pitt and the Great War* (London, 1911), p. 336. Camelford was not, however, present at the duel, as was claimed by Thomas Wright and R. H. Evans, *Historical and Descriptive Account of the Caricatures of James Gillray*, p. 201.

11 Archives Nationales, F⁷ 6339, BP 7155; James Greig (ed.), *The Farington Diary*, II, p. 202.

12 The Duchess of Cleveland, op. cit., p. 22.

Chapter X: *The Prisoner in the Temple*

1 H. F. B. Wheatley and A. M. Broadley, *Napoleon and the Invasion of England*, I, pp. 271–7.

2 Addn. MS. 59493, 188–91.

3 Compare anon., *Journal of a Party of Pleasure to Paris ... in 1802*, pp. 11, 13, 109; Joshua Done, 'The Prisoner of War', *The New Monthly Magazine and Humorist* (London, 1841), LXI (I), p. 69; M. T. S. Raimbach (ed.), *Memoirs and Recollections of the late Abraham Raimbach, Esq.* (London, 1843), p. 105.

4 For the Temple Prison cf. *Journal of a Party of Pleasure to Paris ... in 1802*, pp. 50–1; J. P. T. Bury and J. C. Barry (eds, *An Englishman in Paris: 1803; the Journal of Bertie Greatheed* (London, 1953), pp. 5, 132–4; Maurice Alhoy and Louis Lurine, *Les Prisons de Paris* (Paris, 1846), pp. 370–402.

5 Compare P. Pinkerton and J. H. Ashworth (eds), *The Reign of Terror* (London, 1898), II, pp. 179–227.

6 Only the passport of the French *chargé d'affaires* was essential, and free. The English one, from the Secretary of State's office, cost £2 5s. 0d., and provided extra respect for the traveller in France (Raimbach, op. cit., p. 38).

7 PROB. 2.1412, 263–4. In his will Lord Camelford stated that he paid de la Brunerie a salary of £240 per annum, and Messrs Drummond's accounts record various payments made between 8 March 1800 and 16 March 1801.

8 Archives Nationales, F⁷ 6307, dossier BP 6386; Addn. MS. 59493, 192–4; Addn. MS. 58873, 10–11; *The Manuscripts of J. B. Fortescue ... at Dropmore* (1910), VII, pp. 154–5; J. G. Alger, *Napoleon's British Visitors and Captives 1801–1815* (London, 1904), p. 55; Bury and Barry (eds), op. cit., p. 123. Fouché was temporarily in disgrace at this time.

9 Compare 1st Lord Camelford's *Narrative and Proofs*, pp. 32–3; the Earl of Rosebery (ed.), *The Windham Papers* (London, 1913), II, p. 198. She had been in Lady Camelford's mother's service.

10 Sir Tresham Lever, *The House of Pitt: A Family Chronicle*, pp. 307–9; Addn. MS. 59491, 24–5; 59493, 1–21. The funeral expenses amounted to £109 15s 1d. (Cornwall County Record Office, Fortescue MSS., D.D.F., 92). Sir Sidney Smith was unable to be present, as he was at sea in the Channel. He was however devoted to his aunt, as was she to him. On 12 December 1801 she gave him £200 (Lever, op. cit., p. 307; Messrs Drummond's accounts). This was Lord Camelford's only recorded visit to Boconnoc since he sailed on the *Discovery* in 1791. On 2 September 1804 Lord Grenville wrote to his brother Thomas from Boconnoc: 'We have found this House & place in a much better state than I could have imagined' (Addn. MS. 41852, 201), which perhaps implied that Camelford had rarely or never been resident there. On the occasion of Lady Camelford's interment, the family solicitor wrote 'to Mr Bennett the Steward to have the Vault and also the House properly prepared' (Addn. MS. 59494, 17), suggesting a similar inference.

11 Camelford House is depicted in two water-colours in the British Museum Crace Collection, folio XXIX, 114, 115. For other details, cf. Addn. MS. 59493, 5, 24. The house was pulled down in 1913, to make way for 'the ubiquitous cinematograph palace' ('A Link with Old Soho', *Soho Monthly Paper*, London, 1913, p. 253). A fine grangerised copy of Reade's *Belgravia* article of 1876, compiled by W. Courthope Forman and now in the possession of my friend Mr John Yeowell, the antiquary, contains a photograph of one of the carved statuary marble mantelpieces designed by Robert Adam in 1780. The source is unidentified, but may be *Country Life* or the *Connoisseur*. A plan of the site of Camelford House, dated 1791, is in the British Museum Crace Collection (X, 63).

12 Barrie MSS.

13 Michael Lewis (ed.), *A Narrative of My Personal Adventures by Sir William Henry Dillon*, K.C.H., I, pp. 439–43.

14 The interior of which is illustrated in John Ashton, *The Dawn of the XIXth Century in England*, pp. 436–7.

15 G. H. Wilson, *The Eccentric Mirror*, IV, pp. 17–18; anon., *The Life, Adventures and Eccentricities of the Late Lord Camelford*, pp. 9–10; 'Lord Camelford, ein

merkwürdiger Englischer Sonderling', *London und Paris*, XIII, pp. 18-19;
John Timbs, *Romance of London* (London, 1865), I, p. 237. For inimitable
descriptions and illustrations of parallel incidents, cf. Pierce Egan, *Life in
London; or the Day and Night Scenes of Jerry Hawthorn, Esq. and . . . Corinthian
Tom*, pp. 184-5, 232-3. A roundhouse is depicted by Rowlandson in 'The
Lock Up' (1790): John Hayes, *Rowlandson: Watercolours and Drawings*, p.
140; and Cavendish Square in Hugh Phillips, *Mid-Georgian London* (London,
1964), p. 248. I am extremely grateful to my friend Tom L. Brock, who
went to great trouble in supplying me with an exact calendar of Captain
Barrie's movements between 1799 and 1804. This makes it clear that the
Cavendish Square episode must have taken place in 1803 or early 1804;
certainly not before.

16 Brian Connell (ed.), *Portrait of a Whig Peer* (London, 1957), p. 462; for the
custom of Sunday strolling in Kensington Gardens, cf. anon., *The Picture of
London for 1802* (London, 1802), pp. 86-8.

17 So it was reported to the authorities in France (Archives Nationales, F⁷ 6307,
dossier BP 6386). For the duel, cf. *The New Annual Register ... For the Year
1803* (London, 1804), pp. 45-6; James Greig (ed.), *The Farington Diary*, II,
pp. 199-200; the *Sporting Magazine* (1803), XXI, pp. 22-8, 45-53, 65-6. The
surgeon present was Mr Heaviside, the same who attended Lady Camelford.

18 Addn. MS. 59491, 33.

19 *London und Paris*, XIII, pp. 16-18. A tailor's fitting is described and illustrated
in Egan, op. cit., pp. 145-8.

20 *The Times*, 23 July 1803; James Smith and Horace Smith, *Rejected Addresses:
or, The New Theatrum Poetarum*, p. 57; Barrie MSS. For the Royal Circus,
cf. *The Picture of London for 1802*, p. 225. It may have been Camelford who
was involved in the gambling contretemps at Brighton a year earlier,
described in the *Sporting Magazine* (1803), XXI, p. 116.

21 In December 1803 Camelford had to find bail after yet another fracas (ibid.,
1803, XXIII, p. 160).

22 His sister Anne had married Lord Clare in 1786 (G. E. Cockayne, *The
Complete Peerage*, III, p. 255).

23 On 22 May, six days after the outbreak of war, Napoleon had ordered *all*
British subjects 'from the ages of eighteen to sixty ... who are at present in
France' to be made prisoners of war, (H. F. B. Wheatley and A. M. Broadley,
Napoleon and the Invasion of England: The Story of the Great Terror, I, pp.
277-8).

24 Another of Whaley's horses was named Bonaparte; cf. Edward and James
Weatherby (eds), *The Racing Calendar ... 1802*, pp. 33, 337. Vivaldi's
pedigree is supplied by W. Pick, *Racing Calendar ... for ... 1801* (York, n.d.),
XVI, p. 178.

25 Archives Nationales, F⁷ 6307, dossier BP 6386; F⁷ 6334, BP 7051; F⁷ 6339, BP 7155; cf. Bury and Barry (eds), op. cit., pp. 160, 183; Michael Lewis, *Napoleon and his British Captives* (London, 1962), p. 144. Camelford had supplied Whaley with large sums of money in 1800 and 1801 (Messrs Drummond's accounts ledger).

26 *Memoirs of the Duke of Rovigo, (M. Savary,) Written by Himself* (London, 1828), I (pt. II), p. 10.

27 French *savants* were regular contributors to *A Journal of Natural Philosophy*. Attention was drawn to the article by the *Sporting Magazine* (1803), XXII, p. 111, and the *Monthly Magazine; or, British Register* (1803), XV, p. 365. The invention of this type of pistol is generally ascribed to Michele Lorenzoni, of Florence, working a century earlier. There was a brief revival of these magazine pistols at the end of the eighteenth century, a particularly fine example being that made for Lord Nelson by H. W. Mortimer of London, now in the Metropolitan Museum, New York. Compare C. Blair, *Pistols of the World* (London, 1968), nos. 490–4, and p. 176. I am much indebted to Mr H. L. Blackmore, Keeper of Firearms at H.M. Tower of London, for this and further information on the background of Lord Camelford's pistol.

28 In Lord Camelford's will, where reference is made to Nicholson's 'private Confidential Labours in my affairs'; also to a 'patent Machine' which perhaps was constructed by Camelford himself (PROB. 2. 1412, 264).

29 The *Monthly Magazine; or, British Register* (1804), XVII, p. 291. Messrs Drummond's accounts ledger records three payments totalling £200 paid to Accum between 7 January and 10 March. For a water-colour by Rowlandson of Accum lecturing on chemistry in 1808, *see* Hayes, op. cit., p. 195. That Lord Camelford had his own laboratory is mentioned in passing in G. H. Wilson, op. cit., IV, p. 30; the *Morning Post*, 14 March 1804.

30 Compare Mario Einaudi, *The Early Rousseau* (Ithaca, N.Y., 1967), p. 150; E. H. Wright, *The Meaning of Rousseau* (Oxford, 1929), p. 57.

31 The *Morning Post*, 21 March 1804.

32 Greig (ed.), op. cit., II, p. 202.

33 Rev. William Cockburne, *An Authentic Account of the late Unfortunate Death of Lord Camelford* (London, 1804), pp. 9–11.

34 Barrie made a small return by ordering coal from Lancashire for the Bond Street lodgings (Barrie MSS.).

35 Addn. MS. 59491, 26–32.

Chapter XI: *A Dangerous Challenge*

1 PROB. 2. 1412, 264; Addn. MS. 59004, 179–80; Addn. MS. 59493, 52. At Boconnoc a tradition has been preserved of an incident in which Camelford

supposedly burst into a room with a drawn sword when his steward was settling accounts, upsetting a rent-table and scattering the money (information kindly supplied by Lady Margaret Fortescue and Lt-Commander John Varley). This story might appear to receive confirmation from the independently attested quarrel between Camelford and Borlinder; in fact, though, it must derive from an almost identical (though good-humoured) incident involving Camelford's great-great-uncle John in 1726 (cf. Sir Tresham Lever, *The House of Pitt: A Family Chroncle*, p. 54). Lord Camelford's rent-table is still preserved by his heirs. He paid large sums of money to Borlinder at different times; between 19 August and 13 October 1801, for example, he paid him a total of £2,109 11s. 6d. (Messrs Hoare's accounts ledgers).

2 Compare the *Sporting Magazine* (1802), XIX, p. 63. Camelford's interest in the sport had not abated. On 23 January 1804 he lost a thousand guineas when his protégé Bourke was beaten by Hen Pearce on Wimbledon Common; while his black servant Mungo (the former parliamentary candidate for Old Sarum) on the same day lasted only three rounds against George Maddocks (ibid., XXIII, p. 216; James Brady, *Strange Encounters: Tales of Famous Fights and Famous Fighters*, p. 41).

3 James Greig (ed.), *The Farington Diary*, II, p. 201; 'Bernard Blackmantle', *Fitzalleyne of Berkeley*, I, pp. 132-3, 189 (where Best appears as 'Mr Optimus'). An amusing illustration of his struggle with a mistress by Robert Cruikshank appeared in 'Bernard Blackmantle' (Westmacott), *The English Spy* (London, 1826), II, p. 16.

4 Greig (ed.), op. cit., II, p. 201; the *Morning Post*, 8 and 9 March 1804.

5 For this coffee house see Bryant Lillywhite, *London Coffee Houses* (London, 1936), p. 458.

6 The *Morning Post*, 9 March 1804. On 5 January 1804 Messrs Drummond's ledger records a payment of £107 to Best. Slight variants of this account appear in Thomas Faulkner, *History and Antiquities of Kensington* (London, 1820), p. 127; H. B. Wheatley, *London Past and Present* (London, 1891), I, p. 220.

7 The evidence is not altogether satisfactory on this point. The *Morning Post* of 8 March, which gave a detailed and seemingly accurate account of the affair, describes the outcome of Barrie's mission to Best, but omits to state whether he returned with Best's explanation to Camelford. Six days after Barrie's talk with Best, a friend of Camelford (the surgeon Carlisle) claimed that 'There had been a grudge, some ill will subsisting between him and Mr. Best for a month or 6 weeks', and that Barrie exacted *then* the promise referred to in the text (Greig, ed., op. cit., II, pp. 202-3). But Carlisle seems to have thought the final quarrel stemmed from this 'ill will', which should

therefore be identified with Mrs Simmonds's provocation, and suggests that he or his informant had unwittingly exaggerated the time lapsing between quarrel and duel.

8 Compare *Memoirs of the Duke of Rovigo, (M. Savary,) Written by Himself,* I (pt. II), p. 18; Charles Meryon, *Memoirs of the Lady Hester Lucy Stanhope,* II, p. 289; Ernest Daudet, *La Police et les Chouans sous le Consulat et l'Empire* (Paris, 1895), pp. 37–8.

9 *Memoirs of the Duke of Rovigo,* I (pt. II), pp. 19–20; Archives Nationales, F⁷ 6339, dossier BP 7155.

10 Anon., *The Life, Adventures and Eccentricities of the Late Lord Camelford,* p. 15.

11 John Leyland (ed.), *Dispatches and Letters Relating to the Blockade of Brest 1803–1805* (London, 1899), I, pp. 325–30. An old friend, Thomas Manby, commanded one of the ships in Smith's squadron (ibid.).

12 *The New Annual Register ... For the Year 1804,* 'Public Papers', pp. 165–6.

13 For accounts of the conspiracy see *Memoirs of the Duke of Rovigo,* I, (pt. II). pp. 9–66; *The New Annual Register ... For the Year 1804,* 'British and Foreign History', pp. 269–84, 'Public Papers', pp. 165–8; Jacques Godechot, *The Counter-Revolution: Doctrine and Action 1789–1804* (London, 1961), pp. 366–83. Quotations from French police reports come from Archives Nationales, F⁷ 6307, dossiers BP 6386, BP 6402.

14 Michael Lewis, *Napoleon and his British Captives,* pp. 72–5, 256–7.

15 *The Morning Post,* 14 March 1804 (letter from J. G. Semple Lisle, for whose erratic career cf. *D.N.B.*).

16 Archives Nationales, F⁷ 6307, dossier BP 6386.

Chapter XII: Pistols for Two

1 Five contemporary views of Soho Square (by T. Hosmer Shepherd) are in the British Museum Crace Collection, folio XXIX, 5, 7, 8, 9, 10.

2 The evidence is difficult to reconcile. At the inquest convincing eyewitness accounts stated that the duellists were twenty-nine yards apart.

3 I have handled these fine weapons, which are still in the possession of Lord Camelford's heirs. Tatham and Egg were in partnership from about 1801 to 1815 (John A. Atkinson, *Duelling Pistols,* p. 72).

4 The foregoing account of the duel and Lord Camelford's death is based on a synthesis of the following sources: the *Morning Post,* 8 March 1804, 9 March 1804, 13 March 1804, 14 March 1804, 16 March 1804, 19 March 1804, 26 March 1804; the *True Briton,* 8 March 1804, 10 March 1804, 13 March 1804, 15 March 1804, 26 March 1804; *The New Annual Register ... For the Year 1804* (London, 1805), 'Principal Occurrences', pp. 25–9; the *Monthly Mirror* (London, 1804), XVII, pp. 212–13; the Countess of Minto (ed.), *Life and*

Letters of Sir Gilbert Elliott First Earl of Minto, III, pp. 313–14; Sir Tresham Lever, *The House of Pitt: A Family Chronicle*, pp. 319–21; anon., *The Life, Adventures and Eccentricities of the Late Lord Camelford*, pp. 10–19; Barrie MSS.; the *Gentleman's Magazine* (London, 1804), LXXIV, pp. 284–6; *London und Paris*, XIII, pp. 19–21; Rev. William Cockburne, *An Authentic Account of the Late Unfortunate Death of Lord Camelford*, pp. 3–17; (Philip Neve), *A Letter to the Rev. William Cockburne occasioned by his Pamphlet relating to Lord Camelford's Death* (London, 1804); James Greig (ed.), *The Farington Diary*, II, pp. 199–204; G. H. Wilson (ed.), *The Eccentric Mirror*, IV, pp. 21–9; Camelford's friends and tenants in the West Country learned of his death in the *Royal Cornwall Gazette* (10 March 1804) and the *Sherborne Mercury*, 12 March 1804; I am indebted for these two references to Mr H. L. Douch, Curator of the Royal Institution of Cornwall. Colourful but quite unreliable versions of events appeared in Major Ben C. Truman, *The Field of Honor* (New York, 1884), p. 186; Charles Mackay, *Memoirs of Extraordinary Popular Delusions* (London, 1841), I, pp. 302–3.

For the topography of the site of the duel, I have used the MS. Survey of Lord Holland's park and enclosures, compiled in 1770 (British Museum Crace Collection, folio XXXVI, 71); also 'A Topographical Survey of the Parish of Kensington, with Plans and Elevations of the Royal Palace and Gardens, Hide Park, and Knightsbridge' (1766) ibid., X, 3. From the accounts of witnesses at the inquest held on 12 March 1804, it seems clear that the field numbered 39 on the 1770 map is that of the contest. For a contemporary view of Holland House, cf. Crace Collection, folio XXXVI, 43. The Coach and Horses was on the north side of Kensington High Street (F. H. W. Sheppard, (ed.), *Northern Kensington, Survey of London*, XXXVII, London, 1973, p. 36).

5 Pierce Egan, *Boxiana*, I, p. 12.

6 Greig (ed.), op. cit., II, pp. 199–201; Alexander Haldane, *Memoirs of the Lives of Robert Haldane of Airthrey, and of his Brother, James Alexander Haldane* (London, 1852), pp. 333–41. Disapproval of the practice of duelling was widespread (cf. the *Sporting Magazine*, 1797, IX, p. 249; ibid., XXII, pp. 69–70) but almost entirely ineffective. Lord Camelford might also have considered with profit the strictures of Rousseau's heroine Julie (M. B. Ellis, *Julie or La Nouvelle Héloïse*, Toronto, 1949, p. 57).

7 Anne Fremantle (ed.), *The Wynne Diaries* (Oxford, 1935–40), p. 108; the Earl of Ilchester, *Chronicles of Holland House 1820–1900* (London, 1937), p. 497; Lady Granville (ed.), *Lord Granville Leveson Gower ... Private Correspondence*, I, p. 455; the Duchess of Cleveland, *The Life and Letters of Lady Hester Stanhope*, p. 47.

8 For an account and engraving of the altar, cf. Faulkner's *History and*

Antiquities of Kensington, pp. 125–6; the fine grangerised edition of this work in the British Library (press mark LR. 271.C.3) contains this marginal MS. note: [The altar] 'has been defaced or removed by the workmen employed in the adjacent Road (Addison Road) or in the new buildings lately erected there. (1827)'. Cf. also the *Gentleman's Magazine* (1821), XCI, p. 325; *Notes and Queries* (London, 1865), VII, pp. 131–2; Henry B. Wheatley, *London Past and Present,* II, p. 328; Edward Walford, *Old and New London* (London, n.d.), p. 176; Sir Walter Besant, *London North of the Thames* (London, 1911), p. 127; Earl of Ilchester, op. cit., p. 497. I am grateful to Mr Melvyn Barnes, Kensington Borough Librarian, for assisting me with information and for instituting (alas, fruitlessly) a search in Holland Park for the fragment mentioned by Lord Ilchester. It may have been built into a rockery or path.

Chapter XIII: Envoi

1 The funeral is described in the *Morning Post,* 19 March 1804; the *Gentleman's Magazine,* LXXIV, p. 286; anon., *The Life, Adventures and Eccentricities of the Late Lord Camelford,* pp. 19–20. The Burial Register of St Anne's records that a fee of 6s. 8d. was paid for holding the service before the statutory hour of 3 p.m., and 2s. 6d. for lights to illumine the North Vault (Rev. J. H. Cardwell, *Men and Women of Soho,* London, 1910, p. 119).

2 Barrie MSS. On 18 March Barrie's mother passed on this news to his stepsister, Frances (letter in the possession of Mr Tom L. Brock).

3 Lady Hester Stanhope's story (cf. p. 92) that Lord Camelford spent £50,000 in breaking an entail that would have handed Boconnoc to Lord Chatham appears to be erroneous. No act of parliament, necessary for such a course, was enacted (information kindly supplied by Mr H. Cobb, Deputy Clerk of the Records at the House of Lords), and Thomas and Anne appear to have been co-heirs of the estate from the beginning. Cf. also 'Appointment of the Estates devised by the will of the Right Honourable Thomas Lord Camelford deced' (Cornwall County Record Office, Fortescue MSS., D.D.F., acc., 516, 6; the rentals of the Cornish estates for 1798 and 1800–04 are to be found in ibid., 92, 141); *General Index to the Journals of the House of Lords* (London, 1832), p. 417.

4 PROB. 2, 1412, 264. Barrie's debts came to £9,000. Lord and Lady Grenville offered to waive the condition under which the annuity was to be paid, but Barrie firmly declined this kindness (James Greig, ed., *The Farington Diary,* II, p. 203; cf. Lord Grenville's letter to Barrie of 11 March 1804, Barrie MSS.). On 15 March Barrie's first debt of £104 11s. 10d. was paid from Lord Camelford's account at Drummond's Bank. Devereux's

dogs and guns are listed and valued (for probate) in Addn. MS. 59494, 31.

5 PROB. 2. 1412, 264. The words unconsciously echo the confession of Rousseau's Saint-Preux: 'J'avois toujours désiré de revoir la retraite isolée qui me servit d'asile au milieu des glaces, et où mon coeur se plaisoit à converser en lui-même avec ce qu'il eut de plus cher au monde.' (*La Nouvelle Héloïse, Oeuvres de J. J. Rousseau* (Paris, 1823), VII, p. 176.

6 Ibid., 44-7, 62. As Trebeck is said to have adopted the child, she may well have taken his surname. An objection that she would have had to have been aged two at her baptism may further indicate that the latter event was registered in 1805 or 1806.

7 Addn. MS. 59494, 50-121. Evidence of Lord Grenville's desire to suppress unpleasant memories may perhaps be found in the disappearance of the logs of so many ships in which Camelford served. The *Sporting Magazine* (1804), XXIV, p. 62, announced abruptly that it was abandoning an advertised monthly biography of the late Lord Camelford.

8 St Anne's *Soho Monthly Paper* (1913), p. 253.

9 *Belgravia*, XXIX, p. 328. This story was uncritically repeated by Sir John Laughton in his *D.N.B.* notice.

10 I am extremely grateful to Mr Bryan C. Burrough, who supplied me with considerable help in identifying the place of Lord Camelford's sepulture.

Index

Abbott, Peter, frightening encounter with Camelford, 88–9, 98

Abershaw, Jerry, highwayman (1773?–95), 108

Accum, Friedrich, scientist (1769–1838), 168, 224

Adams, Edmund, Dover boatman, 75

Adamson, sailor, 51

Addington, Henry (1757–1844), 107, 111

Alaska, 23, 25

Alexandria, 30, 31, 147

America, 17, 21, 23, 40, 103, 124, 186

Anderson, Captain Alexander, 48, 49, 50, 51

Andreossi, General Antoine (1761–1828), 150, 155

Antigua, 51, 52–65, 99; Plate 17;

Antraigues, Emmanuel, Comte d' (1775?–1812), royalist conspirator, 178

Australia, 14, 20, 25, 154

Babet, H.M.S., 53

Baker, Lieutenant Joseph, 19

Baker Street, Camelford resides in, 84, 88, 89

Barbados, 46–52, 58, 63, 67, 210, 211

Barras, Paul (1755–1829), 74, 77, 78, 87, 122, 219

Barrie, Captain Robert, on *Discovery*, 18, 23, 25; 35, 36, 39, 71, 79, 142; visits Hester Stanhope, 147; wild life with

Camelford in London, 159–61; intermediary after Circus fracas, 165; 170; arrests Borlinder, 171; 172; intermediary in Camelford's quarrel with Best, 173; 180; searches for Camelford, 182; at Camelford's deathbed, 185–6; 187; at funeral, and bequest from Camelford, 191; 214, 223, 224, 225, 228; Plate 14

Belcher, James ('Jem'), pugilist (1781–1811), 102; fights Bourke at Wimbledon, 108–10; 111, 116; prevented from attending fight at Enfield Wash, 117–18; final fights with Bourke, 134–40; becomes Champion, 140; 220 ;Plate 23

Belcher, Tom, pugilist, 136–7

Bennet and Tolson, tea-dealers, 113, 122

Bennett, steward at Boconnoc, 222

Bessborough, Lady (Frances) (1761–1821), 188

Best, Captain Thomas, 144–5; challenges Camelford to a duel, 171–4; 178; 179; duel with Camelford, 180–4; 185; 188; 225; Plate 28

Bienne, Lac de, 11–13, 127, 158, 191

Bitton, Elias, pugilist, 108

Bligh, Captain William (1754–1817), 22

Boconnoc House, 2, 4, 6, 7–10, 12, 13, 17, 22, 25, 31, 79, 96, 98, 119, 144, 158, 170, 204, 206, 222, 224, 228; Plate 4

Bonaparte, Napoleon, First Consul (1769–1821), invades Egypt, 68; 69, 81;

231

returns to France and offers peace overtures, 85; 98; makes peace with Britain, 111; interest in Camelford's moves, 121; fear that Camelford intended to assassinate, 123, 156, 165–8; 127; holds court in Paris, 128–9; Camelford denies attempt to assassinate, 131–2; 133, 150, 153, 155; agrees to Camelford's release, 156; 157; life menaced by Cadoudal, 175; 176, 179, 193, 223

Bond Street, 33, 34, 100–2; Camelford's house in, 113; riot in, 114–17; 118, 119; French spy visits, 122; 154, 159, 160, 168, 170, 172, 173, 181, 182

Bond Street Loungers, 100–2

Borlinder, John, sent to find Camelford in Paris, 119–21; baffled, 121; 127, 128; Camelford quarrels with, 171, 225

Bosset, Charles Philippe de, 69–72, 76, 77

Boulogne, 120; search for Camelford at, 122, 123; Camelford's arrival at, 124–126; 130, 133, 157

Bounty, H.M.S., 22

Bourke (or Berks), Joe, pugilist, fights Belcher at Wimbledon, 108–10; 111, 116; fight at Enfield Wash frustrated, 117–18; final fights with Belcher, 134–140; 225; Plate 22

Bourrienne, Louis Antoine de (1769–1834), writes to Fouché concerning Camelford, 121

Brenan, Captain, 124

Brest, 73

Brilliant, H.M.S., 171

Brock, Admiral P. W., 61

Brown, Catherine, fruit-seller at Drury Lane, 80

Brown, James, Camelford's servant, 64

Brummell, George, 'Beau' (1778–1840), 90, 147

Brunerie, Monsieur de la, 82, 84, 133, 157, 191

Buckingham, George, Marquis of (1753–1813), 17, 106, 119

Burdett, Sir Francis (1770–1844), 104–5, 147

Burton Pynsent, 102, 119, 146

Cadoudal, Georges, royalist conspirator (1771–1804), 174–9

Calais, 74, 151, 166

California, 23, 24

Camberwell Fair, 135–6

Camelford, Lady (*née* Anne Wilkinson), marries Lord Camelford, 5–6; 9; in Rome, 17; 25, 27, 31, 35, 36, 39, 50, 64, 66, 67, 68, 87, 113; learns of son's disappearance, 119; 141; illness, 150; 151, 154; death and funeral of, 157–8, 159, 162; 170, 207, 212, 222; Plate 3

Camelford, Thomas Pitt, 1st Baron (1736–1793), 3; upbringing and character, 4–5; created Lord Camelford, 5; marriage, 5–6; 7, 9, 11, 13, 15, 16; in Rome, 17; 18; death of, 25, 26, 84, 168, 204, 206; Plate 5

CAMELFORD, Thomas Pitt, 2nd Baron (1775–1804), birth, 6; childhood, 7–10; at school in Neuchâtel, 10–13; at Charterhouse, 13; joins Royal Navy, 13–14; voyage in *Guardian*, 14–17; voyage in *Discovery* to Pacific, 17–25; sails to Australia from Hawaii, and succeeds to title, 25–6; sails to Malacca, 26–7; on board *Resistance*, 27–8; sails to Ceylon, 28–30; returns to Europe, 30–1; challenges and attacks Vancouver, 1, 31–6; serves as lieutenant on board *London*, 36–39; takes seat in House of Lords, 39; quarrel with Charles Vancouver, 39–41; present at Spithead mutiny, 41–2; at Leeward Islands station, 42–4; posted to *Favorite*, 44; attacks shore battery at Grenada, 44–5; eccentric appearance, 45–6; press-ganging at Barbados, 46–52; fatal quarrel with Lieutenant Peterson at Antigua, 52–8; court-martial arising from Peterson's death, 58–63; subsequent altercations and departure for

England, 63–5; desire for new posting, 66–8; appointed to command *Charon*, 68; plans to join Sidney Smith in Mediterranean, 68–9; private schemes, 69–72; an adventure at Dover, 72–8; obliged to leave Royal Navy, and dabbles in politics, 79; violent behaviour at theatre, 79–81; travels on Continent, 81–3; supports Stanhope in anti-government motions, 84–7; terrifies radicals and his friend Abbott, 87–9; relationship with Hester Stanhope, 89–93; threatens to murder Prime Minister, 94–5; charity to London poor, 95–7; mutual attachment with Hester, 97–8; misunderstood character, 99 100; checks menace of Bond Street Loungers, 100–2; clothes, 102, 216; installs Horne Tooke as M.P. for Old Sarum, 103–7; present at fight between Belcher and Bourke at Wimbledon, 107–10; fights with mob in Bond Street, 113–17; boxing match at Enfield Wash frustrated, 117–18; secret expedition to France, 119–33; pleasures in England, 134; concluding contest between Belcher and Bourke, 134–40, buys 'Belcher', 140; relationship with boxers, 141; appears as 'Lord Chiltern' in Trollope's *Phineas Finn*, 142–9; relationship with Hester Stanhope, 146–148; held in Temple prison in Paris, 150–157; mother dies, 157–8; escapades with Robert Barrie, 159–60; wild life in London, 161–5; French fears of his intention to murder Bonaparte, 165–8; versatile interests, 168–9; charity and kindnesses, 169–70; quarrel with Borlinder, 171; and with Best, 171–4; French suspicion that Camelford was connected with conspiracy of Cadoudal, 174–7; possibility that duel with Best was engineered by French, 178–9; duel with Best, 180–4; death of, 184–6; verdicts on character, 187–8; funeral, 190–1; will, 191–2; possibility that he had an illegitimate daughter, 192–3; frustration of desire to be buried in Switzerland, 193–4; Plates 1, 15, 16, 19, 21, 28

Camelford House, Oxford Street, 7, 25, 31, 70, 84, 113, 119, 157, 158–9, 188, 190, 213, 220, 222; Plate 20

Canary Islands, 14, 19–20

Canterbury, 73

Cape of Good Hope, 14, 15, 20, 79, 214

Caravigis, Marquetti, 147

Carlisle, Sir Anthony, 102, 134, 168, 182; assessment of Camelford's character, 187; 225

Cattaro, 31

Cavendish Square, irresponsible incident in, 160

Cayley, Captain William, 59

Ceylon, 29–30, 69, 70

Charles I, King of Great Britain and Ireland (1600–49), 9

Charles, Archduke of Austria (1771–1847), 81–2, 157

Charon, H.M.S., 68, 69, 71, 72, 88, 176

Charterhouse, 13, 14, 22–3, 105

Chatham, H.M.S., 18, 19, 35

Chatham, Lady (Hester), 7, 102, 119; death, 146

Chatham, John Pitt, 2nd Earl of (1756–1835), 15, 16, 26, 36, 76, 92, 93, 98, 105, 146, 228

Chatham, Lady (Mary), 92, 93, 146

Chatham, William Pitt, 1st Earl of (1708–1778), 4, 70, 90

Chevening, 86, 91, 96, 102, 146

Chile, 20, 71

Clayton, Mrs Dorothy, 159, 165, 191, 228

Cleghorn, Professor Hugh, secret agent, 29–30, 69, 70

Cobbett, William (1762–1835), 117

Cockburne, Rev. William, 169, 180, 185, 186

Collingwood, Captain Cuthbert (1750–1810), 25

Collins, John, waiter, 180–1

Colombo, 30

Colpoys, Admiral Sir John (1742?–1821), 38, 39, 41, 42, 44, 60

Colquhoun, prize agent at Antigua, 51, 63–4, 212

Conant, magistrate, 180–1

Conduit Street, 1, 33–5, 36, 39, 40, 70, 101, 102, 172; Plate 15

Conolly, sailor, 47

Cook, Captain James (1728–79), 18, 20, 21, 22

Cornwallis, Charles, 1st Marquis of (1738–1805), 131

Cowper, Charles, 97, 192–3

Cox, Captain, 49–50

Craven, William, 1st Earl of (d. 1825), 134

Crawford, master of the Perdrix, 54, 55, 56, 58

Cribb, Tom, Champion of England (1781–1848), 140

Cruikshank, Isaac, artist (1756?–1811?), 103

Cuxhaven, 81, 82

Daedalus, 25

Darnley, John, 4th Earl of (d. 1831), 188

Dartford, 72–3, 77

Davies, Lieutenant John, 30, 31

Dawes, undertaker, 190

Despard, Colonel Edward, (1751–1803), 155

Devereux, Hon. Henry (d. 1843), 171; acts as second to Camelford in duel, 180–4; 191; and question of translation of Camelford's body, 193–4, 228; Plate 28

Discovery, H.M.S., voyage to Pacific, 18–25, 26, 31, 32, 34, 35, 36, 39, 68, 70, 71, 76, 79, 84, 170, 207, 222; Plates 11, 12

Dixon, Frank, 7

Dover, 72, 74–5, 77, 79, 157

Dropmore, 32, 67, 98, 112, 152, 157, 170, 185

Dundas, Henry (1742–1811), 30

Duroc, Géraud de (1772–1813), urged by Fouché to protect Napoleon from Camelford's machinations, 123

Egerton, Mr and Mrs, accompany Hester Stanhope to Continent, 146

Enfield Wash, proposed fight between Belcher and Bourke at, 117–18, 135, 218

Enghien, Louis Antoine, Duc d' (1772–1804), 178

Fahie, Captain, 53, 60

Falmouth, 18

Farington, Joseph (1747–1821), 188

Favorite, H.M.S., 44, 46, 48, 49, 50, 52, 53, 54, 55, 57, 58, 59, 64, 65, 207, 212

Flaxman, John, sculptor (1755–1826), 208

Florence, 25

Ford, magistrate, 118

Forster, Rev. Benjamin, 7, 204

Fouché, Joseph (1759–1820), orders capture of Camelford, 121; fears for Bonaparte's safety, 123; 126, 127, 128, 130, 131, 132, 133, 178, 179

Fox, Charles James (1749–1806), 10, 85, 102

Gamble, Andrew, Irish pugilist, 117

Geneva, Camelford at, 120

George III, King of Great Britain and Ireland (1738–1820), 5, 15, 16, 73, 74, 76, 85, 112, 154, 155, 181

Gibbon, Edward (1737–94), 11, 205

Gibbons, Bill, pugilist (1757–?), 137

Gibraltar, 13

Gillett, John, Dover boatman, 75

Gillray, James (1757–1815), 34–5, 102–3, 107, 151

Godoy, Manuel, Duke of Alcudia (1767–1851), 26

Gower, Lord Granville Leveson (1773–1846), 77

Granger, William, master's mate, 54

Green, Charles, Governor of Grenada, 44–5

Grenada, Camelford's piratical conduct at, 44–5

Grenville, Lady (née Anne Pitt) (1772–1864), birth, 6; 9, 10; portraits of, 17,

206; 19; marriage to Lord Grenville, 26; 32, 38, 42, 50; description of, 68; 84, 113; 119, 141, 145, 158, 162, 163, 170; at Thomas's deathbed, 185; 191, 228, 229, Plate 8

Grenville, William Wyndham, 1st Baron (1759–1834), 17–18, 20; marriage to Anne Pitt, 26; 27, 31; intervention in quarrel between Camelford and Vancouver, 31–6; 38, 39, 50, 51, 64, 67; description of, 68; 76, 79, 84, 85, 86, 89, 91, 105, 106; misgivings over peace treaty, 112; 113; learns of Camelford's disappearance, 119; sends Borlinder to Paris, 119–20; 121, 128, 132, 133, 145; warning to Camelford, 150–1; learns of Camelford's danger, 151, 152; 153, 156, 157, 158, 170, 171; at Camelford's deathbed, 185–6; 191, 192–3; opposes translation of Camelford's body, 193–4; sells house, 218; 222, 228; Plate 6

Grewelthorpe, fight between Bourke and Belcher at, 135

Guadeloupe, 52, 63

Guardian, H.M.S., 14–17, 18, 19, 20, 98, 205–6, 207; Plates 9, 10

Hamburg, 31, 71, 72; Camelford visits, 132–3; 178

Harding, Thomas, alarmed by Camelford's conduct, 94–5

Harriett, 47, 48, 49, 50

Harvey, Admiral Sir Henry (1737–1810), 44, 45, 51, 52, 58, 60, 61, 65, 210

Harwich, 17, 82

Hawaii, 24, 25, 35

Hawke, Martin Bladen, 2nd Baron (d. 1805), 67

Hawkesbury, Charles, 1st Baron (1770–1828), 111, 112, 155

Hayes, Dr, 188

Heaviside, Dr, 158, 223

Hermione, H.M.S., 53, 60, 92

Highgate, 94, 215

Hoare, Messrs, bankers, 119

Hoche, 73, 76

Holland, Henry, 3rd Baron (1773–1840), 87, 184; erects monument to Camelford, 188–9

Holland House, 182, 189

Holroyd, Mrs, 158, 170

Howe, Richard, Admiral Earl (1726–99), 41

Hugues, Victor, 63, 65, 121

Humphrey, Mrs Hannah (d. 1818), 34

Humphries, assaulted by Camelford, 80–1, 99

Hurley Bottom, fight between Bourke and Belcher at, 134–5

Invincible, H.M.S., 59

Iris, H.M.S., 82–3

Italy, 7, 82, 85

Jackson, actor, 110

Jackson, Francis, British minister in Paris (1770–1814), 120, 127

Jackson, 'Gentleman' John, pugilist (1769–1845), 109

Jafna, 29

Jamaica, 13

Jenkinson, British diplomat, 155

Jones, Tom 'Paddington', pugilist, 108

Junot, General Andache (1771–1813), 128, 166

Kamehameha, King of Hawaii (d. 1819), 35, 209

Kenyon, Lloyd, 1st Baron (1732–1802), tries Camelford for assault, 80–1

King, Peter, 7th Baron (1776–1833), 87

King, Hon. Richard, heads riot at Drury Lane, 80

Kittoe, George, brutally treated by Camelford, 64, 99

Kitty, 47, 48, 49, 50

Knowles and Parker, innkeepers at Boulogne, 124

La Ferté, Camelford's stay at, 126–7

La Martelière, French *émigré*, 176
Langley, hanged for attempting to cross Channel, 76
La Pensée, 52, 63, 211
Laubeypie, French agent, 156
Laughton, Sir John, 60, 229
Lausanne, 11, 127, 157
Lever, Sir Tresham, 158, 207
Lillybourn, John, landlord of the Granby's Head, 72, 77
Limoëlan, Joseph Picot de, 123; attempts to assassinate Bonaparte, possibly in collusion with Camelford, 132–3, 176
London, H.M.S., 13, 36, 37, 38, 39, 41, 209
Loughborough, Alexander, 1st Baron (1733–1805), 33–4, 35, 40, 67, 76, 87
Louis XVI, King of France (1754–93), 153
Louis XVIII, King of France (1755–1824), 130, 174

MacCarthy, Felix, Irish fabulist, 99
Macnamara, Captain, duellist, 161–2, 171, 185
McQuin, John, sailor, 52
Madras, 2, 26, 30
Mahon, Philip, Lord (1781–1855), 102, 146
Mainwaring, Captain Jemmett, 53, 54, 60, 61, 211
Maistral, Captain Désiré de, 73–4, 75, 77, 78
Malacca, 27, 28
Malmesbury, James, 1st Earl of (1746–1820), 105
Manby, Captain Thomas (1769–1834), 35, 36–7, 39, 68, 71, 76, 77, 78, 142, 226
Manchester, William, 5th Duke of (1768–1843), 134
Margate, 110, 112, 217
Martinique, 45, 52, 59, 64, 65, 179, 210
Masséna, General André (1756–1817), 81, 84, 128
Matavai Bay, 20–2; Plate 11
Matilda, H.M.S., 58
May, Captain Matthew, 47, 48, 49, 51
Mediator, H.M.S., 25

Melbourne, William, 2nd Viscount (1779–1848), 87
Mellish, Colonel, sporting patron, 140
Mendoza, Daniel, pugilist (1764–1836), 109, 110, 118
Mengaud, *commissaire* at Calais, arrests Camelford, 151–2; discovers Camelford's true purpose, 154–5
Meryon, Dr Charles (1783–1877), 97, 147
Meuron, Colonel Count Charles de (1738–1813), 29–30, 69
Meuron, Henri de (1752–1813), 10–11, 12, 29
Mexico, 24, 26, 210
Michel, French banker, 166
Milward, Lieutenant, 54, 55, 56, 57, 58, 59
Minto, Gilbert Elliott, Earl of (1751–1814), 77, 105
Mitford, Captain Henry, 58, 59, 61, 63, 212
Mitford, Sir John (1748–1830), 106
Mohun, Charles, 5th Baron (1675?–1712), 2, 144
Montagu, George Conway, swindler, 67
Montgomery, Colonel, 161–2
Moore, General Sir John (1761–1809), 147
Moreau, General Jean (1763–1813), 175
Mudge, Lieutenant Zachariah, 19, 22, 24, 25, 26
Mulach, ? Swiss agent of Camelford's, 127, 130
Mungo, negro pugilist, 106, 178, 225

Nelson, Horatio, Viscount (1758–1805), 39, 68
Neuchâtel, 10–11, 12, 29, 30, 69, 74; Plate 7
Newport, Peter, collector of customs at Dover, 75–6
New Zealand, 20
Nicholson, Dr, 184, 187, 188
Nicholson, William, scientist (1753–1815), 168, 171, 181, 190, 224
Nihell, second to Best in duel, 180–4; Plate 28
Nootka Sound, 18, 24, 186

Nore, mutiny at, 42, 60

Old Sarum, election of 1801 at, 103–7; borough sold by Camelford, 107; 225; Plate 21
Otley, 184
Otto, Louis Guillaume, French envoy, 111, 112, 122, 123, 124, 150
Owen, Rev., 28, 29, 30
Owen, Tom, pugilist, 137, 140
Oxford, 5th Earl of (1773–1849), 104

Pakenham, Captain Edward, 27–8, 35, 36, 44, 142
Paris, 72, 98; Camelford reported to be imprisoned in, 119–20; his stay in, 126; 127; Camelford returns to, 128–32; 133, Camelford imprisoned in Temple, 152–157; 165, 166, 174, 177, 178
Parsons, Lieutenant, 47, 48, 54, 55, 57, 211
Paul I, Tsar of Russia (1754–1801), 84, 131
Perdrix, H.M.S., 52, 53, 54, 55, 56, 57, 58, 59, 61, 62, 212
Petersham, 7, 9, 32, 52
Peterson, Lieutenant Charles, 44, 47, 48, 49; fatal dispute with Camelford, 53–63, 92; 121, 155, 179, 212; Plate 16
Phineas Finn, 142, 148, 221
Pichegru, General Charles (1761–1804), 175, 178
Pigot, Captain Hugh (1769–97), 53, 92
Pitt, Anne, see Grenville, Lady
Pitt, Robert (1680?–1727), 3–4
Pitt, Thomas, Governor of Madras (1653–1726), 2–3, 26, 103, 144, 204
Pitt, Thomas (1706–61), 3–4
Pitt, William, Prime Minister (1759–1806), 5, 26, 76, 84, 85; praises Hester Stanhope, 90; 91; avoids Camelford, 92; Camelford threatens to murder, 94–5; 105, 111, 132; invites Hester Stanhope to live with him, 146; difference with Camelford, 148; 153, 154, 155, 203, 221
'Pitt Diamond', 2

Plymouth, 13, 205
Porcher, Josias Dupre, buys Old Sarum, 107
Port Jackson, 14, 25–6
Portland, William, 3rd Duke of (1738–1809), 76, 77
Portsmouth, 35, 36, 41, 147
Prince of Orange, 17
Prince of Wales Coffee House, 70, 101, 113, 172, 173, 180
Prince of Wales Island (Penang), 28
Puget, Lieutenant Peter, 19

Querel, informer, 177

Rainier, Admiral Peter (1741?–1808), 28, 36
Ramsden, Piccadilly optician, 39, 40
Ranelagh Gardens, 134, 219
Reade, Charles, novelist (1814–84), 142, 194
Régnier, Claude, Grand Judge (1746–1814), 131, 152, 153, 154, 155–6, 166, 167, 175, 178, 179
Reid, Fletcher, sporting patron, 138
Resistance, H.M.S., 27–8, 39
Rêveries du promeneur solitaire, 11–12
Richmond, Bill, negro pugilist (1763–?), 116
Ricketts, Governor of Barbados, 49, 51
Riou, Captain Edward (1758?–1801), 14, 16, 98
Robust, H.M.S., 73
Rome, 17; Camelford stays in, 127
Rousseau, Jean-Jacques (1712–78), 11–12, 168, 227, 229
Royal Charlotte, H.M.S., 41
Royal Circus, fight in, 164–5
Rumbold, Sir George (1764–1807), 178
Russell, Captain Thomas Macnamara (1740?–1824), 42, 44, 60, 120–1, 142, 210
Rutley, Dover clerk, 75–6

St Amand, French royalist, 176
St Anne's Church, Soho, 181, 191, 193, 194

St Kitts, 42, 44, 53

St Nicaise, rue de, attempt to blow up Bonaparte in, 123

St Pierre, Île de, 12–13, 28, 158; Camelford's desire to be buried on, 192, 193–4; 205; Plate 29

St Vincent, John, 1st Earl of (1735–1823), 67

Savary, General Anne (1774–1833), fears assassination of Bonaparte, 167, 175

Scott, Sir William (1745–1836), 194

Scourge, H.M.S., 210

Sharp, Major, 165

Shaw, Lieutenant, fights with Camelford, 164–5

Shea, Henry, sailor, 52

Sheridan, Richard Brinsley (1751–1816), 102, 104, 107

Simmonds, Fanny, 172–4, 178–9, 180, 188, 225

Smith, Bobus, 87

Smith, James and Horace, 165

Smith, Captain John, 5–6

Smith, Captain Sidney (1764–1840), 6, 13–14; imprisoned in Paris, 66, 153; sent to aid Turks, 68; Camelford visits ship of, 69; 71, 78, 79, 81, 82, 85, 88, 132, 159, 177, 185, 212, 213, 222

Smith, Spencer, 68, 177

Spencer, George, 2nd Earl (1758–1834), 36, 41, 67, 79, 112, 207

Spithead, 14; mutiny at, 41–2; 53, 60, 69

Stafford, Lady, 105

Stanhope, Charles, 3rd Earl (1753–1816), votes against government motion, 85–7; harsh treatment of children, 91; Hester flees home of, 102; 105, 112, 131, 154, 168; Plate 19

Stanhope, Lady Hester (1776–1839), character and appearance, 90–1; account of Camelford, 91–3; forthright character, 93–4; 95; relationship with Camelford, 97–8; 99; takes refuge with Lady Chatham, 102; influences Camelford to place Horne Tooke in parliament, 105–

106; 119, 120, 122, 127, 142; ends relationship with Camelford and retires to Lebanon, 146–8; 149; mourns death of Camelford, 188; Plate 18

Stanhope, Lady Lucy, 91

Stewart, John, 19, 25

Stowe, 98, 119

Suez, 30, 147

Sumatra, 27

Suvorov, Field-Marshal Alexander (1729–1800), 81, 82, 84

Swift, 30

Switzerland, 10, 11, 29, 30, 72; campaign of 1799 in, 81–2; 84, 157, 191; Camelford a good friend to, 194

Tahiti, 20–2, 24

Talleyrand-Périgord, Charles Maurice de (1754–1838), 85, 178, 204

Temple of Stowe, Richard Earl (1776–1839), 89; leads move to eject Horne Tooke from parliament, 106–7; Plate 21

Temple prison, 152–3, 156, 175, 177, 178

Terror, H.M.S., 65, 207, 212

Thomson, Lieutenant, 28

Thomson, surgeon, 184

Thurlow, Edward, 1st Baron (1731–1806), 104

Tigre, H.M.S., 69, 213

Tisiphone, H.M.S., 36

Tobago, H.M.S., 13, 205

Tom's Coffee House, 87, 90, 112–13

Tone, Theobald Wolfe (1763–98), 73

Tooke, John Horne (1736–1812), 103–4; and Old Sarum election of 1801, 104–7; 131–2; Plate 21

Toulon, 68, 72

Townsend, police officer, 89, 118

Trebeck, Charles, 192–3, 229

Tremlett, Lieutenant Richard Stiles, 64, 179, 212

Trincomalee, 29

Trollope, Anthony (1815–82), 142–5, 159

'Trusty', formerly 'Belcher', bull-terrier, 140, 220; Plate 24

Tufton, Hon. Mr, 110, 217
Tuileries Palace, 123, 126, 128–9, 131
Turnbull, James, robber, 75

Union, 28–9, 208

Valparaíso, 20, 71
Vancouver, Charles, 32, 33, 34, 35; quarrel with Camelford, 39–41; 67, 209; Plate 15
Vancouver, Captain George (1758–98), voyage on *Discovery*, 18–25; challenged and attacked by Camelford, 31–6; death of, 35; 207, 219; Plates 13, 15
Vancouver Island, 23–4
Vengeance, H.M.S., 42, 210
Vigée Le Brun, Marie-Anne (1755–1842), 17, 206
Vincejo, H.M.S., 178
Vivaldi, racehorse, 166, 223

Wales, George, Prince of (1762–1830), 102
Ward, Joe, pugilist (1751–?), 137
Warren, Admiral Sir John Borlase (1753–1822), 73

Weldon, 171
Westmacott, Sir Richard (1775–1856), 188
Whaley, Colonel William, 166–7; tries to kill informer, 176–7; 179, 223, 224
Whidbey, Joseph, master of the *Discovery*, 22, 23, 35, 36
Whitworth, Charles, Earl (1752–1825), 150; intervenes to save Camelford, 156
Wilkinson, Mary, 5, 6
Wilkinson, Pinckney, 5, 6; M.P. for Old Sarum, 103; will, 203
Williams, Colonel, 82, 124, 126, 155
Wilson, Richard, solicitor, 181, 191
Wimbledon, 104, 105, 107–9, 225
Woolwich, 68, 72
Wright, Commander John (1769–1805), 177, 178
Wyat, clergyman, 9
Wynne, Eugenia, 188

Yonge, Sir George (1731–1812), 79, 214

Zante, 31
Zürich, 81, 82